AF179746

Politicizing Business

The Chinese state has never granted businesses full autonomy, even amid efforts to establish market-supporting institutions. Instead, the state and its officials often view business as political actors, demanding political services from firms to advance political objectives. *Politicizing Business* demonstrates that the politicization of firms is rooted in authoritarianism, often harming business interests and undermining China's efforts to attract and retain investment. Explaining the seemingly arbitrary state takeover of sectors and firms, this book uncovers previously overlooked forms of politicization and demonstrates how politicizing business often creates conflicts between the state and firms, particularly private firms, leading to a state-dominated market in many sectors. Combining academic rigor with exceptionally rich data and analysis, including hundreds of in-depth interviews with government officials and business leaders, original datasets and case studies, *Politicizing Business* offers fresh insights into China's political economy model and explores what the Party-state demands from companies, how compliance is enforced, when and where firms are politicized, and the impact of politicization on China's development.

Ning Leng is an assistant professor at Georgetown University's McCourt School of Public Policy. She holds a PhD in political science from the University of Wisconsin–Madison. She is an expert in Chinese politics, Chinese economy, authoritarian control, and China in Latin America. Her research is supported by numerous organizations, including the National Science Foundation.

Politicizing Business

How Firms Are Made to Serve the Party-State in China

NING LENG
Georgetown University

CAMBRIDGE
UNIVERSITY PRESS

CAMBRIDGE
UNIVERSITY PRESS

Shaftesbury Road, Cambridge CB2 8EA, United Kingdom

One Liberty Plaza, 20th Floor, New York, NY 10006, USA

477 Williamstown Road, Port Melbourne, VIC 3207, Australia

314–321, 3rd Floor, Plot 3, Splendor Forum, Jasola District Centre, New Delhi – 110025, India

103 Penang Road, #05–06/07, Visioncrest Commercial, Singapore 238467

Cambridge University Press is part of Cambridge University Press & Assessment, a department of the University of Cambridge.

We share the University's mission to contribute to society through the pursuit of education, learning and research at the highest international levels of excellence.

www.cambridge.org
Information on this title: www.cambridge.org/9781009662291

DOI: 10.1017/9781009662277

© Ning Leng 2025

This publication is in copyright. Subject to statutory exception and to the provisions of relevant collective licensing agreements, no reproduction of any part may take place without the written permission of Cambridge University Press & Assessment.

When citing this work, please include a reference to the DOI 10.1017/9781009662277

First published 2025

A catalogue record for this publication is available from the British Library

A Cataloging-in-Publication data record for this book is available from the Library of Congress

ISBN 978-1-009-66229-1 Hardback
ISBN 978-1-009-66230-7 Paperback

Cambridge University Press & Assessment has no responsibility for the persistence or accuracy of URLs for external or third-party internet websites referred to in this publication and does not guarantee that any content on such websites is, or will remain, accurate or appropriate.

For my parents, Wei Leng and Su Zhang

Contents

Figures

Figures

Tables

Acknowledgments

I started research for this book in 2015 as a PhD student at the University of Wisconsin-Madison. This journey ultimately became a sobering learning experience about China. Over the years, I spoke with hundreds of people in government and the business community – conversations that are now nearly impossible to have. Because of these conversations, what began as a focus on infrastructure politics and public service provision expanded into an inquiry into how authoritarian institutions shape the decisions of government officials and businesspeople, and how those decisions affect the business landscape, development quality, and sustainability in China. Research for this book has left me deeply concerned about China's trajectory under its current political economy model, though it has also strengthened my respect for the remarkable resilience of the Chinese people.

I am thus deeply grateful to all of my interviewees – more than two hundred in total – for candidly sharing their experiences and views, often at personal and political risk. I also thank those who generously connected me to them, including colleagues in Chinese academia, journalism, and nonprofit organizations. Given the political climate in China today, I will not name them here – but they know who they are, and I am indebted to each and every one of them for their help.

This book would not have been possible without the guidance of a group of outstanding scholars at the University of Wisconsin-Madison. Melanie Manion – my PhD advisor, and the academic "godmother" of the "Madison mafia" – is the most generous and supportive advisor one could hope for. She introduced me to political science, taught me how to conduct research, and encouraged me to pursue topics I was passionate about. Her steady guidance and advice at every stage of my intellectual journey were crucial to my transformation from a green PhD student into an independent scholar.

Edward Friedman, a towering figure in the China field with unparalleled insight, offered nothing but encouragement over many lunches. My later research interests in global China were sparked by conversations with Ed and my time as his teaching assistant. David Weimer, wise and warm-hearted, guided me through the otherwise intimidating world of causal mechanisms during countless office hours and introduced me to the literature on public management. Aseema Sinha played a key role in my conversion from development economics to political science. She also encouraged me to study India as a comparative case, even though it ultimately didn't make it into the final book. Yoshiko Herrera, Scott Gehlbach, and Rikhil Bhavnani all patiently helped me revise my dissertation until I could finally be happy with it. Nadav Shelef, Nils Ringe, John Ahlquist, and Ian Coxhead were mentors who supported not just my intellectual development but also cared about me as a person. Russel Dimond at the Social Science Research Services practically gave me free lessons in statistical modeling and was instrumental in building my quantitative skills. This book owes much to the guidance, patience, and generosity of these remarkable scholars.

The Madison mafia – a group of political science PhD students at the University of Wisconsin-Madison with a shared interest in China – offered camaraderie and an intellectually stimulating environment for discussion and debate throughout my PhD years. Meina Cai, Charles Chaoyi Chang, Dominic DeSapio, Brandon Lamson, Ruoxi Li, Leah Larson-Rabin, Kerry Ratigan, Kristin Vekasi, Samantha Vortherms, and Vera Cai Zuo each gave me friendship and support, and all helped sharpen my thinking about China through countless seminars, lunches, and dinners organized by Melanie Manion and often attended by Sida Liu. To this day, we still celebrate each other's successes – big and small.

I also made lifelong friends with brilliant and kind people I met in Madison. Jing Lu is more like a sister than a friend; we've faced tough times together. David Ohls, Leticia Bode, and Charles Taylor – fellow political scientists and enthusiastic cooks – kept me company through the ups and downs of graduate school. Now, they and their growing families continue to share food and laughter with me in Washington, DC. Camilla Reuterswärd, Delgerjargal Uvsh, and I bonded over our shared experiences as international students and comparative political scientists conducting research in difficult environments. Our sisterhood continues to thrive over Zoom, despite the distances between us. A writing group with Bo Wang and Frank Lefeng Lin kept my dissertation on track – and Bo and his husband Sam made some of the best hotpots I've ever had. Maayan Mor and Yang Gu were always a joy to be around, and we shared so much laughter together.

I had the fortune of being a postdoctoral fellow under the mentorship of Anthony Saich at Harvard University during the 2018–2019 academic year. Tony is one of the most generous people I've met in academia – and he also happens to make a great shepherd's pie. His depth of knowledge and unwavering support for junior scholars have set an example I aspire to follow. Edward Cunningham, who shares my interest in de-privatization, offered invaluable feedback on my work. Elizabeth Plantan was the best officemate one could ask for; our shared concern for academic freedom in China led us to coauthor another exciting project. Saul Wilson read my work more times than I can count and is still not bored with it – something I admire, along with the fact that he gets to live in India. Joshua Freedman, Jundai Liu, and Christopher Carothers were all at different stages in their writing, but we bonded over a healthy dose of groans about our progress. It was also during this year that I got to know Yasheng Huang and Yuhua Wang, both of whom generously shared their insights on China and academia.

At a critical stage in writing this manuscript, a group of scholars, teachers, and friends generously offered their time, expertise, and encouragement, helping me to significantly strengthen this book. Edward Cunningham, Bruce Dickson, Martin Dimitrov, Yasheng Huang, Edmund Malesky, Andrew Mertha, Margaret Pearson, Anthony Saich, Kellee Tsai, and Yuhua Wang attended my book workshops at Harvard and Georgetown, read the entire manuscript with great care, and offered invaluable feedback that shaped both its content and structure. Jérôme Doyon also read the full manuscript and shared thoughtful suggestions. Lynette Ong, Samantha Vortherms, Kerry Ratigan, Rebecca Perlman, and Douglas Fuller each took time from their busy schedules to read individual chapters and offered suggestions and insights. Denise van der Kamp and Diana Fu shared their book proposal with me and provided invaluable feedback. Kristen Looney shared her own writing experiences to help me improve my own. Martin Dimitrov, Carole Sargent, Yuhua Wang, and Yasheng Huang advised me on publication strategies, and Vivian Jing Zhan offered insights into the book publication process. Hiroki Takeuchi stayed in conversation with me over the years and never wavered in his belief in my work.

At the McCourt School of Public Policy, my kind and brilliant colleagues provided much-appreciated support during the final stages of this book manuscript. Kent Weaver read multiple versions, offered thoughtful feedback, and generously treated me to ice cream and lunches to discuss the work. Whenever I needed a second opinion – on anything from research to teaching – Kent was the person I turned to for guidance. William Gormley kindly volunteered to host my book workshop at Georgetown University. When I struggled with key decisions about the manuscript, Bill weighed each option with great care and talked through them with me as if it were his own book. George Akerlof even started sketching out formal models in case I wanted to incorporate a mathematical approach into my theorizing. When it became clear that his Nobel-attested insights exceeded what I could feasibly include, he instead helped me sharpen some key concepts in the book. Raphael Calel asked probing questions that helped me organize my thoughts and patiently listened as I talked through ideas over many coffees and lunches.

Other McCourt colleagues cheered me on and celebrated every milestone, no matter how small. I am grateful to Michael Bailey, NaLette Brodnax, Jacobus Cilliers, Maria Cancian, Jishnu Das, Thomas DeLeire, Eugene Dionne, Nada Eissa, Judith Feder, Gaël Giraud, Nora Gordon, James Habyarimana, Andrea Headley, Pamela Herd, Harry Holzer, Karen Huang, Sebastian Jilke, Wesley Joe, Rebecca Johnson, Dan Kelemen, Andreas Kern, Adriana Kugler, Jonathan Ladd, Jean Mitchell, Donald Moynihan, Nuku Ofori, Evelyn Patterson, Eva Rosen, Krista Ruffini, Lutz Sager, Barbara Schone, Adam Thomas, Jennifer Tobin, and Andrew Zeitlin, among others – for their kindness, camaraderie, and support.

At Georgetown University at large, I benefited from a collegial environment marked by vibrant academic discussions and the exchange of ideas. Nita Rudra and Apichai Shipper offered mentorship and friendship over the years, helping me navigate a wide range of issues. Many colleagues contributed to my growth as a scholar in one way or another, among them are Tariq Ali, Laia Balcells, Jenny Guardado, Arie Kacowicz, Diana Kim, Marko Klasnja, Joanna Lewis, Lizhi Liu, Kristen Looney, Dennis McNamara, James Millward, Abraham Newman, Irfan Nooruddin, Ken Opalo, Dennis Quinn, Mark Richardson, George Shambaugh, Joel Simmons, Yuhki Tajima, Yuye Tong, and Erik Voeten. I am grateful for their feedback, insights, and encouragement.

Research for this book is generously funded by the National Science Foundation, the Chiang Ching-kuo Foundation, the Institute for Humane

Studies, and the political science department at the University of Wisconsin-Madison. These grants made possible the fieldwork that was essential to this book.

I dedicate this book to my parents, Wei Leng and Su Zhang, who opened the world to me. Both artists, intellectuals, and veterans of China's movie industry – a field constantly under political scrutiny – they have always defined success as personal growth and freedom. They cherished curiosity as one of the most precious human qualities, urging me to pursue the joy (and occasional shock) of learning anything and everything new, as long as it was interesting and enlightening. They instilled in me the conviction that one should not be bound by societal expectations or political constraints – for better or worse. My decision to pursue research as a career and to make a life in the United States was no accident. These paths were only possible because of their unwavering support, in every sense.

Brandon Lamson, a longtime partner and cheerleader, played a crucial role in my journey. A man of remarkable intellect and having the biggest heart I've ever known, Brandon taught me countless valuable life (and music) lessons and always brought me back down to earth whenever I went too far. His steady support and unwavering faith in me were essential to the completion of this book.

The animals who have been an integral part of my life growing up taught me how to be human. Over the years, my dogs and cats showered me with unconditional love and helped me see the world from an entirely different perspective – often from the ground level. It is their quiet, unspoken humanity that continues to inspire me to be a better person. In gratitude, the royalties from this book will go to nonprofit animal conservation organizations.

Writing a book – and learning about the world in the process – is incredibly fun. I am so fortunate to be able to do so.

1

The Hidden Political Roles of Firms in China

> The economy is secondary to politics in this country. We'd give up economic growth without hesitation for political needs.
>
> Teaching from a Communist Party study session in Beijing, 2015

How does an authoritarian state see firms? Engines of growth and employment? Sources of rents and clientelism? If firms fulfill these widely recognized roles, do they consequently experience a stable business environment and maintain a stable relationship with an authoritarian state?

Not necessarily. Even in China, where the legitimacy of the authoritarian state largely stems from economic growth resulting from its liberal market reforms, the fate of private firms is often subject to the whims of the state, even when these firms deliver economic outcomes and play by the political rules.

If one casually browses through Chinese economic news since 1978, the year China began its economic reform, it is easy to get lost in the abundance of news about China's commitment to a market economy and the increasingly vital roles played by private firms, both domestic and foreign. The Chinese state and private firms, it would seem, have found a mutually beneficial way to coexist. But if one reads carefully, every once in a while, there are noticeable discordant stories of the Chinese government encroaching on yet another private sector. By encroachment, I am not referring to regulations, but rather to drastic measures including nationalization, forced merger with and acquisition by state-owned enterprises (SOEs), forced state buyout of shareholders, forced issuance of new shares to SOEs, forced establishment of party cells in a company, direct state interference with business operations, and even the shutdown of an entire private sector.

A recent wave of state encroachment that unfolded at the national level in several prominent sectors can shed light on this phenomenon. In 2021, China's Ministry of Education suddenly shut down the multibillion-dollar industry of private tutoring for schoolchildren, ordering over half a million private firms to turn into nonprofit organizations. That same year, the Publicity Department of the Central Committee of the Communist Party of China (CCP) denounced video gaming as "opium for the mind" and ordered online gaming companies, including internet giants such as Tencent, to enforce gaming curfews and increase monitoring of users with facial recognition technology. Also in that same year, companies affiliated with the Chinese government took equity stakes and board seats in Weibo and the Chinese entity of ByteDance. Weibo is China's largest microblogging platform, and ByteDance is the parent company of TikTok, the most popular short-form video hosting service in the world.

These events were a continuation of actions taken a year prior, in 2020, when the government cracked down on the fourteen largest tech companies in China, including Alibaba, Baidu, and ByteDance. The government ordered these conglomerates to change their data privacy policies and halt their overseas initial public offering (IPO) plans. All these firms are successful in business and are considered major contributors to China's economic growth. They have also adhered to the state–business norms in China, or, one might say, the norms of crony capitalism. Alibaba, for example, has deep ties with the CCP elites, with some of its major investors being families of officials at the highest level of Chinese politics.[1] Likewise, the founder of Tencent is called an "ambassador of the Chinese state" and actively participated in CCP's key policies, and Tencent has invested generously in government relations.[2] Additionally, all of these tech companies have made substantial donations to social

[1] On Alibaba's ties with top Chinese leaders, see, for example, "Alibaba's I.P.O. Could Be a Bonanza for the Scions of Chinese Leaders," *New York Times*, 2014-07-20, https://archive.nytimes.com/dealbook.nytimes.com/2014/07/20/alibabas-i-p-o-could-be-a-bonanza-for-the-scions-of-chinese-leaders/.

[2] "Tencent rugu zhongjin gongsi, weishenme shuo Ma Huateng shen'an zhengshang guanxi," *Sohu News*, 2017-09-23, www.sohu.com/a/193958328_99967267; "Tencent executive earned more than HK$274 million in annual salary, filings reveal," *Southern China Morning Post*, www.scmp.com/tech/article/1939584/tencent-executive-earned-more-hk274-million-annual-salary-filings-reveal.

programs launched by the CCP to maintain good relations with the Chinese government.[3]

Therefore, this wave of high-profile state encroachment into some of China's most successful private sectors took many by surprise, and is often seen as a mark of the times, with increasingly powerful private firms suffering under the personalistic rule of President Xi Jinping, a strongman whom many suspect wants to bring back Marxism or at least a stronger form of state capitalism.[4] This assertion holds some truth considering Xi is tightening societal control on multiple fronts, but it does not fully explain similar crackdowns on the private sector before Xi's ascension to power and at the local level.

State encroachment into the private sector has been happening in various industries since China's 1978 economic reform, and the particular forms of encroachment that we observe today in the national events already mentioned can be traced back to 1993, the year the CCP formally incorporated a "socialist market economy" into China's constitution and recognized the private sector as an integral part of the Chinese economy. It is less that the CCP is turning against the market than that we are seeing the same pattern of state–business relations previously observed at the local level being played out in some high-profile sectors. Through the years, similar stories gained prominence as they do today, sparking anxious debates on whether China is scaling back its commitment to building a market economy. Eventually, they then gradually fade into a larger narrative of the growing pains of economic reform, forgotten amid another round of reassurance from the Chinese government regarding its unwavering support for the private sector, until the next wave of state encroachment arrives somewhere else.

Based on an open-source search for state encroachment in its narrowest forms, including nationalization, merger with and acquisition by SOEs, sale of control to SOEs and local governments, and administrative shutdown of an entire sector,[5] state encroachment into the private sector

[3] "BAT Zhengshang guanxi ju niubi," *IT Time*, 2014-10-27, www.ittime.com.cn/news/news_2518.shtml.

[4] This is a popular claim by some China watchers – see, for example, "The Return of Red China: Xi Jinping Brings Back Marxism," *Foreign Affairs*, 2022-11-09, www.foreignaffairs.com/china/return-red-china, and "Xi Jinping Is Reinventing State Capitalism. Don't Underestimate It," *The Economist*, 2020-08-13, www.economist.com/leaders/2020/08/13/xi-jinping-is-reinventing-state-capitalism-dont-underestimate-it.

[5] Other "softer" forms of state encroachment can include the government purchasing minority stakes in a company, as the central government did in the technology sector mentioned at the beginning of the chapter, or the CCP setting up party cells in a

has happened at least in the following sectors and years in different locations:[6] gas stations (1998–2012), urban transportation (1999–2018), airlines (2002, 2009–2010), the publication industry (2003–2004), trust funds (2004–2005), steel (2004–2010), rare earth minerals (2002–2011), coal mining (2006–2009), online streaming platforms (2009), online payment systems (2018, 2021), food manufacturing (2005, 2009), real estate (2009, 2021–2022), paper manufacturing (2006–2010), city gas supply (2010), hog farms (2011–2012, 2018–2023), the seed industry (2010–2018, 2023), and others. (See Appendix for Chapter 1.)

These incidents exhibit a sector-specific pattern, happened at the local government level, and did not always have identifiable central government guidance, often appearing to be uncoordinated actions by local governments. These patterns of state encroachment are different from those prior to 1993, when the entire private economy was considered a potential threat to socialism and was operating in a legal grey zone in China's socialist economy. State encroachment into the private economy before 1993 happened in the form of two waves of national crackdowns indiscriminately across all private entrepreneurs in all sectors, investigating and charging them for economic offenses that were later decriminalized, and confiscating or nationalizing private property.[7]

A few examples can help us better understand the nature of state encroachment into private sectors after 1993. An example of forced merger with and acquisition by SOEs is the case of Rizhao, a steel manufacturer. Rizhao was relatively profitable and one of the largest private steel companies in China, but in 2008 it was forced by the provincial government of Shandong to merge with the Shandong Iron and Steel Group, a loss-making provincial SOE. Rizhao initially refused this deal, and to compel the

company. Because it is difficult to discern whether these state interventions make the state the dominant actor in the private sector, I do not include them in this list.

[6] Appendix 1 offers a comprehensive chronological account of these incidents compiled from academic and news sources from 1993 to 2024. All the articles collected can be accessed through this online depository: https://drive.google.com/drive/folders/11YHwSh7a_mLVR-QUnKU7tm9OI_AIrxTw?usp=drive_link. The keyword for my search is "Guo jin min tui" ("国进民退"), a term commonly used in Chinese to describe state encroachment. Of all the results I find in this search, I only include those events in the narrow forms of state encroachment as explained in the text. This means there are many more incidents of state encroachment than the list I compiled.

[7] The central government of China launched two waves of indiscriminate crackdown on the private economy between 1982 and 1984, and then again between 1989 and 1992. These crackdowns took the form of investigations and charging of private entrepreneurs for economic offenses, which were later decriminalized. These episodes are detailed later in this chapter.

merger, the Shandong government suspended Rizhao's ongoing investments and procurement deals until the company agreed to it.[8] In a similar vein, within the airline sector, the Wuhan city government suspended the operations of Dongxing, a private airline, to pressure it into acquisition by Air China, an SOE, at a value much lower than its market price.[9]

Occasionally, local Chinese governments would use the extreme form of state encroachment – shutting down an entire private sector, as the central government did to the tutoring industry in 2021. Between 2006 and 2010, provincial governments of Shanxi, Henan, Hebei, and Inner Mongolia, China's main coal-producing provinces, forced private coal mines to shut down, some of which were later reopened by SOEs. Similarly, multiple local governments shut down the paper manufacturing industry throughout the 2010s. And as this book will detail, local city governments across China forced private firms in the urban bus sector to exit, starting in the early 2000s.

These examples of state encroachment, then, are inherently distinct from typical government regulation, and they consistently result in private firms ceding ground to SOEs in a certain sector. This outcome and its cause – the underlying rationale behind state encroachment – are what this book sets out to explain. I show how firms in China have been systematically politicized by the state and government officials to provide political services, and these political services often put private firms at a disadvantage to SOEs. I reveal two particular forms of political services provided by firms that have thus far remained under the radar: contributions to authoritarian officials' careers and assistance with societal control. When private firms refuse or fail to provide these services, state encroachment may follow. But before I elaborate on this mechanism, let me first introduce the research questions and the motivation for this book.

THE PUZZLE AND RESEARCH QUESTIONS

When and *where* does the state encroach into the private sector? And *why*? The encroachment behavior of various levels of Chinese

8 "Chongzu rigang buneng qiangmai qiangmai," *Zhonghua gongshang shibao*, 2009-08-07, https://finance.sina.cn/sa/2009-08-07/detail-ikkntiam4397474.d.html?from=wap.

9 "Dongxing hangkong zuo bei tingfei gaoguan cheng zao yeman shougou," *Guangzhou Daily*, 2009-03-16, https://finance.sina.com.cn/chanjing/b/20090316/07595979647.shtml; "Wuhanshi chuli dongxing tingfei shiyi, zhonghang fouren qiangzhi shougou," *Securities Daily*, 2009-03-17, https://business.sohu.com/20090317/n262841630.shtml; and "Dongxing hangkong pochan," *Sina News*, https://finance.sina.com.cn/focus/eaststar_tf/index.shtml.

government across different sectors and localities presents two puzzles. First, it goes against the central state's stated policy goals since 1993 that have been consistently pro-market. *Why* the inconsistency? Second, the existing literature cannot fully explain the pattern as to *when* and *where* state encroachment happens. What can China tell us about the rationale of state encroachment on the private sector?

The first puzzle is an empirical one, embedded in the contradiction between the Chinese state's behavior and its own mantra of promoting the private economy. Xi Jinping has openly stressed the CCP's continuing strong support for market liberalization and private entrepreneurs every year since 2013, promising to further expand the private sector.[10] Even among the most recent waves of high-profile state encroachment, the Chinese state has continued to stress its support for private firms. In his 2022 Party Congress speech, which was intended to set the tone for China's trajectory, Xi Jinping said, "China will unwaveringly encourage, support, and guide the private economy, and let the market play a decisive role in resource allocation."[11] In 2020, the central government vowed to level the uneven playing field between private firms and SOEs and improve competition law.[12] In 2013, the CCP published a decision to deepen economic reform, detailing sixty specific reforms to further promote the market economy and the private sector, and to reduce the role of government in the economy.[13] Numerous laws and policies have since been passed to reduce administrative burdens for companies, reduce taxes and fees, protect intellectual property, increase private companies' access to credit, and simplify procedures for companies to get listed on stock markets.[14] These policies are very much in line with the CCP's

[10] For example, "Xi Jinping de gaige zuji – xinshidai zaichufa!," *China Media Group*, 2018-12-15, https://news.cctv.com/2018/12/15/ARTIUltBoC69BzK2N8x7qUye181215.shtml.

[11] "Xi Jinping: Opening Speech at the 20th Party Congress in China," *Xinhua News*, www.news.cn/politics/cpc20/zb/xhwkmh1016/wzsl.htm.

[12] "Zaici jujiao minying jingji, zhongyang pinfan fasheng youhe shenyi," the State Council, 2020-09-18, www.gov.cn/zhengce/2020-09/18/content_5544516.htm; and "Niandi qian shixian gongping jingzheng shencha zhidu zai guojia, sheng, shi, xian sijizhengfu quan fugai," *People's Daily*, 2019-04-03, www.gov.cn/zhengce/2019-04/03/content_5379226.htm.

[13] "Zhonggong zhongyang guanyu quanmian shenhua gaige ruogan zhongda wenti de jueding," *Xinhua News*, 2013-11-15, www.gov.cn/jrzg/2013-11/15/content_2528179.htm.

[14] For example, "Zhonggong zhongyang guowuyuan guanyu yingzao genghao fazhan huanjing zhichi minying qiye gaige fazhan de yijian," the State Council, 2019-12-22, www.gov.cn/zhengce/2019-12/22/content_5463137.htm; "Foreign Investment Law of the People's Republic of China," adopted at the second session of the Thirteenth

official stance toward private entrepreneurs since 1993. The CCP even granted private entrepreneurs political legitimacy in 2002 by accepting them into the Party; they then became one of the fastest growing groups among CCP members.[15]

All in all, the Chinese state has not formally moved away from its commitment in the constitution to "build a socialist market economy," a goal in place since 1978. There is a scholarly consensus that the Chinese state has partially but substantially tied its own hands and made credible commitments to the private sector, and Chinese officials are believed to respect quid-pro-quo relationships, which reduces the risk of government expropriation and creates a market environment conducive to investment.[16] These policies allowed private firms to be the main pillar of China's economy and an important source of performance legitimacy for the CCP. In 2022, private firms accounted for over 90 percent of all firms in China, over 90 percent of urban employment, over 80 percent of total employment, over 80 percent of exports, over 60 percent of gross domestic product, and over 50 percent of tax revenues.[17]

For an authoritarian state that had been touting market reform as one of its greatest achievements, the CCP presumably does not want to risk stifling its private sector. But then what explains the sporadic state advances that break from the state's own commitment to the private sector and a market economy?

The second puzzle is one regarding the incompatibility between the pattern of state encroachment in China and existing academic explanations for state encroachment. When it comes to reasons for state intrusion on the private sector, the political science and economics literature

National People's Congress, 2019-03-15, www.gov.cn/zhengce/content/2019-12/31/content_5465449.htm; "Xuejian 1/3 shenpi shixiang mubiao yiwancheng," 2014-12-13, www.gov.cn/zhengce/2014-12/13/content_2790388.htm; and "Guowuyuan guanyu yinfa 2016 nian tuijin jianzheng fangquan fangguan jiehe youhua fuwu gaige gongzuo de tongzhi," the State Council, 2016-05-24, www.gov.cn/zhengce/content/2016-05/24/content_5076241.htm.

15 The number of private entrepreneurs who are CCP members increased from 590,000 in 2012 to 1.65 million in 2020, representing an increase of 250 percent: www.xinhuanet.com/politics/2020-11/10/c_1126691339.htm.

16 See, for example, Nee 1992; Yang 2004; Wang 2015; Ang 2020.

17 "Xi Jinping: zai minying qiye zuotanhui shang de jianghua," Organization Department of the Chinese Communist Party, 2018-11-01, www.12371.cn/2018/11/01/ARTI1541079015074692.shtml; "Woguo gelei shichang zhuti huoli jingxiang bengfa," *China Economic Network*, 2022-02-02, https://k.sina.cn/article_7517400647_1c0126e4705902n9ja.html?from=news; and "Woguo minying qiye shuliang shi nian fan liangfan," *People's Daily*, 2022-03-23, www.gov.cn/xinwen/2022-03/23/content_5680738.htm.

offers four groups of explanations: national security, economic predation, political gain, and the difficulty of writing complete contracts.

National security is often cited as a reason for nationalization of strategic sectors that are at risk of foreign dependency, such as railways, oil, banking, and telecommunications (Shafer 1983; Kobrin 1984). Keeping the control of these sectors in a national government's hands reduces dependency on, and the risk of expropriation by, foreign governments. Economic predation is a second reason for state intrusion. A sector that harbors valuable assets or can generate large cash flow could fall prey to a predatory state and experience state takeover, especially when product prices rise in these sectors. This is often seen in oil, mining, and other resource extraction sectors (Shleifer and Vishny 2002; Guriev, Kolotilin, and Sonin 2011). Third, the decision to nationalize could be triggered by politicians' desire for political gains. Since public ownership tends to employ more workers, a politician could nationalize a sector and increase its employment size to gain support from the labor union or to attract voters (Hart, Shleifer, and Vishny 1997). Similarly, when a dictator feels insecure about their rule, they could nationalize resource extractive sectors to distribute the windfall for political support (Mahdavi 2020). Lastly, the state might have incentives to intrude and take over a sector where the state lacks the ability to create a complete contract with private companies, particularly in monopolistic public service sectors. In these sectors, the private providers could exploit the incomplete contract through the bargaining power they amass from their monopoly status, creating various problems such as de facto soft budget constraint problems, lack of innovation, high product prices, and insufficient supply of services or goods (Hart and Moore 1990; Holmstrom and Milgrom 1991; Vickers and Yarrow 1991; Hart 1995, 2003; Ohemeng and Grant 2008). The state might then resort to nationalization to solve these problems.

Within the Chinese context, a few more China-specific explanations of the outsized role of the state in the economy are relevant to understand state encroachment. One centers around interest groups. Some scholars suggest that the legacy institutions of socialism that support China's SOEs, such as the State-Owned Assets Supervision and Administration Commission of the State Council, led to the growing power of central SOEs and their expansion in the market (Nolan 2001; Naughton 2008). The other explanation centers around the model of state capitalism, which is akin to the concept of the developmental state (Wade 1990; Evans 1995). State capitalism sees the state's role to be directing industrial development and increasing global competitiveness, and the state might expand into sectors that can help the state reach these goals. Lastly, and more recently, scholars have started to discuss the role of economic nationalism and domestic security in the Chinese state's expansion into the market. The Chinese state might be expanding into certain sensitive sectors to both reduce the power of a rapidly rising private sector, such as in the airline industry, and to protect sensitive sectors from foreign competition, such as in the telecommunications sector (Eaton 2015). And the CCP is increasingly emboldened in controlling private sectors crucial to domestic security, including social media and technology companies (Pearson, Rithmire, and Tsai 2021).

Together, this existing scholarship offers credible explanations for the Chinese state's encroachment into certain sectors. Economic predation could be an incentive for the Chinese state to encroach into real estate, gas stations, and finance sectors – sectors that generate high profit margins. The Chinese state might also want to control private firms in sectors of strategic importance to China's national security, which could explain the merger and acquisition of private companies in the rare earth sector, a product key to many strategic manufacturing sectors, including defense, green energy, and technology; or the seed industry, which matters for food security in China. The Chinese state is also increasingly worried about domestic security and stability, and therefore has become more intrusive in the business operations of social media and technology companies. Finally, in a new industry where a few dominant companies could form a cartel, such as in the ride share app sector, the Chinese government might find it difficult to write complete contracts with those companies that act like a monopolist, and that could be why the state forced shareholder sales of these companies to SOEs to increase state control. In general, for sectors that hold significant political and economic importance for the state, and sectors that could present serious challenges for the state to manage and to regulate, existing scholarship offers compelling explanations for state encroachment into these sectors.

But existing explanations do not fully explain state encroachment into many other sectors that do not possess strategic importance, and they do not fully explain local variations in state encroachment within each sector. For example, why do China's local governments want to encroach into paper manufacturing, city gas supply, urban buses, and other businesses that lack geopolitical or domestic security significance, are not pivotal to China's global strategy, are not monopolistic, do not appear to suffer from more regulatory failures than other sectors, and yield only slim profit margins? Moreover, how do we explain the local variations of state encroachment into the same sector? For example, why do some local governments shut down private paper manufacturing factories or take over hog farms and urban buses, while others do not?

Leveraging variations in state encroachment across sectors and localities, this book explains state encroachment with the hidden political roles of firms in China. Drawing on some of the most mundane sectors, such as urban buses and solid waste treatment, as well as variations in state encroachment in these two sectors across localities, I show how firms in China have been systematically politicized by the state and government officials to provide political services, not just to the Party-state as a whole but also to individual politicians. This book reveals two particular political services provided by firms: contributions to officials' careers through *visibility projects*; and acting as a supplement to the state in direct *societal control* beyond surveillance and monitoring of the public.

The outcome of politicizing firms is a deepened preference for SOEs by the Chinese government. A hidden arena for firm competition, these political services imposed on firms further separate private firms and SOEs by political competitiveness. In any sector with both private firms and SOEs present, private firms fall behind SOEs on provision of most types of political services, particularly in the long term. When politicians need political services, this lack of political competitiveness, while not necessarily lacking economic or technological competitiveness, is an important reason for private firms to lose favor with the state.

This book further explains the political origin of the politicization of firms. The first service, visibility projects, stems from the incentive structure that the Party-state uses to keep its government officials in line. The second service, societal control, stems from the need to keep societal grievances under control. Fundamentally, politicization of firms is the result of two key imperatives for the authoritarian Party-state: the constant tradeoff it must make between encouraging private investment and preventing organized opposition of private entrepreneurs; and the constant struggle of an authoritarian state to select government officials who are both loyal and competent. The first imperative creates the conditions for politicization of firms, and the second imperative creates incentives for government officials to use firms for risky and unpopular projects and policies. These institutional roots of firms' political roles exemplify the difficulties of the Chinese state in juggling between the goals of maintaining authoritarian rule, attracting and retaining private investments for a market economy, and pursuing sustainable development.

THE POLITICAL SERVICES DEMANDED OF FIRMS BY AUTHORITARIAN OFFICIALS

Firms engage not only in production and transactions but also in other economic and political activities to stay in business and to generate profits. Through these activities, all firms, intentionally and unintentionally, voluntarily and involuntarily, create potential economic and political benefits for both the state as a whole and state officials as individuals (Table 1.1).

We are most familiar with the economic functions of firms. Firms directly benefit the state by creating growth, tax revenues, and employment. Firms can also directly benefit individual state agents, providing them and their family with rents and job opportunities. These economic functions of firms are universal across firm types and regime types, and they can create indirect political impacts. For example, a strong economic growth record is an important source of a government's performance legitimacy, and corruption almost always hurts legitimacy.[18]

What can firms provide to the state and politicians beyond the benefits listed here? When it comes to firms' direct political services to the state and its agents,[19] our best developed knowledge is on firms' policy impacts and, in electoral contexts, their political impact through campaign donations. Policy impacts can come from lobbying, consultation, and associational activities where firms use their information advantages to promote favorable industrial and regulatory policies. Campaign donations by firms are an important source for politicians' careers in electoral

TABLE 1.1 *Economic and political services of firms*

		Direct beneficiary	
		State officials	**State**
Firms as providers of:	Economic services	Rents and job opportunities	Growth, tax, and employment
	Political services	*Contributions to political career*	Information, policy input, policy feedback, and *societal control*

[18] See, for example, Rose-Ackerman and Palifka (2016) and Manion (2004).

[19] Another dimension of firms' roles in society is their social roles, such as impact on the environment, labor, welfare, and equity.

contexts, and they also have indirect effects on policymaking.[20] In nonelectoral contexts, lobbying and associational activities also exist but to a lesser extent, depending on the regime's receptiveness to business and tolerance for organizational activities (Frye 2002; Kennedy 2009). But beyond these better-known phenomena, in authoritarian states, firms provide two more political services that are understudied so far: contributions to state agents' political career through *visibility projects*, which are an element of *selectoral campaigns*; and supplements to state functions of *societal control* by being the state's allies or scapegoats.

Selectoral Campaigns and Visibility Projects

Firms directly contribute to the political career of authoritarian officials. Authoritarian officials routinely launch what I call *selectoral campaigns* to promote themselves to their superiors. Selectoral campaigns, a group of strategies to promote oneself in a nonelectoral context, serve as an informal supplement to the formal government personnel system that selects politicians and bureaucrats. One better known form of selectoral campaigns is office buying, often with firm contributions. In publicized corruption cases in China, firms, particularly private firms, were found to supply the money that government officials used to bribe for promotion.[21] Another form of selectoral campaign is media campaigns, where officials sing the praises of their superiors or talk about their own achievements on TV and other media outlets (Shih 2008; Zhu and Wang 2013). In this book, I introduce another way for firms to contribute to selectoral campaigns: *visibility projects*, a safer, legal, inconspicuous, and therefore more common albeit more costly approach for authoritarian officials to promote themselves.

Visibility projects are projects launched to showcase competence and improve the career prospects of government officials. They include highly visible infrastructure, public projects, and government activities that can be readily noticed by higher-up government leaders. Examples include building industrial parks, malls, bridges, and other "signature" infrastructure projects; hosting sports events and government galas; and winning national titles such as "the cleanest city in China." For visibility

[20] For example, Powell (2012).

[21] "Maiguan Maiguan Qianguize," *Xinhua News*, 2014-11-17, http://finance.china.com.cn/roll/20141117/2792897.shtml; and "Zhaidiao minqi zanzhu de guanmao haiyao zhuihui liyi," *Hunan Rednet*, 2014-11-18, http://news.sina.com.cn/o/2014-11-18/000831159272.shtml.

projects, form dictates function. The purpose of visibility projects is to showcase one's governing capability to the higher political echelons to improve one's chance of promotion, and therefore these projects must be noticeable and are often large in scale. These concepts are defined and developed in more detail in Chapter 2.

Societal Control: Allies and Scapegoats of the State

The second political service that firms directly provide is to supplement state functions of societal control. Firms either become an ally of or a scapegoat for the state in performing this function. As an ally, firms can supplement government functions where the state lacks capacity, such as providing surveillance for the state, and help the state appease or suppress the public during state–society conflicts. As a scapegoat, firms can take on the full responsibility for a failed policy, project, or event to help the state and state agents deflect blame. This political service directly benefits the state but also indirectly benefits government officials, agents of the state.

This political service by firms is particularly difficult to observe, and we only occasionally get a glimpse of it at the national level. During the Suharto era, two of Indonesia's richest businessmen and allies of Suharto, Liong and Hasan, donated to Suharto's private foundations that launched police and military operations to suppress his political opponents and the public (King 2000). More recently, after the Russian occupation of Crimea, one of Putin's closest business allies, Arkady Rotenberg, built the Kerch Strait Bridge in 2015 that connected Russia to Crimea. The three billion dollar bridge symbolized Putin's rule and helped to solidify Russian control of the region. Out of concerns of fragile security and the dim prospect of profitability from this bridge (which was bombed during the Russian invasion of Ukraine in 2022), few other businesses were willing to invest, leaving Rotenberg alone to build it.[22]

In China, providing this political service has been a common but rarely documented role of firms. It is now widely known that social media and technology firms provide monitoring and surveillance of the society for the Chinese state (King, Pan, and Roberts 2013; Huang and Tsai 2022). But that is not the only way for firms to participate in societal control. Firms can be allies of the state by providing "hush money" and

[22] "Putin's Shadow Cabinet and the Bridge to Crimea," *The New Yorker*, 2022-05-09, www.newyorker.com/magazine/2017/05/29/putins-shadow-cabinet-and-the-bridge-to-crimea.

employment opportunities to protesters, or even directly participating in suppression, either by providing manpower or by bringing in political support to legitimize local government suppression. And firms sometimes serve as scapegoats, shouldering blame for failed policies or projects in the place of the state. These functions are further elucidated in Chapter 3.

These two direct political roles of firms, providing contributions to visibility projects and supplements to the state for societal control, are often dormant. They become activated when a sector or a firm is designated by government officials to provide political services. Firms can take up these political roles voluntarily or involuntarily, and intentionally or unintentionally. But once these political roles of firms are activated, state–business relations start to change. Such change can be good news for firms, but it frequently is not.

WHY DO OFFICIALS NEED THESE POLITICAL SERVICES, AND WHY ASK FIRMS?

As in all countries, there is no shortage of ambitious politicians and bureaucrats in China. In an authoritarian Party-state, power is not only an end but also a means to share the resources controlled by the state. To climb up the political ladder, Chinese officials must outcompete each other on loyalty and competence. But they also need to be careful to not fall off the political ladder, meaning they must avoid grave political mistakes. That is, they must engage in both credit-claiming and blame-avoidance.[23] Unlike in systems of open electoral competition, Chinese officials are subject to evaluation not by the public, but by their political superiors and the "scorecards" in China's personnel evaluation system. Operationally, this would mean any ambitious Chinese official needs to excel in a set of formal evaluations designed by the CCP, and they must avoid stepping over the Party's red lines, including losing control of the mass public and appearing defiant by making policies or conducting local governance differently from the CCP's guidance.

These conditions for career advancement are tricky to grasp for a Chinese official. While the formal evaluations seem clear and transparent, Chinese officials are disillusioned with the effectiveness of the system. They find that excelling at formal evaluations is at best a prerequisite

[23] "Blame avoidance" is a key incentive for politicians in making policy decisions. This concept is developed by Kent Weaver (1986), who observes that politicians are primarily driven by blame avoidance for unpopular actions rather than claiming credit for popular ones. See also Hood (2010).

for promotion. The quantitative evaluations that assess the competence of a government official in delivering policy outcomes, designed to select the most competent, suffer from rigidity, gaming behavior, and under-the-table negotiations that allow too many officials to get good evaluations (Gao 2015; Leng and Zuo 2021). Doing well in this system will grant a pass, but not an A on one's report card.

Realizing that simply doing well in the formal evaluation does not guarantee promotion, ambitious Chinese officials seek to stand out in other ways. It is with this incentive that they have developed selectoral campaigns – visibility projects, media exposure, and office buying. Like high schoolers eyeing Ivy League universities, doing well on the SAT and having a good grade point average – quantitative evaluations – are considered just a minimum threshold; they also endeavor to show "extracurricular" achievements akin to selectoral campaigns, including sports and community services, in their application to improve their prospects for admission. Within the Chinese state, officials similarly create selectoral campaigns to supplement their formal evaluations for a better chance to stand out in the cut-throat competition for promotion in the Party-state.

The high costs of selectoral campaigns give rise to the demand for firm contributions. Visibility projects, a major type of selectoral campaign, can be very expensive. Many involve excessive investment in large infrastructure, projects, or events, which often incurs financial losses and is not sustainable. Because the whole point of visibility projects is to go beyond the top-down requirements and to get extra credit, it is hard to justify paying for these projects within government budgets. Always trying to avoid blame for imprudent spending, government officials find it safer to have firms cover the costs. This combination of officials' incentives to balance credit claiming and blame avoidance creates the first political role of firms – contributions to authoritarian officials' selectoral campaigns and visibility projects that will aid their political career. This mechanism is discussed in detail in Chapter 2.

The demand for the second political service, supplementing state capacity for societal control, has a more direct political logic: blame deflection. When controversies and public opposition arise in relation to government policies and projects, it is in the government officials' interests to distance themselves from the policies and projects to avoid blame from both the public and their superiors. It is also in the officials' interests to avoid dealing with the public directly to reduce political ramifications. These blame avoidance incentives lead to the incentive of blame deflection, with firms that carry out the controversial or failed projects being blamed rather than the state itself. Firms become the natural choice to take on blame and to exercise part of the societal control function, either appeasement or coercion, so that the legitimacy of the state is preserved and local officials are not blamed for social disturbances by the Party.

HOW DO FIRMS PERCEIVE POLITICAL SERVICES? REGULATION VERSUS BRIBE

Firms, both SOEs and private firms, often comply with political service provision to maintain a good relationship with state officials, as they have strong incentives to stay in the good graces of the Party-state. But compliance is often reluctant. Providing political services to an authoritarian state is a risky and inefficient way for firms to benefit themselves. Unlike other corporate political activities such as lobbying, network building, or bribery, providing direct political services – contributions to officials' career and supplements to societal control – has a distinctive feature: Firms do not have full control over the *costs* of these political services.

Firms do not have full control over the costs because firms do not have full control over almost all aspects of political services – the timing, the scope, and even the type of political services are dictated by government officials. Sometimes, firms do not even have a choice over whom the political services are benefiting. Compare political services with lobbying, for example. Firms have control over when to lobby – crucial moments in legislation; and whom to lobby – key politicians in the legislative process. Compare political services with bribery, and firms still have more control over when to bribe – at the time of tendering or licensing; the target of bribery – specific government officials that matter for sealing the deal; and how much to pay – based on the "going rate" and negotiations. But when it comes to political services, firms might not have options over any of these aspects. In the end, political services cater not to business interests, but to politicians' incentives, which are shaped by China's political institutions. This is a key difference between political services and other corporate political activities.

Consider this tricky scenario I observed in one Chinese city. A top city leader asked a local wastewater treatment company to build a "museum of water." This museum was not going to be profitable for the company, but it would showcase the city leader's dedication to water quality and public education, both considered important by the CCP. Should the company build the museum? How can the company recoup the costs? Can the company be sure that it will be rewarded with other government contracts or subsidies, as was implied by the city leader? What if this leader is reposted before the firm can get any returns? But then if the company refuses to build this museum, will there be coercion or retribution from the city leader? Knowing their business success depends on the state, can the company say no? There is no clear answer to any of these questions, rendering the situation more like a high-risk gamble than a low-risk investment for the firm.

In certain situations, firms do get payoffs for their political services. This can be seen in several publicized corruption cases of Chinese politicians, including the former vice Party secretary of Sichuan province, Chuncheng Li; and the former Party secretary of Lüliang city, Chunyu Nie. In Nie's case, he asked an entrepreneur to cover the costs of bribes to upper-level officials for office buying. Owing to the secrecy of the matter, Nie only asked one entrepreneur, his longtime business ally. In return, Nie provided various government support to this entrepreneur's business. Even though the entrepreneur could not set the price for office buying, which is dictated by the market for government positions, the entrepreneur happily obliged because he (correctly) expected returns for his contributions, including purchasing a small state-owned coal mine priced below market value and getting preferential loans from state-owned banks.[24]

In former Sichuan Vice Party Secretary Li's case, one real estate developer benefited from contributing to Li's loss-incurring visibility project, the New Century Global Center in the provincial capital of Chengdu. Opened in 2013, the Global Center is the largest single-building by floor space in the world; it incorporates shopping, entertainment, hotels, and conference centers. According to my interviews with officials in Chengdu who participated in the project,[25] the Global Center was meant to showcase Li's ability to introduce consumption-driven economic growth, a model advocated by Beijing. The Global Center was estimated to be loss-incurring owing to its location and enormous size, and the Chengdu city government could not afford building it with an estimated government debt level at over 100 percent of the budget.[26] Li turned to one of his

[24] An example of a private entrepreneur paying for a city mayor's office buying can be seen here: "Nie Chunyu zhuzheng xia de Lvliang: meilaoban chuqian maiguan guanyuan bangmang pingshi," *Beijing News*, 2014-11-09, http://politics.people.com.cn/n/2014/0901/c1001-25575863.html.

[25] Interview 20151022a, b, c.

[26] "Zhaiwulv chao 100% de jiuge shenghui chengshi hui shi shei?," *Reuters*, 2013-07-29, www.reuters.com/article/idUSL4S0G00SG/.

closest business allies. The businessman agreed to build the Center but proposed a smaller scale to limit loss. Li vetoed the idea, but to coax this reluctant businessman into a loss-incurring project, he promised a separate land development deal elsewhere, and the businessman agreed.[27]

In these two cases, political contributions from firms are similar to a *bribe* in nature, where the firms could differentiate themselves from other firms in providing a unique political service and thereafter claim credit for this service. Therefore, the firm agreed to the demanded contributions. But when the political services in question are closer to *regulations* in nature, meaning that firms cannot differentiate themselves from other firms in providing these political services, because every firm has been providing them, they are less likely to welcome these political services and would only agree to provide these services out of concern for political retribution and coercion.

Take one visibility project I observed as an example. A city leader decided to "build a verdant city," a response to the central government's call for environmental protection. The city leader insisted on turning the city "green" within three months, with part of the plan being to install green walls (also called vertical gardens) on the outer walls of major buildings in a busy tourism area. Seeing as this was a very expensive project, the city government "invited" all the relevant buildings' owners and business occupants to "voluntarily" pay for the green walls. Business owners were reluctant because it was unclear how they could recoup the costs. Having a green wall would not necessarily attract more customers, and more importantly, because all businesses in the area were asked to participate, no business could stand out as the hero in realizing the leader's vision and get preferential treatment. Quite the opposite: Any business objecting to this plan would stand out as obstructing the leader's vision and might invite retribution such as tax audits and unannounced health and safety inspections. All businesses eventually contributed, and green walls were installed. This project was quickly abandoned a few months later when the top leader was promoted and

[27] This information comes from both my interviews and is corroborated with news articles. See "Li Chuncheng liyi shusong duoshe tudi xiangmu," *Beijing News*, 2014-05-08, http://epaper.bjnews.com.cn/html/2014-05/08/content_510592.htm?div=0; "Corruption and the World's Biggest Building," *The Telegraph*, 2013-09-13, www.telegraph.co.uk/news/worldnews/asia/china/10308029/Corruption-and-the-worlds-biggest-building.html; and "Amid Probe, Chinese Moguls Vanish," *Wall Street Journal*, 2013-09-26, www.wsj.com/articles/SB10001424052702303983904579092990279667928.

moved to another city. Not making any extra income from these green walls, the businesses had no incentive to keep up with the expensive maintenance and the walls died.

Another example is the societal control services demanded of internet firms in China. In 2010, an official Google announcement revealed that Google China had been censoring search results for the Chinese government since it entered the Chinese market.[28] This is essentially a societal control service Google provided as the Chinese state's ally. The censorship service was requested by the Chinese state of all internet companies, and it did not bring Google extra benefits. Instead, it increased the costs for Google to operate in China. Providing this service led to reputational losses and potential legal consequences outside China for Google. It was accused of "sickening collaboration" with the Chinese state in a US congressional hearing and was criticized by numerous American news media and nongovernmental organizations (NGOs).[29] Google was probably also vulnerable to the EU Data Protection Directive, predecessor of the General Data Protection Regulation. This law would later become the strictest privacy and security law in the world, imposing fines on companies operating in Europe for any breaches of privacy and security, regardless of where they occur in the world. When providing this political service for China, Google had little ability to negotiate the terms of censorship, as it constitutes one of the foundational pillars of the CCP's rule. Google also could not secure additional benefits over other internet companies, as this political service is mandated for all tech companies.

Therefore, this political service is in nature closer to *regulation* of the firm rather than a *bribe* from the firm. Google cannot differentiate itself from other internet companies by providing this political service because every internet company must provide it, and this makes it difficult for Google to negotiate with the state for compensation for providing this service. Years after entering China, Google still had only around 30 percent of the search engine market share in 2010, far behind the largest domestic company, Baidu, which controlled almost 70 percent of the

[28] "A New Approach to China," Google Official Blog, 2010-01-12, https://googleblog.blogspot.com/2010/01/new-approach-to-china.html.

[29] In terms of reputational costs, Google was criticized by NGOs and media all over the world. See, for example, "Google to End Censorship in China over Cyber Attacks," *The Guardian*, 2010-01-12, www.theguardian.com/technology/2010/jan/12/google-china-ends-censorship.

market.[30] This political service of being the state's ally did not yield additional business returns, and so when the associated costs became too high and led to reputational loss and increased risks of losing other markets, Google exited China.

Providing political services, therefore, is not the most efficient means for firms to gain favor from China's politicians. If the political services demanded are in nature closer to a bribe, meaning firms can differentiate themselves in claiming credit from these political services, then firms are more likely to comply to gain favor of the state or individual leaders. If the political services are in nature closer to regulations, meaning the firms cannot easily differentiate themselves from others by providing these services, then a firm's response would depend on the foreseeable costs of these political services. If the costs are bearable, then firms might agree to prevent government retribution. But when the costs become too high, many firms would not be able to afford the political services demanded of them. The nature of the political service demanded of a firm, and the ability of a firm to bear the costs of political services, are what eventually set firms apart in the eyes of the state. Some firms are better providers for certain political services, and this often correlates with the firm's ownership type.

POLITICAL SERVICES, THE HIDDEN UNEVEN PLAYING FIELD FOR PRIVATE AND STATE-OWNED FIRMS

Political service provision is a hidden battleground for firms in China, an authoritarian country. Firms not only compete over efficiency, market shares, and networks with political elites, but they also must compete on their capability to provide political services for the state and its agents. Facing the high uncertainty of returns over political service provision, firm competition comes down to two dimensions: budget constraints and political capital.

Budget constraints are particularly important for a firm's capacity to contribute to visibility projects. When it comes to budget constraints, on average, private firms lack the financial capacity to sustain expensive political services for an extended time. Unlike SOEs, private firms have hard budget constraints and they are profit driven. SOEs, on the other

[30] "Google Loses Chinese Market Share," *Wall Street Journal*, 2010-04-27, www.wsj.com/articles/SB10001424052748703465204575207833281993688.

hand, have relatively soft budget constraints.[31] Even though they are supposed to have a fixed budget in theory, loss-making SOEs often get bailed out by the government with subsidies, write-offs of bad loans owed to state-owned banks, and other financial instruments often not available to private firms. This means that SOEs depend much less on profits to stay in business compared with private firms. When political services require large investments that do not promise acceptable returns, private firms are more likely to refuse to provide these services than SOEs, or they are more likely to fail at providing the demanded services if they cannot recoup the costs. This difference in budget constraints creates the first uneven playing field between SOEs and private firms in political service provision. Private firms' refusal or failure to shoulder the high costs of political services is an important reason for a sector to experience the exit of private firms, sometimes voluntarily, and at other times owing to state coercion.

Political capital is another important dimension for firm competition, and this is particularly important when exercising societal control for the state. Like the concept of social capital, which refers to capital gained from social networks (Coleman 1988; Putnam 2000), political capital is often understood as capital gained from relational ties with politicians. In the literature, a firm's political capital is often operationalized with the firm owner's political positions, the number of board members, shareholders, and top officers with a political background, or a firm's expenditure on government relations. This literature has focused on how political capital matters to companies and has produced a rich body of works. In general, companies that have more political connections tend to have higher company values on the stock market or revenue across different political contexts (e.g. Fisman 2001; Faccio 2006; Goldman, Rocholl, and So 2009; Kostovetsky 2015; Szakonyi 2018) and are more likely to obtain bank loans and have higher leverage (Li et al. 2008; Firth et al. 2009). However, they also suffer from a weakness that comes from dependency on political connections: Once the politicians that lend political capital to these firms lose power, these firms are more likely to experience a sharper drop in their value and profitability compared with firms with fewer political connections (Fisman 2001; Faccio 2010). After all, a

[31] Kornai (1979) developed the concept of soft budget constraints by observing SOEs in Hungary. Kornai, Maskin, and Gerard (2003) provide a comprehensive review on the development of this concept, its historical contexts, and enabling conditions.

state–business relationship built on individual ties is precarious and is more likely to collapse (Rithmire 2023).

The stability and reliability of political connections, therefore, is key to any company's political capital, and this is exactly where an SOE's political capital fundamentally differs from that of private firms, even if an SOE has an equal number of connections with politicians as a private company has, based on these commonly used measures of political capital. In most sectors, private firms' political capital comes from a selected set of individual politicians that the firm owner is able to cultivate. These ties are vulnerable to change in politics. Once the connected politicians lose power, private firms' political capital plummets. But SOEs, extensions of the state's economic function, have ties with not only a selected groups of individual state agents, but also with the state as a whole. In other words, SOEs are *always* connected to a set of politicians in power, and their political capital does not depend as much on specific politicians as is the case with private firms. SOEs' political capital, therefore, does not fluctuate nearly as much as that of private firms. This direct and more stable tie with the state is what differentiates SOEs from private firms in political capital.

This fundamental difference in the nature and stability of political capital between SOEs and private firms is what sets them apart in providing the political service of societal control in the eyes of the state. In general, government officials find it easier to "conscript" private firms for societal control functions unwelcome by the firms. Private firms, understanding their ability to do business depends on individual government officials, are more likely to comply with government officials' demands. In a local leader's own words, "private firms are the most motivated to work with us [local government officials]. It's not that SOEs won't work with us, but we find them difficult to deal with. They [SOE managers] are like government officials."[32] Another local official made a similar comparison, noting that "private firms are easy to work with. SOEs are so bossy, so bureaucratic ... we need to negotiate with them on every decision, and every decision takes such a long time in their super bureaucratic structure. They are even more bureaucratic than us [the government]!"[33]

But this does not mean private firms can outcompete SOEs in providing societal control functions. Rather, they each have their comparative advantages. It is easier for government officials to use private firms as scapegoats. Dependent on relations with government officials, private

32 Interview 2015102.

33 Interview 20151018.

firms are more likely to agree to shoulder blame for unpopular or failed projects and be publicly punished. But SOEs, particularly large SOEs, are better political allies when controversial projects invite large scale public opposition. If public opposition is high and requires suppression, SOEs can not only participate in suppression but also bring in extra political support to justify and support the decision of suppression. Depending on what government officials need from a firm, they would prefer firms of different ownership types.

All in all, when one observes a change in the landscape of firms in a sector, it is important to examine the political services demanded by the state in that sector. On average, private firms lag behind SOEs on financial capacity, and while they are better scapegoats, private firms are not better allies to the state. Depending on the costs and types of political services needed by the state and its agents, firms of different ownership types will be favored. State encroachment into a sector can happen when private firms fail at providing political services.

REVISITING CHINA'S MARKET REFORM: CONTAINING ECONOMIC PREDATION, BUT NOT POLITICAL PREDATION

Throughout China's market reform, economic actors never gained full autonomy from politics. Despite the progress in limited institutionalization, the Chinese state always reserves its ability to politicize economic actors, bestowing on them political roles and making them part of authoritarian politics.

Politicization of business, to borrow from Boycko, Shleifer and Vishny (1996), is to have businesses "pressured or bribed to bring their objectives in line with those of the politicians" (1996: 318). By showing how government officials demand political services from firms, and how these political services create an extra dimension of firm competition that often benefits SOEs rather than private firms, this book shows in detail how the politicization of firms distorts China's state–business relations and changes the landscape of firms in different sectors. In the process of market reform, the Chinese Party-state neither reduced the incentives of its officials to politicize firms, nor completely tied the officials' hands to prevent them from politicizing firms.

This is not to say that China did not curb state predation – it did curb economic predation to a certain degree. In the quest to answer why authoritarianism did not deter China's economic growth and investment attraction, scholars generally agree that a key factor is the Chinese state tying its own hands to limit economic predation, perhaps partly incentivized by an early form of public–private partnership, collectively owned enterprises, that gave Chinese officials a mindset of "corporatism" (Oi 1999). On the legal side, the Chinese state has launched several legal reforms since the 1980s. These include laws allowing private parties to sue government agencies (Pei 1997; Yang 2004). The state also institutionalized legal dispute resolution processes to restrict government officials from overtly distorting market outcomes or biasing them toward SOEs (Clarke, Murrell, and Whiting 2008). While China still does not have robust property rights institutions and faces challenges in enforcing contract law, competition law, labor law, and other laws governing the economic realm (Peerenboom 2002; Williams 2005; Du, Lu, and Tao 2015), it has nonetheless strengthened the legal aspects of transactions (Nee 1992; Zhang 2008), improved judicial fairness in the commercial realm (Wang 2015), regularized enforcement of laws and regulations in selected areas (Dimitrov 2016), and established a legal framework for labor without granting extensive labor rights (Gallagher 2011). Many argue that even though China does not have rule *of* law, it nonetheless has rule *by* law (Lubman 1999; Peerenboom 2002; Clarke 2003).

The Chinese state has also tied its hands on the administrative side to some degree. For instance, China reined in the discretionary tax authority of local governments (Naughton 2008). A centralized regulatory bureaucracy has been created to prevent local protectionism and to standardize policy enforcement with partial success (Mertha 2005). The capacity of Chinese regulatory agencies has increased as well, though they remain weak and not independent (Pearson 2005; Yasuda 2017). While China has never fully curbed corruption, and some argue that corruption is part of the system (Pei 2016), the state did launch anti-corruption campaigns that kept corruption from spiraling out of control (Wedeman 2012; Manion 2016). This has been particularly notable in mitigating low-level corruption, though not high-level corruption (Wedeman 2005). Some argue that the dominant type of corruption in China today is high-level corruption, which, although not ideal, may have a stimulating effect on investment (Ang 2020). These administrative reforms, along with the legal reforms, enabled China to attract robust investment without undertaking political reforms.

But these same measures are less effective at containing the politicization of economic actors. For one thing, these measures to tie the government's hands are only partial efforts rather than complete institutionalization, which requires political reform that some convincingly argue is extremely difficult to achieve (Fewsmith 2013). As previously outlined, much of this scholarship, while acknowledging the Chinese state's efforts to improve property rights protection, also notes the limits of these reforms. This partial nature of China's economic reform is particularly salient when taking on a sectoral perspective. Examining deregulation patterns in China, for example, Hsueh (2011) points out that China was never fully committed to pursuing a sweeping liberal market reform. In sectors that concern national interests such as telecommunications, the Chinese state would reintroduce sectoral regulations after pursuing macro-level deregulation in compliance with the World Trade Organization. Similarly, by studying the information technology sector, Fuller (2016) observes that, unlike Japan or Korea, China can only be best described as having improved, but never fully developed, the market institutions necessary for technological innovation. Examining China's financial sector, Shih (2007) reaches similar conclusions – that the market reform in this sector is only partial, with the state retaining control over it.

Therefore, China has surely increased predictability and security for firms by building up "intermediate institutions" (Rodrik 2000), just as China for a period of time increased predictability and security in politics with partial political reforms (Nathan 2003). However, these substitutions for market-supporting institutions are not fully credible commitments, much like China's limited political reforms (Fewsmith and Nathan 2019). They leave room for government intervention in the economy, which allows politicization of business to happen.

And politicization of business does happen, because the incentives of the Chinese government officials to politicize firms are rooted in two authoritarian logics essential for the survival of the Party-state that outweigh economic growth: the Party-state's needs for loyalty from its government officials, and its needs for controlling the society without undermining its legitimacy.

The first authoritarian logic, to make sure government officials are loyal, is translated into a top-down personnel system that controls all government officials in China and attempts to strike a balance between loyalty and competence in selecting officials. This system, with its pros and cons, motivates government officials to use firms when they adopt unconventional political strategies to advance their careers. This mechanism is explained in detail in Chapter 2. The second authoritarian logic, to mitigate significant grievances from its citizens without sabotaging legitimacy, motivates the Party-state to use third parties such as firms for societal control. This mechanism is explained in Chapter 3. The incentives to politicize firms are thus present as long as these authoritarian logics are in place, and these authoritarian logics carry a higher degree of importance to the CCP's survival than that of economic growth. Therefore, the incentives to politicize firms are not bounded by, and cannot be weakened by the aforementioned state efforts to curb economic predation by state officials.

The Party-state even provides direct justification to politicize firms for its government officials. The CCP's official documents on building a market economy contain statements such as "the private sector will continue to be the pillar of China's economy" and private entrepreneurs are "our [the Party's] own people."[34] But they also contain statements that the private sector needs to "be consistent with the Party" and be "politically sensible."[35] Both are sincere messages from the Party, stemming from the Party's fear that capitalists could become an organized opposition. And this fear has a history as long as China's economic reform since 1978.

In 1982, a mere four years after China's economic reform began, the CCP had its first crackdown on the private economy in the reform era. This was directed by Deng Xiaoping himself, the very person who initiated China's economic reform. Speaking at a meeting of the CCP Politburo on April 10 that year,[36] Deng cautioned that there was a risk of regime change resulting from rapidly growing capitalism in China. He demanded every provincial government to prosecute several large cases of economic offenses within two months. Deng's order started a wave of investigations into the economic crime of "speculation and profiteering."[37] Loosely defined in the 1979 Criminal Law, this offense encompasses any behavior that involves selling products for substantial profits that could potentially disrupt the market, with no specific criteria for what constitutes "substantial."

By the end of 1982, courts across China had investigated more than 164,000 cases of "speculation and profiteering," sentenced nearly 30,000 people, and confiscated over 320 million yuan.[38] This led to a heavy blow

34 "Guanyu jiaqiang xinshidai minying jingji tongzhan gongzuo de yijian," General Office of the Chinese Communist Party, 2020-09-15, www.gov.cn/zhengce/2020-09/15/content_5543685.htm.

35 Ibid.

36 "Deng Xiaoping: jianjue daji jingji fanzui huodong," Deng Xiaoping wenxuan dierjuan, 1982-04-10, www.reformdata.org/1982/0410/5291.shtml.

37 In Chinese, this offense is called "tou ji dao ba (投机倒把)."

38 "Zhongguo gongchandang dashiji (1982)," *Xinhua News*, 2006-06-26, https://news.sina.cn/sa/2006-06-26/detail-ikftssap2649518.d.html.

on China's economic growth. Take Wenzhou city in Zhejiang province, for example. Wenzhou is known as a cradle for entrepreneurship and, unrelatedly, Christian house churches. It made national headlines in this wave of crackdowns when the Wenzhou city government sentenced eight of its most successful private entrepreneurs to jail for "speculation and profiteering," spanning sectors from manufacturing screws to coils. The result was the retraction of the city's private firms and the city's industrial output dropping by 53 percent at the end of 1982.[39] Seeing this devastating effect on the economy, the CCP reversed course in 1984 and restarted encouraging private entrepreneurship, and the crime of "speculation and profiteering" was removed from China's 1988 Criminal Law.

After a few quiet years, in 1989, after Tiananmen, another wave of crackdowns on private sectors began. This wave of crackdowns began with the CCP's associating private entrepreneurs with the student protesters at Tiananmen. At a Party study session in December 1989 that was later published in *People's Daily*,[40] the then head of the CCP's Propaganda Department summarized the lessons of Tiananmen. Specifically, he stated that the financial backing for the student protesters originated from China's private entrepreneurs. Moreover, he asserted that these entrepreneurs, empowered by their newfound wealth, were actively seeking political agents in the government to participate in politics. This statement prompted local governments across China to engage in the politically motivated targeting of private entrepreneurs and scrutinizing of the tax records of private enterprises.

Consequently, between 1989 and 1992, a trend of nationalization of private firms emerged across the country. Some private firms voluntarily sought to change their ownership type by merging with SOEs, while others were subject to forced mergers and acquisitions, and some went so far as to "donate" their private companies to the state (Zhang 1993), which were then transformed into "Township and Village Enterprises," an early form of local public enterprise.[41] Some of China's most successful entrepreneurs explained the rationale of voluntary nationalization later in interviews. For instance, the founder of Geely Auto, one of China's largest car manufacturers in the 2020s, relinquished ownership of his

39 "Wenzhou 1982 nian zaoyu badawang shijian," *Changchengwang*, 2011-06-24, www.reformdata.org/2011/0624/15658.shtml.

40 "Wang Renzhi: guanyu fandui zichanjieji ziyouhua," *People's Daily*, 1990-02-22, www.reformdata.org/1990/0222/6145.shtml.

41 See Oi (1999) for a detailed account on these enterprises and how they contributed to China's economic growth.

then refrigerator company to a local government in 1989 owing to fears that he would be thrown into jail for being a successful capitalist.[42] The founder of New Hope Group, China's largest agricultural products company, also offered to surrender his enterprise to a local government in 1990 to avoid political troubles.[43] Likewise, the founder of China's largest cable company, Far East, was forced to relinquish the company to a local government in 1992.[44] In the second half of 1989 alone, the number of self-employed individuals and microenterprises decreased by 15 percent, and the number of private enterprises decreased by 50 percent nationwide.[45] Again, fearing these crackdowns were hurting the economy too much, Deng Xiaoping went on his famous 1992 southern tour to reverse course and reaffirm the CCP's commitment to economic reform and capitalism.[46]

This earlier history of the CCP's distrust in entrepreneurs set the tone for a partial reform that tries to strike a balance between attracting private investments and not empowering private entrepreneurs politically. And the CCP was probably right to think that private entrepreneurs could potentially challenge the regime. After all, the bourgeoisie or the middle class, many of whom were business owners, were considered a driving force behind democratization in many parts of the world (Lipset 1960; Moore 1966),[47] and so the CCP has always sought to keep China's rising entrepreneurs in line. Regarding this goal, the CCP has largely succeeded. Survey research throughout the years shows that private entrepreneurs in China do not generally demand democracy (Pearson 2000; Dickson 2003; Tsai 2007; Chen and Dickson 2010). This is probably

[42] "Qiche jie de nian yu: Li Shufu," *Workers' Daily*, 2008-12-16, www.chinanews.com.cn/auto/kong/news/2008/12-16/1489069.shtml.

[43] "Liu Yonghao: chuangye shengya zhong wuge jingxindongpo de gushi," *Zhongguo qiyejia wang*, 2013-12-17, https://finance.sina.com.cn/leadership/crz/20131217/075617655931.shtml.

[44] "Dianlan dawang Jiang Xipei: cong xiubiao jiang dao jituan zhuxi," *Zhongguo Cishanjia Zazhi*, 2018-03-05, https://finance.sina.cn/chanjing/gsxw/2018-03-05/detail-ifxipenm9276265.d.html?from=wap.

[45] Private enterprises are those employing more than eight people in 1989. Source of data: Dong (1999: 429–30).

[46] This back-and-forth reflects the uncertainty among Chinese elites regarding the direction of China's economic reforms. For those interested in seeing the debates among China's top political elites on economic reforms in the 1980s, see Fewsmith (2016).

[47] Modernization theory claims economic development will lead to democratization, largely as a result of a rising middle class that will demand political rights. This theory has been widely debated ever since: See, for example, Przeworski and Limongi (1997), which shows its limits, and Marsh (2014), which argues for its validity.

because many entrepreneurs perceive themselves as winners in China's partial reforms, and we know from the Soviet Union experience that winners of partial reforms often resist further, full liberal reforms to maintain their advantages in the existing system (Hellman 1998).

Therefore, the CCP will continue to, as stated in its documents, make sure entrepreneurs remain "politically sensible." This very incentive is what leaves open the possibility to politicize firms. In today's China, the CCP probably views private entrepreneurs as less of a threat to the regime than in the 1980s, but they continue to view private entrepreneurs as political servants to the Party-state. And thanks to a partial reform process that did not empower private entrepreneurs, the CCP is able to call for firms to provide political services when they see fit, because the firms are required to be "politically sensible." This creates conflicts between the state and firms, leading to oscillations in state–business relations that persist to this day.

But what is being "politically sensible"? What does it mean to the private sector? Is it regarding a firm's production? Investment? Competition? This vagueness around the Party's "bottom line" for private firms, intentional or not, deprives firms of full autonomy as economic actors. Such a statement leaves open the possibility for any government official to rein in firms in the name of political needs. Adding onto this justification handed over by the Party, the stealthy nature of political services makes it a relatively safe act for government officials. Compared with economic predation such as demanding bribes, it is more difficult to detect or convict politicization. Asking firms to provide political services does not often produce direct evidence against a government official individually, because political services, such as visibility projects or societal control, are easily framed as genuine efforts to carry out Party agendas and benefit society, and do not produce piles of cash or arms full of expensive wristwatches. When these favorable conditions for politicization of firms meet the incentives to demand political services from firms, we see firms turned into political actors by the state.

As a result, China's economic reform has focused on containing economic predation but not political predation. Politicization of firms is both of lesser concern to the CCP and a more challenging issue to tackle. The CCP certainly enjoys performance legitimacy from economic growth brought by firms, but it is also wary of potential organized opposition from the private sector. If the Party tells its officials to leave the private sector alone, how can it make sure the private sector stays only in the economic lane? But then how does the Party define the proper scope of monitoring and guidance of the firms to be in line with the Party, without overstepping into regular business operations? When asking an official in Beijing in 2015 whether the government might be concerned that using firms for political services, such as asking companies to contribute to the aforementioned green walls or to share customer data with the state, might go too far and deter future investments, he gave me the quote at the beginning of this chapter, from Party learning sessions: "The [Party's] teaching is clear. The economy is secondary to politics in this country. We'd give up economic growth without hesitation for political needs."[48]

The impossibility of defining the Party line in business operations therefore provides government officials political leeway when they use firms for political services, since most of these political services can be framed in the name of executing Party agendas. Consequently, despite all the institutional building efforts to tie the state's hands, the CCP has left open the possibility of politicization of firms. This facilitating condition, combined with the built-in incentives of Chinese officials to use firms for political goals, has created a market reform process in which the state has reduced its economic predation of the private sector but retained its power to politicize them.

The politicization of firms, as depicted in this book, thus extends our understanding of state–business relations in China in two ways. First, it shows the limits of firms' efforts to reduce political risks in an authoritarian environment. It is well documented that firms in China are adept at protecting and advancing their interests through engaging in corruption, building ties with important government figures, joining government bodies and representative institutions, and forming business alliances and coalitions (e.g. Dickson 2003; Tsai 2002; Kennedy 2009; Cai, Fang, and Xu 2011; Hou 2019; Dimitrov 2020). These measures, while indeed improving their business environment by compensating for weak market institutions, nonetheless fall short in protecting them from political predation in an authoritarian state. Political predation by the authoritarian state stems from the state's need to prevent regime change, a political logic of a higher order than to enhance regime legitimacy through economic growth. Therefore, all the political ties with the state accumulated by firms, regardless of their depth or extent, are not sufficient to shield them from political demands of the state.

[48] Interview 20150428.

The companies depicted in this book, whether private (including foreign) or state-owned, are sophisticated economic actors that understand how to operate in an environment lacking full protection of property rights. These firms have undertaken the necessary actions, some of which they are proud of and others less so, to establish a mutually beneficial relation with the Chinese state. They are not oblivious to the complicated environment they operate in, and they are skilled and seasoned economic actors that are often quite ready to work with an authoritarian state and its officials when such cooperation aligns with their business interests.

However, the demand by the state to provide political services is different from the average state–business exchange of interests. It is often when conscripted to provide political services that businesses realize the limits on their end to protect their business interests. Even the winners of China's partial reform who are adept at building ties with the state discovered the often unbearable costs associated with political demands by the state. And the high costs associated with providing political services is what often puts private companies at a disadvantage compared to SOEs in a sector with both types of ownerships, and which may lead to their exit from a sector, sometimes voluntarily, other times not.

Second, this book reminds us that *all* sectors, including the most mundane, can be politicized by the state. If we only focus on the central government of China, then it would seem as if the Chinese state tends to exert statist control over highly profitable sectors for economic predation, or strategic sectors for developmental purposes or out of national and domestic security concerns. But sectors of less strategic importance could still have political value to the state. This book, through studying some of the most mundane sectors, such as urban buses and waste treatment, shows how the political values of a sector are separate from its strategic values. Firms are beyond economic actors in the eyes of the authoritarian state. They are considered an integral part of the Chinese political system, and authoritarian politics can pull all firms, strategic or not, into politics.

So, returning to the driving question of this book: When and where does the Chinese state encroach into a private sector? Not only when the state needs to directly control an industry for economic gains, national development trajectory, or geopolitical and security reasons, but also when the authoritarian machine requires private firms to cooperate with the state for deeply political reasons.

RESEARCH DESIGN

This book uncovers the phenomenon of politicization of firms in China, traces its institutional origins, and examines its outcome in state–business relations and ownership change in a business sector. I adopt a mixed method design involving quantitative analysis of original datasets I compiled on two sectors, over 200 semi-structured interviews with government officials, businesspeople, and various stakeholders in fifteen cities, and in-depth case studies and process tracing in four cities across China. The outcome of interest is an extreme form of state encroachment, deprivatization, an outcome not easily confused with standard government regulation of a sector. I leverage both sectoral variation and local variation within each sector on the outcome of deprivatization to tease out the effect of politicization of firms on state–business relations.

I select two sectors – urban buses and municipal waste treatment – to fulfil this analytical purpose. Both sectors were open to private investors in the early 1990s and experienced notable success in initially attracting private companies, and the Chinese central government continues to call for more private provision of both services to this date (2025). Both sectors experienced intense politicization nationwide. Firms in the urban bus sector were asked to contribute to visibility projects, and firms in the waste treatment sector were asked to provide societal control over protests against waste incineration projects, and in some locations also to provide visibility projects. Nonetheless, the outcomes faced by private companies vary between these two sectors and across different cities within each sector. In the urban bus sector, private firms in the majority of Chinese municipalities were forced to exit the sector by local governments. Conversely, in the waste treatment sector, local governments did not systematically coerce private firms to exit as they did in the bus sector. Private firms in some localities continued to thrive and in other localities started to lose ground to SOEs, opting to voluntarily exit or form joint ventures with SOEs at a later stage.

This variation in outcomes by sector and locality of the private firms allows me to tease out several alternative hypotheses generated in the literature for nationalization or deprivatization of a sector. Unlike oil and telecommunications, both urban buses and waste treatment sectors are mundane foot soldiers of urban life that are not crucial to national security or geopolitics. Furthermore, both urban buses and waste treatment are semi-public service sectors with price regulations, and between these two sectors, the waste treatment sector has a higher profit margin than that of urban buses. Some scholars optimistically estimated that the return on investment of waste-to-energy plants in China is about 18 percent in 2015 (Zhao et al. 2016), and my interviews revealed a range of profitability percentage between 10 percent and 12 percent between 2009 and 2018. While systematic data on profit margins do not exist for the urban bus sector, my collection of data shows the range of profitability percentage of bus firms between 2009 and 2016 to be between 1.48 percent and 13.22 percent.[49] These differences exclude the possibility that local governments might force private companies out of the urban bus sector for economic predation incentives. In particular, if state encroachment was driven by economic predation, we should observe coerced exit of private firms in the waste treatment sector rather than the urban bus sector.

Similarly, the difficulty for the government to write complete contracts with these sectors does not well explain the outcome of privatization in these two sectors. Around the world, services in these two sectors are successfully provided by the private sector in many countries. A large literature describes how public transportation is an ideal sector for privatization and contracting out, and private provision of public transit is often more efficient and effective than government-provided public transit across the world. Privatization introduces competition into the urban transit sector, and this sector has easily measurable services, therefore making it easy for local governments to come up with specified contracts with private providers. As a result, privatization in the bus sector often leads to efficient private provision of high-quality services (Perry and Babitsky 1986; Gomez-Ibanez and Meyer 1993; Finn and Mulley 2011). In the solid waste management sector, privatization and contracting out would often initially save costs compared with service under public ownership. In the long run, however, the experience of privatization of waste management in North America and Europe did not show significant change in cost savings for the government, mostly because the waste treatment sector is naturally more concentrated and has little competition within a city (Bartone et al. 1991; Dijkgraaf and Gradus 2007; Bel and Warner 2008; Bae 2010; Bel, Fageda, and Warner 2010).

[49] The figure of 13.22 percent is the revenue percentage of one of the busiest bus routes in China's capital city (Liu et al. 2018). The profitability percentage for the bus company that owns this route is certainly lower than 13.22 percent.

In China, both sectors have been privatized for more than twenty years, and there has been more competition in the urban bus sector than in the waste treatment sector. On average, each Chinese city had 8.0 bus companies and 3.9 waste treatment firms following privatization.[50] If the difficulty associated with writing complete contracts and regulation in sectors with limited competition were the rationale behind deprivatization, then we should expect the local Chinese governments to deprivatize the solid waste sector before the urban bus sector, but the reality is the opposite.

I also leverage local variations within each sector to control for the different nature of political services demanded in these sectors, as well as sectoral factors related to strategic importance, profitability, ease of contract writing, and regulations, all of which are difficult to compare quantitatively between sectors. For each sector, I first conduct statistical analysis of trends across Chinese cities with original data I compiled, revealing a correlation between politicization of firms and sectoral ownership change. I then delve deeper into the causal mechanisms at work with a most-similar case comparison using process tracing of ownership change in two cities in each sector. These cities would be similar in respect to key variables other than politicization of firms, but experienced different outcomes in ownership change in a sector, allowing me to identify the impact of politicization on state–business relation outcomes.

An original quantitative dataset was compiled for the statistical analysis component. State–business outcome data are collected and coded from news reports and government documents. Data on protests are collected and coded from news reports; People's Congress documents; the Wickedonna blog; the Social Unrest Database of the Chinese Academy of Social Sciences; the Global Database of Events, Language, and Tone (GDELT); and the China Labour Bulletin. The qualitative evidence comes from two waves of over 200 in-depth interviews conducted between 2015 and 2019 in fifteen cities across China, as well as in-depth case studies and process tracing based on government documents, news reports, and academic journal articles. The first wave of interviews included thirty-four loosely structured interviews to generate hypotheses and develop a question bank, while the follow-up wave consisted of semi-structured interviews across all fifteen cities to test the hypotheses. Of all the interviewees, 41 percent are city government officials in charge of a public service sector, 46 percent are business executives and

50 Author's data collection.

managers providing these public services, and 13 percent are academics, NGO managers, and journalists. The selection of interview cities follows the principle of stratified sampling, with the cities varying along the dimensions of population size, economic development level, and industry composition. In each city, I use the snowball sampling method to select interviewees.

Through this cross-sector and cross-locality comparative study utilizing mixed methods, I explain the different state–business outcomes in the two sectors with the different nature of politicization these sectors experienced. In the urban bus sector, political services of visibility projects resemble regulations that increased costs for all private firms beyond their capacity. This led to the private firms, but not SOEs, to eventually refuse to provide more political services and led to deprivatization of the noncooperative private companies. In the waste treatment sector, political services of societal control resemble bribes. Only those private companies unable to afford the "bribe," especially those lacking political competitiveness relative to SOEs in providing societal control, exited the sector one way or another, and other private companies remained.

BOOK STRUCTURE

The rest of the book is organized as follows. Chapter 2 explains the first political service provided by firms' contributions to visibility projects. This chapter provides a definition of visibility projects and distinguishes it from other public projects, including development projects, white elephant projects, Potemkin projects, and performative governance. The chapter then proceeds to outline the motivations driving Chinese officials to launch visibility projects, elucidates how firms are enlisted to provide this political service, and underscores the disadvantage faced by private firms compared with SOEs in providing this political service. This mechanism is empirically tested in Chapters 4 and 5, which respectively use quantitative and qualitative analyses in the urban bus sector to show this process across Chinese cities.

Chapter 3 describes the second political service provided by firms: supplementing the state in societal control. It details how Chinese officials respond to public opposition when launching controversial projects, and how the officials use private firms and SOEs differently to appease or suppress protesters. This mechanism is tested in Chapters 6 and 7. I use the municipal solid waste treatment sector to show how waste incineration plants act as allies or scapegoats in the face of public protests, and how private firms and SOEs have different advantages in providing this service. Eventually, based on the nature of societal control that a city needs, private firms either remain in the sector or lose their competitiveness and become replaced by SOEs.

Chapter 8 concludes by discussing how China's prospect of attracting and retaining private investments can be diminished by the state's politicization of firms. It also raises concerns about the quality of China's sustainable development, which is an important goal in both the urban bus sector and the solid waste sector. The chapter ends with a reflection on how China's authoritarian institutional arrangements might compromise the country's effort to attract and retain investment and to build a market economy, and to break from a model of economic growth at all costs to one of sustainable development.

2

Visibility Projects, the First Political Service

All development in this country has to happen in a form that benefits some leader.

A Chinese local government official, 2018

Jade City, in a beautiful mountainous area in southwest China, built a third wastewater treatment plant in 2012. This was not your usual wastewater treatment plant – some boring and messy industrial site covered by crisscrossed pipelines and large water tanks – it is beautiful. Covering 11 acres of land in this small city of 600,000 people, the new plant is the largest in this part of China, an area covered by rivers but lagging behind in economic development. This new plant has a state-of-the-art facility building, neatly arranged pipelines connecting rectangular sedimentation tanks, and six huge water pools. At the end of the facility, a lovely little pond collects the effluent before releasing it into the local waterways. Goldfish swim around the waterlilies in the pond, and a bird watches with great interest. Pebbled stone paths zigzag around the plant, dotted with trees and flowers, providing a lovely walk for anyone so inclined.

Proudly showing me around, the plant manager said, "We look just like a park."[1] This plant will treat 150,000 tons of wastewater per day and raise the city's wastewater treatment rate from 61 percent to 93 percent, a number on par with some of the most developed cities in the world, such as London and Hamburg. It should greatly improve the water quality of the two rivers running through the city. Jade City's government also did not need to pay the full amount of this project, which

[1] Interview 201548.

cost 100 million RMB. Using a public–private partnership, Jade City signed a build–operate–transfer (BOT) contract with a private firm, which financed the construction and will operate this wastewater plant for the next thirty years. Jade City just needed to pay wastewater treatment fees to the firm during this period.

An impressive public facility that received considerable media attention, this wastewater plant was a response to the Chinese central government's call for sustainable development. The CCP elevated sustainability to be a political priority and encouraged local governments to use the marketization of public sectors to finance projects in areas of public transportation, waste treatment, wastewater treatment, water supply, internet, dams and ports, irrigation, health, education, elderly care, and more. "Sustainable development" (*kechixu fazhan*) has been on the CCP's agenda since 2003, with slogans such as "green development" (*lvse fazhan*) (2003), "ecological civilization" (*shengtai wenming*) (2007), and "beautiful China" (*meili zhongguo*) (2012). Of these, "ecological civilization," which stresses that environmental preservation should be as important as economic growth, was incorporated into the Constitution of the CCP in 2013, and later into the Constitution of the People's Republic of China in 2018. Jade City's wastewater treatment plant was a direct response to these environmental agendas.

Jade City's wastewater treatment plant also responds to another set of central initiatives that continued to call for the private sector's "decisive role" in building public projects and providing public services. In the hope of relieving the financial burden of debt-laden local governments, China's central government issued at least one policy directive every other year from 2013 calling for the private sector to enter various public sectors,[2] and for the local governments to develop pro-market policies in these sectors. When choosing a firm to build and operate this wastewater treatment plant, Jade City's leaders deliberately chose a private firm "because the central policies suggested so ... that we are a market economy. It's good to have a private firm to build and operate public services. Private firms are more advanced [than state-owned enterprises, SOEs] in both technology and management, and they are more efficient and save us [the local government] money."[3]

[2] The first one of these initiatives was "Zhonggong zhongyang guanyu quanmian shenhua gaige ruogan zhongda wenti de jueding," 2013-11-15, www.gov.cn/jrzg/2013-11/15/content_2528179.htm.

[3] Interview 37292015.

Touting the double success in environmental protection and public–private partnership, the city government stated in an internal government document to the upper-level provincial government:

> under the leadership of the city's Party committee, our city showed uncompromised resolution in following the Party center's instruction to preserve green water and verdant mountains.[4] … an exemplary model of public–private partnership, and equipped with cutting-edge technology, this plant will raise the city's wastewater treatment rate to 93 percent, above other cities in the province. This plant reflects the city's history of emphasizing sustainable development, and our goal of reaching harmony between economic development and nature.[5]

However, when taking a closer look at Jade City's new plant, unnerving facts emerge. This wastewater treatment plant is neither necessary nor doing its job. To begin with, there is simply not enough wastewater to be treated. Like most Chinese cities, Jade City has a severe lack of sewerage network to collect and transfer wastewater, and the scattered and disconnected sewer pipes in place are outdated and narrow, often blocked (I was told that a mysterious couch blocked a section once), corroded, and constantly leaking. The other two wastewater plants in the city, built within the past fifteen years, were only operating at 21 percent and 70 percent respectively of their full capacity before the third plant was built, and the city government had to negotiate with the other two plants to divert some of the wastewater to the new plant. Once the new plant was in place, the other two plants' operating level dropped even further to 10 percent and 50 percent respectively of their full capacity, and the new plant was only operating at 41 percent of its capacity at the end of 2017.

There is also little prospect of population growth to increase wastewater supply in the future. Jade City is a small city, and its population growth has stagnated at an annual rate of 0.31 percent since 2010, making the city's total wastewater treatment capacity more than three times its actual needs. Even if the city's population and per capita water consumption grow at a rate equal to that of Beijing, it would still take over forty years to reach the plants' full capacity, exceeding their lifespan of thirty years. In other words, this new plant will be operating at only partial capacity for its whole lifespan. If the only income source were

[4] The slogan "green water and verdant mountains" (*lv shui qing shan*) comes from the Chinese president Xi Jinping.

[5] Author's data collection of local government documents.

wastewater treatment fees, as stated in the BOT contract, the plant would be always running at a loss.

Asking the firm why it built at overcapacity, the manager said, "the [city] leader wanted something grand. The size must match [his] resolution in environmental preservation." But how does the firm expect to make ends meet? The Jade City government promised two things. They planned to develop a new residential area near the wastewater plant, which would eventually increase the amount of wastewater that required treatment. They also agreed to provide subsidies to meet the gap between received wastewater treatment fees and the operating costs. The plant manager said, "It will be hard for the first few years, but as long as the government is giving us subsidies as promised, it should get better afterwards." What if the government reneges?

> Well, but this is the way you do business with governments in China. You can't worry about it. If you want everything written in the contract, then you would never win the bid [for public projects]. The norm is you do things for them [the government] first, and they would not mistreat you afterwards. It [government reneging] is a risk but it's out of our control. We simply can't worry about it unless we want no business opportunity at all.

The government also turned a blind eye to cost-saving measures pursued by this plant and the other two wastewater plants in the city. It turns out the new plant, like the other two, had been secretly releasing untreated wastewater into the river nearby, and the firm never built the sludge treatment facilities to treat the most toxic components of the wastewater. Instead, they dumped sludge on nearby farmland at night, killing the crops. Angry residents and farmers led protests in front of the wastewater treatment plant demanding the plant be shut down and insisting on government supervision. The city government promised the crowd they would work on it, and issued a fine to the wastewater plant, but never enforced it. Meanwhile, the government identified the protest leaders and arranged for the firm to pay them off. When the unappeased residents tried to contact local media to expose these matters, the city government warned the journalists to stay away.

This new plant operated smoothly for another four years, until the city leader who approved this plant was promoted. A new city leader came in and asked the firm to build another wastewater plant with a treatment capacity of 350,000 tons per day, two and a half times the current plant's capacity, having wrongly concluded that clearly three plants were still not enough to make the rivers clean. The plant manager angrily reflected on this demand:

> Why don't they [the leaders] just shut down those polluting factories instead? We were just beginning to make ends meet and now we will operate at a loss again, dumping in more new investment ... Every new leader means a new set of conditions and another round of negotiations. What do they expect us to do? That's why all three plants in the city are garbage![6]

A year later, not willing to build a fourth plant, the private firm sold its plant to an SOE and left Jade City, when there was still twenty-five years left on the contract. The city's wastewater treatment plants are all publicly-owned again.

But why build a third plant at all? And then a fourth, without the capacity to collect and transfer wastewater to them? Why not instead, as suggested by so many industry experts, first build up the sewer pipes essential to effective wastewater treatment, and then fully utilize the other two semi-idling wastewater plants? And equally important, if Jade City genuinely wanted to encourage private investment in wastewater treatment, why would unrealistic demands be made of the private firm, with the risk that future public–private partnership opportunities with other private firms would be lost?

These questions are not only pertinent to Jade City's wastewater treatment, but also to many other emerging projects and infrastructure plans all over China. In eighteen months of fieldwork in fifteen Chinese cities, I observed misbegotten projects spanning localities rich and poor, and sectors big and small. They include public transportation system upgrades, waste treatment facility upgrades, river cleaning projects, hog farms, bamboo farms, data centers for internet companies, and more. Like Jade City's wastewater plant, the final selected projects are often ill-conceived, short-lived, or replaced quickly. So why are they built?

VISIBILITY PROJECTS

I call these projects *visibility projects*. Visibility projects are public projects that prioritize appearance and scale over practicality, cost-effectiveness, and sustainability. Their primary purpose is to enhance the project initiator's political visibility and reputation in the system rather than to promote local development or to seek rents. They are launched for credit claiming rather than blame avoidance. The target audience of visibility projects is those who control the careers of the project initiators.

[6] Interview 20170534.

Visibility projects aim to make visible upgrades to infrastructure and the general physical environment as quickly as possible.

In the context of China, visibility projects are launched to signal both government officials' competence and loyalty to the CCP. The target audience of visibility projects is the higher-up officials in the Party-state echelon rather than the public. Visibility projects are the origin of firms' first political role in this book. Contributions from firms to government officials' careers often go to visibility projects.

As a phenomenon, visibility projects themselves are nothing new. Chinese local officials have been using them for career advancement since at least the 1990s. Scholars had previously documented some visibility projects, but discussed them within the conventional framework of government officials seeking promotion through promoting economic growth. For example, earlier scholarship documented the popular local government projects of excessively fancy government buildings, malls, and hotels, but called them "development projects" (O'Brien and Li 1999) or "political achievement projects" (Cai 2004; Guo 2009), viewing them mainly as responses to formal and quantitative policy targets of gross domestic product (GDP) growth and investment attraction. While these explanations certainly have their merits, as these projects also bring in GDP growth and investments, they do not fully explain why some local projects are preferred over other projects that could bring in similar levels of economic benefits or rents.

Consider the decision of building a bridge over a bay versus an undersea tunnel in Qingdao city.[7] Qingdao is a city hugging Jiaozhou Bay, with districts scattered along the bay's shorelines. In 2000, Qingdao had a new mayor, Shicheng Du, who later became the city's Party secretary. Du proposed a vision for the city called "Big Qingdao," which included a plan to connect the two major districts situated on opposite sides of the bay inlet. There were two possible solutions: a bridge over the bay or an undersea tunnel.

Du preferred a bridge, but almost everyone else preferred an undersea tunnel. The bridge would be cheaper to build, but it would not be as feasible or sustainable as a tunnel. To begin with, constructing the bridge at the bay inlet, which is the shortest distance, was not possible.

[7] "Rezhong 'Xingxiang Gongcheng' zi hui qiantu," in "Gongcheng jianshe lingyu fubai dianxing anli pouxi," China Fangzheng Publisher (the CPC Central Commission for Discipline Inspection), 2010-03; "Du Shicheng zhengji gongcheng de mingyun," Oriental Outlook (*Xinhua News*), 2008-04-03, http://news.sohu.com/20080403/n256084720.shtml.

Jiaozhou Bay is the third busiest commercial port in China, and if a bridge were to be built at the inlet, it would restrict the size of cargo ships that could pass through. As a result, the bridge had to be built further into the bay. However, this meant that the bridge would be significantly longer, which led to other problems. Engineers cautioned that building a longer bridge over the bay, which became the world's longest bay bridge upon completion, would increase its susceptibility to the typical weather hazards in this northern city, including wind, snow, and ice. Consequently, the annual maintenance costs of the bridge would be significantly higher than those for an undersea tunnel, and the number of days in a year when the bridge could be used would be limited. By contrast, a tunnel would not be affected by adverse weather conditions and could be utilized year round. Additionally, a tunnel could be constructed at the bay inlet, reducing the distance covered and resulting in lower maintenance costs, despite the per-kilometer construction cost being higher than that of a bridge.

Du insisted on building the bridge, but decided that both the bridge and an undersea tunnel would be built. This would result in duplicate projects and unnecessary expense, and it was not primarily driven by corruption. In fact, Du encountered considerable difficulties in finding companies willing to undertake the construction of the bridge, causing the construction start date to be postponed by over a year. In contrast, the undersea tunnel had no issues attracting companies to participate in the bidding process, which would be a source of bribery. According to the published records of a later corruption case against Du, his sources of bribery were primarily from real estate developers and the oil industry in the city, not the bridge.[8] So why was he so persistent in building the bridge?

The CCP essentially concluded that this bridge was Du's visibility project without using the term. In the records of Du's corruption case, the Party accused him of wasteful spending, stating that this bridge

> did not serve any real purpose, and it was not used a lot by the public. It [the bridge] is evidence that Du was not thinking about local demands, but only wanted to showcase his competence in urban planning. Du went against expert opinions on this bridge ... because it [the bridge] can attract more attention for him and can better display his achievement.[9]

[8] Ibid. and "Yuan Qingdao shiwei shuji Du Shicheng bei mianzhi neimu," Dongnan Kuai Bao, 2006-12-27, *The Law Year Book of China*, 2009: 919.

[9] Ibid.

Visibility projects such as this bridge have a primary focus on appearance and scale, rather than economic development, rents, or good governance. They often result in wasteful spending on nonessential functions without consideration of cost-effectiveness. But how can we tell whether a project is a visibility project? After all, most public projects address a mix of incentives of government officials, including good governance, rent-seeking, and career advancement. Visibility projects primarily serve the purpose of career advancement, but they can also generate developmental effects and rent-seeking opportunities.

Four defining features can help us identify visibility projects: They are extra efforts beyond requirements; they are borne out of ambiguous, rather than well-defined, policy directives; they cater to top-down demands rather than bottom-up demands, and therefore often draw resources away from local needs; and they are often quickly launched and short-lived because maintenance is not a key factor in the decision. I will now explain these features in the context of China.

First Feature of Visibility Projects: Extra Efforts beyond Requirement

Visibility projects are efforts that go beyond the job description. To use a metaphor that draws on Chapter 1, ambitious Chinese local officials who seek promotion are like high school students who apply to a top university (seeking promotion). Having a high SAT score (meeting required goals) might not be sufficient to get admitted. Students also put their awards, community service, or volunteer experience on applications for better chances of admission. Visibility project are like these extra efforts. Visibility projects are not the efforts of an ambitious government official to meet what is required of everyone in the government evaluation system; rather, they are extra efforts intended to showcase competence, claim credit, and differentiate oneself from others.

For conceptual clarity, this key feature can be better understood by comparing visibility projects with Potemkin village projects and performative governance. All of them serve the purpose of signaling, but they serve fundamentally opposite incentives: Visibility projects are extra efforts to show competence, while Potemkin projects and performative governance are efforts to conceal incompetence. This difference in incentives leads to different contents and costs of visibility projects compared with the other two.

The original Potemkin village refers to a myth suggesting that Potemkin, lover of the Russian empress Catherine II, set up mobile fake villages along the Dnieper River to hide his failure to establish resettlement villages for Russians in the 1780s. This term was subsequently applied to describe analogous behavior, such as the Soviet Union's government showcasing a model worker's affluent home to foreign delegations or the Romanian government presenting demonstration farms to foreign delegations to hide the actual desolate situation in the country (David-Fox 2011). In the same vein, performative governance, detailed by Ding (2022), refers to actions such as the Chinese government dispatching investigative teams to polluting factories, ostensibly to signal government accountability to the public when lacking the actual capacity to enforce environmental regulations. These projects and behaviors are essentially to conceal incompetence and to avoid blame when under scrutiny. They would not occur if no one were paying attention. To conceal incompetence, the actors only need to leverage the minimum input possible to attain the maximum output of preserving their reputation.

Visibility projects, on the contrary, are invented to attract attention and to show off competence. This means that they often include highly visible and marketable components that entail significantly higher costs than necessary, at the expense of cheaper alternatives. The aforementioned case of bridge versus tunnel is a good illustration of this. Visibility projects are not results of low capacity; they are the results of an ineffective evaluation system that creates incentives for the competent to stand out. They are, therefore, extra efforts above and beyond the basic requirements in order to claim credit and attract attention. Consequently, visibility projects often involve unnecessarily high costs.

Second Feature of Visibility Projects: Engagement with Ambiguous Policy Directives

Visibility projects are often launched to engage with ambiguous policy directives. By ambiguous, I mean that either the policy goals, the means to achieve them, or both, are unspecified or poorly defined. Xi Jinping's call to "preserve green water and verdant mountains" mentioned earlier in this chapter is a great example. This call is a broad and ambiguous goal relating to environmental preservation. Without specific guidance on how to achieve it, government officials have numerous potential approaches to choose from, such as deindustrialization, shutting down mines, reducing agriculture, cleaning water bodies, restricting wastewater emissions, planting trees, and establishing natural preservation areas. Ambiguous policy directives often represent policy agendas that the national government has yet to establish a clear direction for, or has not accumulated sufficient information and experience to define a policy goal and provide specific policy recommendations. Therefore, both the policy goals and the means to reach them as yet lack clear evaluation standards.

Ambiguous policy directives thus allow for creativity, which is a valued opportunity to differentiate oneself from others in the competition for attention. Moreover, because there are no specific measures to be evaluated on and to compete over for ambiguous policy directives, government officials turn to *verifiable* efforts to pursue these policy goals, and *visible* efforts such as physical infrastructure or an event are the easiest to verify. Therefore, ambiguity gives rise to visibility projects.

This observation that ambitious Chinese government officials choose to engage with ambiguous policy directives goes against the findings in the literature of principal–agent theory and public management. Scholars notice that when choosing between multiple tasks from the principal, agents only engage with measurable and well-defined tasks and ignore the unmeasurable tasks, because the principal cannot monitor the enforcement of these tasks (Holmstrom 1979). Public management scholars call this phenomenon "goal displacement." When the evaluation of agents includes quantitative and standardized measures for specific organizational goals, such as evaluating school teachers based on their students' standardized test grades or assessing hospital managers according to patient wait times, agents tend to divert effort toward these well-specified goals. Consequently, efforts are directed away from broader, more complex goals such as fostering critical thinking in education or enhancing the quality of medical services (Gormley and Weimer 1999; Grizzle 2002; Hood 2006).

This is inconsistent with what I observe in China, and the inconsistency likely stems from a scope condition within this literature: The agents must believe that the formal evaluation system is effective in identifying competence and does not fail to recognize it. In other words, the agents must believe that their efforts within the formal evaluation system, whether through hard work, gaming behavior, or even fraud, will result in corresponding rewards from the principal. The Chinese evaluation system does not effectively function in this sense, for reasons I will elaborate later in this chapter. Local government officials do not believe that the CCP's evaluation system can identify the most competent or avoid overlooking the truly competent, and as a result, ambitious local officials in China actively engage with ambiguous and unspecified policy directives to open up new opportunities for attention from the Party-state, while the not so ambitious local officials continue to focus on well-defined and measurable policy directives.

With the limited financial resources every local government faces, we may even observe a phenomenon contrary to what is described in the literature: resources are diverted away from measurable but invisible goals toward visible but unmeasurable or unmeasured goals. For example, to engage with the ambiguous and broad policy directive of water quality improvement in China, government officials created a distorted wastewater treatment system across Chinese localities: a surplus of wastewater treatment plants but a shortage of underground sewer pipes to collect wastewater for these plants (Jin and Xu 2022). And even among the sewer pipes that are built, the focus was clearly on construction and not management or maintenance, rendering many of these sewer pipes unsustainable (Wang et al. 2021).

The rationale here is simple: Local government officials engage with this ambiguous policy directive with visibility projects in wastewater treatment. Wastewater treatment plants are above the ground and highly visible, but the volume of water treated in the plant is difficult to measure and can be easily gamed. Sewer pipes, on the other hand, are easy to measure in terms of length and coverage, but they are underground and invisible.

Engaging with ambiguous policy directives not only allows for creativity, but also further contributes to the high costs often associated with visibility projects. Given that the purpose of visibility projects is to signal competence and attract attention, typically the costs associated with such projects heavily prioritize presentation and scale. The more visible, the larger in scale, and the more impressive the presentation, the more likely that a visibility project will be noticed. Ambiguous policy directives thus become even more attractive because clear standards for policy goals or implementation are not yet established, meaning there is a lack of benchmarks for acceptable or reasonable costs. It is therefore easier to justify unorthodox or wasteful methods to pursue an ambiguous policy directive.

Here it would be helpful to distinguish visibility projects from rent-seeking projects.[10] Ambiguity is an attractive feature for both the officials who seek attention for career advancement and those who seek rents. It is easier to justify wasteful spending as miscalculation in the process of

[10] Also called "boondoggle" projects (Keefer and Knack 2007).

"experimenting" with different approaches to reach an ambiguous policy goal. However, the secretive nature of corruption dictates that projects launched for rents should be as invisible as possible to escape scrutiny. Back to the wastewater treatment system example: The invisible, underground sewer pipes are obviously a better choice if one's primary incentive is corruption, because it is more difficult to audit construction costs of underground pipes than that of a very visible wastewater treatment plant above ground. Therefore, while both visibility projects and rent-seeking projects engage with ambiguous policy directives, they differ fundamentally in the focus of the efforts.

Visibility projects, therefore, favor ambiguous policy directives. Ambiguity allows for creativity, attracts attention, and is more forgiving of the unreasonable costs often associated with visibility projects.

Third Feature of Visibility Projects: Prioritize Principal's Preferences over Bottom-Up Demands

Visibility projects cater to the preferences of the principal to attract the principal's attention for career advancement. When the principal's preferences are inconsistent with bottom-up and local demands, or require resources be directed away from meeting local demands, projects catering to these preferences are often visibility projects.

In the context of the Chinese government, this would mean that visibility projects rise to respond to the Party-state's preferences, not bottom-up and local demands from the public. This is associated with two features of authoritarian rule. First, upward accountability, a defining feature of authoritarianism, dictates that if the priorities of the Party-state are incongruent with local public demand, the Party-state's demands will be given priority. After all, local government officials are primarily agents of the Party-state, not the public. Secondly, authoritarian government officials are not allowed to have individual political agendas, as this can be viewed as a challenge to the Party-state. Responding to the Party-state's policy directives signals loyalty and can signal competence if one succeeds. Responding to local demands that are not the priorities of the Party-state, on the other hand, can at best signal competence if one succeeds, but it does not signal loyalty when the Party-state does not prioritize these local demands.

It can even be risky for local officials to launch projects that respond to bottom-up demands without knowing the Party-state's stance on the issue. An extreme example of this is the free universal healthcare reform in Shenmu county, Shaanxi, in 2009.[11] The then Party secretary of Shenmu county, Baoxiong Guo, decided to invest 150 million RMB into the public healthcare system, providing all Shenmu residents with free healthcare. This daring local reform drew national attention and started a debate on why other local governments would not do the same, particularly considering that Shenmu county is not even that rich. The Party-state eventually called off this bottom-up program, and Guo was demoted in 2010.[12]

Therefore, it is politically safer to engage with the Party-state's preferences. It not only reduces the risk of being blamed for potential failures, but it also reduces the greatest risk for Chinese government officials: to be perceived as too autonomous, too confident, and overstepping the Party line by independently determining which policy areas are important.

Visibility projects, thus, rise only in response to the Party-state's preferences. The preferences of the Party-state are exemplified in two ways. In the formal cadre evaluation system that dictates the career prospects and bonuses of every Chinese government official, high priority policy goals carry the most weight in evaluating a government official's performance.[13] Alternatively, the Party-state reveals its preferences through national policy directives, speeches of the Party leaders, reports and suggestions by China's nominal legislature, and occasionally, government subsidies and grants.

Visibility projects respond to the preferences of the Party-state, often at the costs of launching projects not suitable to the local situation or even in conflict with local interests. Whether these projects cater to the local situation is at best a secondary consideration. This is because the preferences of the Party-state in China are often inconsistent with local demand, or at least do not align with the demand of every locality. The inconsistency is partly due to the intrinsic difficulty for an authoritarian state to obtain information from the public, and partly due to the large size of China and its heterogeneous localities.

An example of the Party-state priority conflicting with local demands is the case of crops versus trees. In 1999, the Chinese national

[11] "Shaanxi shenmu quanmin mianfei yiliao," *Yangzi Wanbao*, 2010-06-04, www.chinadaily.com.cn/dfpd/2010-06/04/content_9933116.htm.

[12] "Shaanxi shenmu yuan shuji zicheng bei bian," 2010-09-19, *Xibu wang*, www.chinanews.com.cn/gn/2010/09-19/2542547.shtml.

[13] See Leng and Zuo (2021) for a list of policy goals based on their weights in the cadre evaluation system.

government launched its "Grain for Green" program in response to soil erosion, dust storms, and other environmental risks associated with the rapidly disappearing woods and forests in China.[14] Under this program, local governments can encourage local farmers to voluntarily retire their farmland and plant trees on the land instead. Local governments typically offer financial compensation equal to five to eight years' worth of income from the original farmland (Xu and Cao 2002), and the farmers are responsible for sustaining the planted trees. This central plan is consistent with demands in some localities that suffered from grave environmental degradation, such as Inner Mongolia, Gansu, and Qinghai provinces, which have experienced severe desertification. But this plan also came into direct conflict with local demands in many other places.

In Tangshan, for instance, a coastal area of Hebei province, ambitious local officials worried that they were falling behind in responding to the "Grain for Green" program because farmers in that area were not interested. Even though the national program is not mandatory, local officials still decided to force local villagers to retire their arable land, the sole income source for many farmers. When villagers refused to cooperate, local government officials had all the spring wheat seedlings cut down during the thirty-minute lunch break local farmers took on a spring day. Infuriated, but without any harvest and income in sight, local farmers finally signed the contract to retire their farmland.[15] An interviewee told me of a similar story in Jiangxi province, where local leaders ordered resistant farmers to cut down their bamboo, a major cash crop, and replace it with trees to respond to the same program.[16]

Scenarios such as this one are illustrations of how visibility projects that cater to the Party-state's preferences can activate conflicts with the public if these preferences go against local demands. Often, such conflict is minor, such as with a common visibility project to build new ring roads in a city that creates impressive urban planning effects but cuts across existing streets and removes pedestrian areas. And some visibility projects, despite being wasteful, can even be entertaining to the public, such as replicating the ancient Austrian village of Hallstatt in Huizhou, Guangdong, or building the world's largest (and probably the only) museum in the vivid shape and color of a giant turtle in Baiyangdian, Hebei.

[14] A revised version of the "Grain for Green" program was issued in 2016: "Tuigeng huanlin tiaoli," 2016-02-06, www.gov.cn/gongbao/content/2016/content_5139491.htm.

[15] "Maimiao bei hui, shubaimu gengdi bei qiangzhi zhongshu," *China Media Group*, 2021-04-19, https://china.huanqiu.com/article/42nK5VSx7s6.

[16] Interview 201906.

This leads to another scenario where the Party-state's preferences would not be in conflict with, but would direct resources away from, local development. Examples include the Chinese state's strategic plan of "Made in China 2025," which is crucial to China's plan of breaking free from the middle-income trap and reducing foreign dependence. While this central plan makes sense for the country as a whole, most technology sectors are unlikely to flourish at random locations in China. Take the robotics industry, part of this strategic plan, for example. The robotics industry requires a highly educated workforce, supporting infrastructure, and cost-efficient logistics. Few localities in China meet the requirements to sustain a robotics sector. As a result, the sector had been concentrated in China's most advanced manufacturing centers in the eastern coastal region.

But local officials whose jurisdiction is not suitable for the robotics industry do not just ignore this policy directive. They see this strategic plan as a great opportunity to showcase their competence and loyalty. They do so not by investing in research, manufacturing, or logistics, but by building an "AI tourism town" with robots chatting with tourists or a tourist park with robot models.[17] These projects are clearly visibility projects, and they come at the costs of investing in other areas more suitable for the locality.

It is important to note that visibility projects do not always come into conflict with bottom-up demands, and the local leaders would prefer that visibility projects do not lead to public grievances. But in general, because visibility, rather than practicality, is the main driver of visibility projects, developmental outcomes are not guaranteed. This does not mean that all visibility projects do not carry any social merit. It is just that their role in local development is secondary to their role in getting attention from the upper-level officials.

Again, here it would be useful to compare visibility projects to other wasteful projects such as "white elephants" (Robinson and Torvik 2005) and "pork barrel" projects (Shepsle and Weingast 1981) for conceptual clarity. All of these projects are economically inefficient, and are launched to serve political purposes. The difference lies in what these different projects offer to their target audience. White elephants and pork barrel

[17] "Tiegemen jiancheng guonei shouge huanbao gangdiao jiqiren zhuti gongyuan," *Xinhua News*, 2012-03-26, www.chinadaily.com.cn/dfpd/shehui/2012-03/26/content_14910485_4.htm. And, "Zhihui funeng Yunnan tese xiaozhen jianshe," Yunan govern ment, 2021-07-11, www.cac.gov.cn/2021-07/11/c_1627588859003660.htm.

projects are launched for electoral or legislative coalition-building purposes; therefore, they are designed to benefit their target audience. A typical white elephant project, for example, is a footwear factory in a locality without the comparative advantage in shoe manufacturing, but the factory nonetheless being launched by local politicians to create jobs for voters (Robinson and Torvik 2005). Pork barrel projects often entail diverting limited budgets not to populations or places most in need, but to localities where they can secure political advantages, such as votes. "A bridge to nowhere" is a classic example, intended to enhance a politician's electoral margins in a remote area, despite the bridge's higher utility in a more densely populated region. Therefore, the target audiences for white elephants and pork barrels are also the populations that will benefit from these inefficient projects, often in suboptimal locations.

Visibility projects, on the other hand, do not have the purpose of providing direct benefits to their target audience – the upper-level officials. Rather, the target audience is often separated from the population affected by visibility projects. Visibility projects aim to signal to the principal, but they are not intended to bring personal benefits to the principal. They are often located far away from where the principal lives and works, and affects a different population. Because of this, the benefits or the costs to the populations directly affected by visibility projects are not the primary concern when launching these projects. And unlike white elephants and pork barrel projects, visibility projects do not have to be launched in a specific location; they can be launched anywhere.

Fourth Feature of Visibility Projects: Not Focusing on Sustainability

Because the primary purpose of visibility projects is not practicality or to benefit a locality, they often ignore sustainability. In other words, future investments to maintain or to sustain these projects are usually not the primary consideration in the design and launching of a visibility project. As a result, visibility projects tend to be short-lived.

The lack of focus on sustainability is best shown in the case of "poplar versus shrubs." Starting in 1978, the Chinese national government continued to call for de-desertification in northern China. This policy directive led to the Three North Shelterbelt Project in northwest China, the world's largest tree-planting project. Chinese citizens and hundreds of local governments participated in this project, and without central guidance on the specifics, many local governments chose to plant poplar trees, and only poplar trees, instead of native shrubs. The rationale was one of visibility: Poplar trees are one of the fastest growing trees in the world. Especially when propagated by cuttings, they can form a forest in months. Planting only poplar trees, instead of mixing them with native but less impressive short shrubs, could result in a visually appealing forest within the shortest time possible, which would quickly show great efforts in de-desertification.

But poplars are not the best trees for afforestation in deserts. In fact, this is an "ecological mismatch."[18] Poplars require much more water to survive than native plants. As a result, planting poplars in deserts further aggravates desertification by depleting groundwater and killing grass that holds the soil together. Moreover, planting only poplars, meaning adopting a monoculture, can easily lead to disease and pest hazards. These lack of considerations for sustainability led to predictable ramifications: Only 15 percent of the planted trees in this entire project survived by 2014. In Ningxia province, a pest wiped out 1 billion poplar trees in 2000 alone.[19] In Hebei province, reports revealed that another direct cause for the premature death of the forest was the absence of management, maintenance, and, most importantly, irrigation, by local governments after trees were planted.[20]

In the context of China, the lack of sustainability in visibility projects is due to two reasons. First, local officials are subject to limited terms in office. Leaders are constantly rotated so that the Party-state can prevent "local lords" from rising. A Party policy dictates that all local leaders above county level are subject to transfer to a different locality after ten years in their post.[21] In reality, their term is even shorter, with the average tenure for Party secretaries and mayors in Chinese cities being less than three and a half years, and the average tenure for provincial

[18] *The Economist* published two detailed reports on the ecological mismatch problem in this afforestation effort in China: "Great Green Wall," *The Economist*, 2014-08-23, www.economist.com/international/2014/08/23/great-green-wall; and "China's desert-taming "green Great Wall" is not as great as it sounds," 2019-05-18, *The Economist*, www.economist.com/china/2019/05/18/chinas-desert-taming-green-great-wall-is-not-as-great-as-it-sounds.

[19] Ibid.

[20] "Sanbei fanghu lin zhangbei duan linmu dapi siwang, xianru wuren guanli jingdi," *Chinese Central Television*, 2013-10-09, http://politics.people.com.cn/BIG5/n/2013/1009/c70731-23132789.html; and "Weihe zhong shu bu jian shu?," *Xinhua News*, 2020-06-29, www.xinhuanet.com/politics/2020-06/29/c_1126172206.htm.

[21] "Dangzheng lingdao ganbu jiaoliu gongzuo guiding" ("Provisions on Exchange of Leading Party and Government Cadres"), *Gongchandangyuan wang*, 2006-08-06, https://news.12371.cn/2015/03/12/ARTI1426126426386172.shtml.

governors being less than five.[22] This mechanism of maintaining stable authoritarian rule unavoidably creates short-sighted officials. Even if we assume that China's central governmental leaders are indeed "stationary bandits" (Olson 1993) who care about long-term development, the state has by choice created a class of potential "roving bandits" on whom it must depend to make and implement their long-term policies at the local level. Short-sighted local officials seek quick political returns, resulting in visibility projects that are planned and launched within a short period of time, which greatly increases the risk of inadequate planning.

Secondly, each new generation of local government officials needs its own visibility projects. Officials cannot claim credit for visibility projects launched by their predecessors. Therefore, there is no incentive to maintain previous visibility projects, and instead new leaders have the incentive to create their own new visibility projects. As a result, compared with regular development projects, visibility projects are more likely to be abandoned, demolished, or rebuilt once the responsible government officials leave their positions.

Here it would be useful to distinguish visibility projects from development projects. Albert Hirschman (1967: 1) describes what makes a project developmental: "The development project is a special kind of investment. The term connotes purposefulness, some minimum size, a specific location, the introduction of something qualitatively new, and the expectation that a sequence of further development moves will be set in motion." Visibility projects fundamentally differ from development projects in that they do not bear the expectation for a sequence of further development moves or the expectation for sustainability. Visibility projects might very well be introducing something qualitatively new, but they are not designed with sustainability in mind. Because the purpose of visibility projects is not primarily development, even though they could still have developmental effects, these effects are not guaranteed to be sustainable. The purpose of visibility projects is to signal competence to improve one's chance of promotion during one's limited tenure at a certain location. Therefore, visibility projects are often quickly launched and short-lived.

To summarize, visibility projects are launched to attract attention and signal competence through extra efforts on visual presentation and scale. Four features together help us identify a visibility project: when a project

[22] Author's data. This is consistent with other statistics such as in Malesky and London (2014) and Choi (2012).

represents extra efforts that go beyond the principal's requirements; when a project engages with ambiguous directives from the principal; when a project caters to the principal's preferences even when those preferences are inconsistent with bottom-up needs and local situation; and when the budget and design of the project does not stress sustainability.

Visibility projects are therefore not economically efficient. They might be launched in a less than ideal location and their costs heavily focus on presentation and scale, often at the costs of developmental potential or sustainability. But again, this does not mean that all visibility projects do not carry any societal merit; they still can, but that is not their primary focus. In the end, most public projects satisfy multiple incentives of the local officials, including good governance, rent-seeking, and career advancement. But projects differ on the primary purpose of their launch, and this primary purpose dictates the nature of the project.

Visibility Projects: Trends in China

Like fashion, visibility projects have trends. After all, the preferences of the principal can change, and new, ambiguous directives can appear. Visibility projects have also evolved to better justify their wasteful nature. In the past two decades, visibility projects in China have become "smarter" and more varied. As the old-style visibility projects such as grand government buildings, bridges, and airports with little usership became alarmingly wasteful in the 2000s, they raised criticism from society and drew central government's attention. In 2004, central government openly criticized and halted some ludicrous and unnecessary construction projects and punished over four hundred local leaders for misuse of public funds on these projects.[23]

This did not stop local officials from launching visibility projects, but it led to two important evolutions. First, local officials learned to choose visibility projects that were strictly in line with the central government's preferences since those projects were less likely to be criticized and better signaled loyalty. What this means is that visibility projects now exhibit a sector-based pattern rather than resulting in the random construction of large infrastructure. With recent calls for sustainable development and environmental protection, local officials are increasingly turning their eyes to sectors that can show visible efforts in sustainability. Examples

23 "Zhengji gongcheng ruhe shouchang?," *Xinhua News*, 2014-10-15, http://politics.people.com.cn/n/2014/1015/c1001-25840389.html.

include a panda-shaped solar farm and planting 6 million flowers in a city within a year. Such projects are usually large in scale and size with the purpose of being seen, but they do not necessarily bring in sustainable development. Secondly, local officials are starting to seek other funding sources to cover visibility projects to avoid being blamed for wasteful public spending. These two evolutions explain how firms became essential to visibility projects, creating the first political role this book describes: becoming donors to authoritarian officials' political careers.

Visibility Projects: A Part of Selectoral Campaigns in Closed Authoritarian Countries

Visibility projects belong to a group of strategies developed by ambitious authoritarian officials to self-promote in a political environment without elections and individual political campaigns. I call these strategies *selectoral campaigns*.

The absence of elections in closed authoritarian regimes does not necessarily mean the absence of political campaigns. While not accountable to electorates, government officials in closed authoritarian regimes have different constituencies: *selectors* – upper-level political elites who have control of personnel in the state and select and promote lower-level officials.[24] Selectoral campaigns can be seen as upside-down versions of electoral campaigns in democracies, with a flipped purpose of winning the approval from selectors rather than voters, and with a narrower set of campaigning strategies available.

Selectoral campaigns are a group of strategies used by authoritarian officials to promote themselves in front of their selectors. Some campaign strategies have been previously documented by scholars without using the term. For example, a few researchers on China noted how junior officials sing "nauseating" praises of senior officials in newspapers to signal loyalty (Shih 2008), and that ambitious rising officials are more likely to appear on television shows to talk about their achievements to signal competence to upper-level officials (Zhu and Wang 2013). While these scholars did not categorize such behavior as campaigning for one's political career, these behaviors are essentially an

[24] I use the word "selector" to distinguish this concept from the popular concept of "selectorate." "Selectorates" refers to political and economic elites in a country who choose leaders, often electoral winners, in a polity (Smith et al. 2004; Bueno de Mesquita et al. 2005). The concept of "selectorate" was first raised in Paterson (1967). Gallagher and Hanson (2015) provide a thorough review of the development of that concept.

upside-down version of electoral media campaigns, albeit targeting selectors rather than electorates.

Similarly, many local policy experiments can be viewed through the lens of selectoral campaigns as well, even though they are traditionally viewed as an outcome of decentralization or pseudo-federalism (Montinola, Qian, and Weingast 1995; Yang 1996; Cai and Treisman 2006). A few scholars observe the connection between policy experimentation and career incentives, where local officials use policy experimentation and innovation to signal incentive alignment with the upper-level officials (Heilmann 2008; Teets and Hurst 2014; Teets 2015; Teets and Hasmath 2020). Paying close attention to the policy innovations in this scholarship, many of them were responding to central directives that had unclear goals and measures and were not yet incorporated into the cadre evaluation system. The lack of goals or measures creates space for local officials to showcase creativity and competence, allowing them to gain reputation beyond the formal cadre evaluation system. For example, the central policy directive of streamlining administrative procedures induced six rounds of experiments from the 1980s until 2010, but none of them were successful (Guo 2017). Most of them focused on policy inputs that were visible, such as producing many policy documents and building new government buildings to concentrate the licensing and permitting services in one place. But there was much less effort to decentralize and restructure administrative power and to reduce interbureaucracy dependence – key to the reform but hard to measure and evaluate. Other works find that once the chance of promotion disappears as a local official approaches mandatory retirement, the official becomes much less likely to innovate (Zhu and Zhang 2016). Evidently, officials connect policy experimentation with their career prospects beyond the pursuit of good policy.

To high-level officials, selectoral campaigns are also useful. The invention of these campaigns caters to the common remedies for ineffective performance evaluation systems and moral hazard induced by information asymmetry between the principal and the agent. Scholars have observed that when facing ineffective performance evaluation, the principal can collect extra, albeit imperfect, information and write it into the contract to monitor agents and incentivize them to engage in unmeasurable tasks (Holmstrom 1979; Holmstrom and Milgrom 1991; Baker 1992). Others observe that the principal could add subjective evaluation for the agents to complement incentive distortions caused by imperfect objective measures, and these subjective evaluations are often based on loose perspectives such as enthusiasm and effort (Baker, Gibbons, and

Murphy 1994; Prendergast 1999). For the higher-up officials in the Chinese Party-state, selectoral campaigns serve as an extra signal of their subordinates' competence, and hence they too welcome these campaigns to some degree.

Nonetheless, selectoral campaign strategies are highly limited in closed authoritarianism, both because of the absence of elections and the paramount requirement of political loyalty. Common campaigning strategies in electoral systems such as individual platform advertising, negative campaigning, and candidate debates are rare if not nonexistent, as they place emphasis on individuals, which could risk looking overly ambitious and threatening to authoritarian rulers. More often, ambitious authoritarian politicians choose campaigning strategies that put less emphasis on personal charisma but more emphasis on their alignment with the Party-state. In this narrow space of campaigning strategies, Chinese local officials invent visibility projects, a popular type of selectoral campaigning strategy.

But why would Chinese local officials need selectoral campaigns and visibility projects, when there is a highly institutionalized process for selecting and promoting officials? The answer lies in a fundamental institution of China's bureaucratic control, the cadre evaluation system.

AUTHORITARIAN ORIGIN OF VISIBILITY PROJECTS AND SELECTORAL CAMPAIGNS: CHINA'S CADRE EVALUATION SYSTEM

China, an authoritarian country without elections, resorts to a top-down cadre evaluation system to evaluate its large body of government officials and select and promote the most capable. China's cadre evaluation system is a mix of the Soviet Union's *nomenklatura* system (Manion 1985; Edin 2003) and the imperial bureaucratic system in which officials enter the system through exams and rise through the ranks over time. This hierarchical structure of bureaucratic control has three components: the target responsibility system, top-down evaluation by one's superiors, and bottom-up evaluation by one's colleagues and subordinates. Together, these evaluations are intended to select loyal and competent Party-state officials to run the country. Under the current Chinese system, government officials at all levels above the village are subject to cadre evaluation for career prospects and income.

Of the three parts of cadre evaluation, the target responsibility system is the newest component, introduced in the mid 1980s. It is intended to institutionalize selection by meritocracy within the Party-state. The system is composed of a set of concrete and quantitative annual targets on a variety of policy areas including economic growth, investment, social stability, social welfare, and, recently, newly added environmental protection targets. It also includes veto targets – targets in policy areas in which the officials must meet the minimum to prevent demotion or punishment. Two long-standing veto targets were family planning (formerly the one-child policy) and social stability. For the former, prior to 2015, local leaders were required to contain population growth rate under a certain number, and social stability includes a ceiling on the number of protests occurring per year. The exact parameters of this ceiling is unknown outside the government. The target responsibility system not only provides quantitative goals to measure and compare performance among local officials, but it is also intended to align local officials' incentives with the preferences from the top.

This system is not unique to China, as quantitative performance evaluation systems are widely used in government bureaucracies, firms, schools, and hospitals around the world. But it has two distinct features in the Chinese state's application. First, the object of evaluation is individual government officials rather than a whole bureaucratic organization, and performance is tied to individual career prospects and bonuses, rather than organizational funding. Second, the Chinese version emphasizes competition among government officials, and promotion decisions are made in a "tournament style." Local leaders who want to move up the career ladder not only need to meet targets, but also need to outcompete others in delivering targets (Zhou 2007). This tournament style of official selection and promotion is much like how some companies incentivize their salespeople with progressive bonuses, pushing them to overachieve targets set by the selectors.

The second component of the cadre evaluation system is top-down evaluations, where one is evaluated by the Party committee one level up. This process is a black box not just to scholars, but to the local officials themselves. In formal documents, standards for top-down evaluations include abstract phrases such as "loyalty to the Party," "political attitudes," and "a spirit to take on responsibility."[25] These standards are vague and highly subjective. In my interviews, no local government officials could specify exactly what the upper-level officials are looking for in

[25] "Dangzheng lingdao ganbu kaohe gongzuo tiaoli," *Xinhua News*, 2019-04-21, www.gov.cn/zhengce/2019-04/21/content_5384955.htm.

the top-down evaluations. Such opaque standards successfully keep the local officials on their toes.

The third and last evaluation component, bottom-up evaluation by one's colleagues and subordinates, is also a subjective process that outside observers know very little about. The formal guidance on bottom-up evaluation simply says, "the leadership must be accepted by the masses" and "adopt democratic centralism" in decision-making.[26] In my interviews with government officials, this evaluation criterion is considered the weakest, without much impact on one's career, because even though the bottom-up evaluation is supposed to be anonymous, there is no formal procedure to guarantee anonymity, making the evaluation almost always positive because no one wants to offend one's leaders and colleagues. This process is also often manipulated, and we have gotten peeks into how bottom-up evaluations operate. In a 2009 documentary *The Transition Period*,[27] a banquet scene recorded how over a toast, the Party secretary and a few top leaders in the county decided that the county mayor would get a bottom-up evaluation of 95 out of 100 points from his subordinates. The fact that these local leaders did not mind doing it in front of a camera reflects how common and accepted such a practice is.

In any case, the combination of the target responsibility system and top-down evaluation are still considered effective in aligning the incentives of officials and should provide a balance between selecting both the competent and the loyal. However, the reality is far from this picture.

The Not-So-Mighty Cadre Evaluation System

The cadre evaluation system instills dual insecurities among China's government officials. The first insecurity arises from problems within the target responsibility system, which is not trusted to identify and promote the most competent of officials. The second insecurity arises from the top-down evaluation system, where loyalty and "political reliability" is key, but few understand what counts as loyalty and reliability. As a result, Chinese government officials are highly anxious about whether they can exhibit either competence or loyalty.

The problem with selecting the most competent starts with the target responsibility system, which in theory adheres to the principle of meritocracy. In reality, it is widely considered to be rife with gaming behavior

[26] Ibid.
[27] *The Transition Period* (*Shu Ji*) by Hao Zhou, 2009.

and fraud. Lower level officials tend to avoid or distort policy tasks in the performance evaluation system and solely focus on the measurable and quantifiable policy goals (O'Brien and Li 1999; Wedeman 2001; Guo 2009). Well-measured policy tasks and those carrying more weight in the target responsibility system, such as economic growth, investment, and (at least prior to 2015) the one-child policy are therefore more strictly followed, and poorly measured goals such as social welfare, burial policies, and environment policies are constantly ignored or distorted (O'Brien and Li 1999; Saich 2008; Gao 2009; Liang and Langbein 2015). Data fabrication in evaluation results is also severe. While there is no way to assess the true prevalence of faking evaluation results across Chinese local governments, a few scholars have shown evidence of it from interviews, archival research, and creative data analysis (Cai 2000; Tsai 2008; Gao 2015; Wallace 2016). On rare occasions, we get a sense of the severity from government approved news reports. For example, in 2016, the national government publicly denounced all cities and counties in Liaoning province for inflating several years of economic and fiscal data by more than 50 percent.[28]

Therefore, be it reality or constructed reality, with a belief that other officials are not entirely honest with their evaluation results, Chinese officials do not believe doing well on one's formal evaluation alone promises a bright political future. In all the fifteen cities where I conducted interviews, government officials commonly held a cynical view about China's cadre evaluation system. One official from the Organization Department (the personnel management department controlling officials' promotion) commented: "It [performance evaluation] is for show. When was the last time you saw someone demoted simply because s/he didn't get a high score in an evaluation?"[29] Another official from a different province mentioned, "The whole point of the evaluation system is it provides a bottom line, that you don't make mistakes on those listed policy targets, that's really it....promotion is not entirely based on it. It [promotion] is a complicated process, [there are] so many things to consider."[30] Such a cynical view is further strengthened by a widely held belief that cadre evaluation results are faked everywhere. When I asked the first official if he really thought the evaluation results were made up, he answered,

[28] "Liaoning sheng shengzhang Chen Qiufa: women dingzhe yali jiya shuifen," *People's Daily*, 2017-01-17, http://politics.people.com.cn/n1/2017/0117/c1001-29030885.html.

[29] Interview 20150708.

[30] Interview 20160204.

"Think about who filled in the performance evaluation forms? Yourself. Everyone made stuff up."[31] This view is resonated by another official in charge of the making of evaluation criteria in a different province, "Of course it [the evaluation system] is serious, but there is a lot of art in making your numbers pretty. It is art."[32]

With such cynical views on the system, Chinese local officials with political ambition turn to focus on top-down evaluation, which, according to all my interviews with government officials, is the deciding factor in one's promotion. One official said, "It all comes down to whether your 'bosses' like you. Your boss controls your future."[33] This view among government officials is supported by a small group of scholars who challenge the dominant view that performance in the target responsibility system is decisive to one's political future in China. Some find performance to have only limited roles in officials' promotion and only for those at the bottom level of the government (Landry 2008; Landry, Lü, and Duan 2018). Some find that political networks and factions play the most important role in one's promotion (Shih 2009; Shih, Adolph, and Liu 2012; Keller 2016). Still others find that merit must be complemented by political networks for political advancement (Jia, Kudamatsu, and Seim 2015), each playing different roles depending on the official's career stage and educational background (Ma, Tang, and Yan 2015). A recent study finds that even the evaluation criteria in the target responsibility system is affected by political networks, where the well-connected get easier targets, compromising the meritocracy principle of the target responsibility system (Leng and Zuo 2021).

But it is not easy to perform well in the top-down evaluation. Designed to be opaque, the system depends on the higher-up officials' experience and judgment to select the loyal. But what counts as loyalty? How does one show loyalty? What are the higher-up officials looking for? This ambiguity is further complicated by how the CCP manages its cadres to guarantee regime stability: Party-state leaders are reposted frequently to prevent local lords from emerging. This leaves ambitious local leaders with limited time to familiarize themselves with upper-level officials and even less time to establish solid networks for promotion before the connected individuals within an official's political network are transferred.

[31] Interview 20150708.
[32] Interview 20150708.
[33] Interview 20181104.

The system of reposting also increases the difficulty of effective network building, as the higher-up officials with different preferences come and go. Everywhere I talked to local officials, there was paramount insecurity and anxiety about the top-down evaluation, and no one was sure how to please their superiors. A government official described the anxiety he observed among his fellow officials: "They are so desperate to find out what they can do [for promotion], so insecure about their future, that they run around like their rear ends are on fire."[34] Another interviewee, an official in the Party committee of the city (the power center at the city level) described the anxiety common to his "middle-aged male colleagues": "They want to get promoted, but how? They did well in performance evaluation but then everyone did well in performance evaluation. This matter [promotion] seems so random, unless one has particularly strong backing from the above, otherwise no one knows if he can get promoted. Why do you think Buddhism and fortune telling is so popular among Chinese officials?"[35]

Therefore, the ambitious Chinese officials who care about promotion – and there is no shortage of the ambitious – suffer from double insecurity. On the one hand, they worry that their competence is unnoticed in the target responsibility system that is ineffective in distinguishing the most competent. On the other hand, they are insecure about making the right impression on their career-controlling selectors, knowing neither how long a new group of selectors will be in place, nor exactly what they are looking for. Visibility projects and selectoral campaigns are borne out of this uncertainty and insecurity among ambitious officials.

VISIBILITY PROJECTS, AN UNEVEN PLAYING FIELD FOR FIRMS

Visibility projects can have a strong impact on firms and the landscape of sectors. When a sector is selected to launch visibility projects, local officials often ask firms to contribute to these projects to avoid blame for wasteful spending.[36] Contributions can be direct investments in, or changing business operations for, visibility projects. Firms, private

[34] Interview 20190326.
[35] Interview 20181109.
[36] Following the 2008 financial crisis, the central government became less tolerant of local government debt (Liu, Oi, and Zhang 2022), likely increasing the need for local governments to rely on company contributions for extra-budgetary spending.

(including foreign) and state-owned, would be elicited, sometimes with persuasion, and other times with coercion. In general, firms do not find visibility projects attractive, and this is not just because visibility projects pursue scale and scope beyond what makes sense from a business perspective.

Visibility projects, in the eyes of businesspeople, are not the best approach to build connections with state officials. Compared with bribery and other forms of interest exchange, as described in Chapter 1, firms do not have nearly as much control over their contributions to visibility projects, including the type, scale, overall costs, and sometimes even the beneficiaries of visibility projects. This lack of control means firms cannot guarantee they will recoup the costs of visibility projects, particularly when these projects do not have practicality as the primary concern. However, if the firm does contribute and can distinguish its contributions from other firms, and therefore can claim credit in front of the local leaders, then there is a chance that it will be rewarded by the local leaders with renewal of contracts, access to loans, government subsidies, and an easier business environment in general. Moreover, if a firm refuses to contribute to visibility projects, it needs to be able to survive potential political retribution for the business and even the business owners. And it is easy for the government to punish businesses. One city official said confidently, "We have at least two ways to get to an entrepreneur: their tax records and their registered capital.[37] I can tell you now, not a single entrepreneur in this city meets these requirements."[38]

Understanding their dependence on the local governments who control key resources, firms of all ownership types usually agree to contribute to city leaders' visibility projects at first. But different firms have different capacity to afford visibility projects, based on their budget constraints. Firms with hard budget constraints will lose out to firms with soft budget constraints in the long run, because they cannot afford visibility projects as easily. In China, this means that private firms have less capacity to contribute to visibility projects than state-owned firms. After all, private firms have hard budget constraints, are profit driven, and have much more restricted access to credit and loans (Tsai 2002; Huang

[37] Registered capital is a requirement for companies in China. Shareholders of a company must declare an amount of capital that they will inject into the company, and they are required by law to inject 20 percent of this amount into a company when it is first founded. Registered capital serves as a reference point for the authorities to assess the scale of the company's operations.

[38] Interview 20171141843.

2003; Firth et al. 2009; Poncet, Steingress, and Vandenbussche 2010). When a visibility project goes so far, or when new leaders come in and start a new wave of visibility projects, it becomes unsustainable for private firms to continue sponsoring the leaders' visibility projects, which boast excessive scale and looks but do not necessarily bring returns. The eventual refusal of private firms to "carry the sedan chair" for the local government is a major reason for the subsequent collapse of marketization in many sectors. Under constant demand for contributions to visibility projects, private firms either leave or are forced out and replaced by SOEs that could continue to sponsor visibility projects, creating sectors dominated by SOEs.

I show this mechanism in Chapter 4 and Chapter 5, with the urban bus sector in China. This sector became popular for the launch of visibility projects from the 2000s, and these projects gradually created a state-dominated sector across Chinese cities without any central coordination, defeating the Chinese central government's continuing call for private investment in this sector. I show the trend and correlation between visibility projects and the exit of private firms with an original dataset in Chapter 4, and illustrate the causal mechanism with process tracing and comparative case studies in Chapter 5.

3

Societal Control, the Second Political Service

> Here is the thing. Usually, local governments have no trouble controlling social unrest. But when they do have trouble, it is best to have a central state-owned enterprise by their side.
>
> A Chinese central government official, 2019

During a long conversation in spring 2015 with a private entrepreneur who owned a manufacturing company with several factories in China, the entrepreneur went on a venting session about why he immigrated to Singapore. He felt as if he did not have full control over his business success in China. "It's so unpredictable," he said.

> My factories have the highest standards in the industry, and I was a *sun-zi* [grandson, a derogatory term to indicate someone is at the service of others unconditionally] to them [government officials]. But what do I get? They go back on their word to cover their own a**. And I have this big belly [from dining], and my liver is on the edge of explosion [from drinking]. What is it all for?[1]

His business may or may not have had the highest standards (his factories had experienced labor disputes and safety violations), but he took it to heart that the competitiveness of business does not guarantee success in China. The fall of his business started with a public protest against an industrial park that one of his factories was situated in. This protest did not hurt his business directly in that he did not lose buyers or suppliers, but it caused fallout between him and the local leaders whom he used to have a cozy relationship with.

[1] Interview 2015904L; all the quotes that follow are from the same source.

Manufacturing chemical products, his plant was located in an industrial park with a few other manufacturing plants, some owned by private firms and others by state-owned enterprises (SOEs). The entire industrial park shares a common wastewater treatment system that collects and treats all the plants' wastewater before it is released, following a basic pretreatment conducted by each plant. In 2017, a public protest took place, accusing the park of releasing untreated wastewater into the river, which had damaged the crops in nearby farms. Confident that his factory created substantial tax revenues and jobs for the city, and that his plant was just one of several in the park, among them three SOEs that were "like family of the government," he was sure that his business would emerge from the turmoil unscathed.

But he was wrong. Once the protest escalated, he quickly realized that the local government was going to offer his plant and that of another private company to the villagers. The government initially announced that the industrial park had met wastewater treatment standards, as proven by a real-time water monitoring system in the wastewater treatment plant. The pollution of the river, therefore, must have come from another hub of factories further upstream. But the villagers rejected this explanation, showing evidence of untreated wastewater coming out from underground "dark pipes" (*an'guan*) suspiciously near the industrial park. The government then changed strategy. They first promised the villagers they would investigate these dark pipes. After this, they asked all the factories in the industrial park to provide hush money to the protest leaders to defuse the situation. The two private companies agreed to pay, but they realized the SOEs were not doing the same. When the leaders of the protest refused the hush money, the government changed strategy again. They decided they needed to use force, as well as offering a head on a plate. The government sent in the special police to disperse the crowd and claimed that an investigation showed that the dark pipes came from the privately owned factories. The government suspended these factories' operations and ordered them to upgrade their pretreatment facilities. They also issued a harsh fine roughly equal to a year's revenue.

This private entrepreneur was infuriated. He was angry not because his factory did not have dark pipes (he never confirmed or denied this), but because when everyone else had dark pipes, including the SOEs, his plant had to take all the blame. He explained that these factories had dark pipes because the new standards for pretreated wastewater were unrealistic. Since 2013, the province mandated that the pretreated wastewater that exits factories must contain less than 60 mg/kg of total nitrogen and total phosphorous, which is an exceptionally stringent requirement, almost as strict as the standard for effluent (treated wastewater). When these factories were built, prior to 2013, their pretreatment facility was set up to meet the old standard of 1,000 mg/kg:

> To meet this new standard would mean that all the factories would each need to have a full wastewater treatment plant. No one has one. The whole point of having a single wastewater treatment plant for the entire industrial park is so that we don't need to invest in this facility ourselves. Tell me, how can any factory reach the new standard without a full wastewater treatment facility?

Therefore, he was certain that the two companies bearing the costs were selected because they were privately owned. He felt betrayed by the city leaders whom he had up until this point had a reciprocal relationship with.

> When the wolves [the public] come, they feed us to them. They never trouble the SOEs. SOEs and them [government officials] come from the same family [the Party-state]. But us [private firms], what are we to them? We are not family, we are servants. They know we cannot get back at them. And so I thought, to hell with it, I quit.

He refused to pay the fines and instead shut down his factory. A few months later, the local leaders offered to retract the majority of the fine and asked him to reopen the factory, but he declined.

His experience is not unique. Private companies often become scapegoats in state–society conflicts. But SOEs have their roles as well, even though this private entrepreneur did not get to observe it. SOEs are not just protected because they are "family" to local officials, but because they often bring in political support to local officials when dealing with public unrest. SOEs have more political capital than private firms, and their political capital goes beyond just political connections with government leaders that successful private firms also have. When the authoritarian state officials look at private firms and SOEs, they see different political capital that are useful in state–society conflicts. They strategically choose firms to help them manage the risks of social unrest, and in the process create a landscape of companies not entirely based on the companies' business competitiveness.

This chapter introduces the second political role of firms in China: societal control. In this book, I focus on the direct roles of firms in dealing with public protests, which is part of a wider range of societal control services provided by firms in China. For example, companies in internet, telecommunications, and financial sectors provide citizen surveillance and tracking, as well as censorship for the state (King, Pan, and Roberts 2013; Huang and Tsai 2022); SOEs can provide employment in times of economic slowdown, crucial to maintaining social stability; and online shopping platforms had an unintentional stabilizing effect by distracting citizens from paying attention to security issues (Liu 2024). But the direct roles of firms in managing public unrest are not well documented and will be a focus of this book.

Similar to the first political role of firms, which involves providing contributions to authoritarian officials' careers, societal control creates an extra dimension of competition between private firms and SOEs, based on their differing political capital. Private firms are good scapegoats. They are the easiest type of firm to control and to punish, because they have a lower level of political capital. SOEs, particularly the large ones and those controlled by the central government, have high political capital and are better allies when the local government faces protests, even though these SOEs are also harder to control. But before we move on to discuss the political service of societal control and how it divides firms in the eyes of the state, I will explain what social unrest means to local officials in China.

PROTESTS ARE FINE, HIGH-PROFILE PROTESTS ARE NOT

The CCP is highly sensitive to protests and considers social unrest damaging to regime stability and legitimacy. To make sure protests are contained, the CCP includes social stability as a one-vote veto target (*yi piao fou jue*), a must-meet task in its performance evaluation of local officials. If local officials cannot contain protests, the resulting social instability will cancel out an official's otherwise outstanding achievements. However, while appearing strict on paper, no one is really certain how strictly this criterion is enforced. While there is a lack of study of the actual impact of social stability on local officials' careers owing to data limits, some scholarship finds that protests do not deter Chinese local officials from launching contentious economic policies (Cai 2008), and as long as protesters do not challenge the ruling party, the government will tolerate protests or even encourage protests to obtain information on local governance (O'Brien and Li 2006; Lorentzen 2013), or to push for policies otherwise resisted by political elites (O'Brien, Li, and Liu 2020; Deng, Yang, and Ma 2022; Ma 2022). These studies generate an indication that having protests alone does not really concern local government officials, otherwise they would do everything within their power to prevent protests from ever happening.

My interviews verify this implication from the literature. All the local officials I interviewed, except for one, were not very concerned about the breakout of mild and issue-specific protests. A city government official, for example, told me that surely no official likes to deal with social unrest, but it is not as threatening as people usually think. He explained, "Protests are everywhere. Everywhere. They are tests of a leader's ability." When asked whether that means having protests in one's jurisdiction will not necessarily hurt a leader's future, he stressed, "It's a test, you understand? They [the Party-state] never explicitly say that it's a test, but if one successfully dealt with collective actions, then it's great news for one's political future. Look at all the leaders high above, all of them had successful experience handling protests."[2] His view is resonated by other interviewees. Officials widely recognize that no one gets demoted solely because of social unrest in their jurisdiction. Rather, if an official is not a high-flyer, or is already on a downward path, or has made powerful political enemies, then being unable to "handle" social unrest could become a justification for sinking their career prospects.

Therefore, while Chinese local officials are not concerned about having protests in their jurisdiction per se, they are careful to contain protests and prevent them from becoming high-profile protests that will attract attention from above. From interviews, I summarize three different but often related signs that a protest has become high profile and is potentially beyond a local government's control, thereby becoming a genuine risk to an official's political future.

The first sign is casualties. Casualties of either protesters or the police is a clear indicator that the local officials have failed to contain the protest, and that it has become high profile. Casualties, particularly deaths of protesters, can greatly damage regime legitimacy. It is also extremely difficult for local officials to hide casualties from the upper-level government, particularly in an era of social media. Casualties guarantee interference from the upper-level government, which is not welcomed by local officials.

The second sign is mobilization of the People's Armed Police (PAP). The PAP is a semi-police and semi-military organization overseeing domestic security. When a protest requires physical suppression, local governments will first resort to the local police and the local urban management forces (*cheng'guan*). If the protest continues to escalate and these local forces are no longer sufficient for suppression, local governments then mobilize the PAP. Using this paramilitary force requires a

[2] Interview 2016084827.

formal application of mobilization by the city government to the PAP's city headquarters, and such an application is always reported to the provincial government.[3] Therefore, mobilization of the PAP signals large-scale protests that are impossible to hide from the upper-level government, and that can make city leaders look incompetent in containing protests within their jurisdiction.

The third sign is coverage of the protest in news media from beyond the city. According to a local official whose job was "maintenance of social stability," only when protests have a large scale and last a long time does it become difficult for the government to hide it from the news media, especially media from outside the city.[4] Attracting journalists from provincial and national media means local leaders failed to contain a protest and created public chaos, which signals incompetence. Indeed, a small body of scholarship finds that local cadres put in a lot of effort to cover up local incidents and prevent them from escalating to the point of being in the national spotlight (Edin 2003; Baekkeskov and Rubin 2016; Lu and Xue 2016).

If one or more of these three signs are present in a protest, local leaders risk looking incompetent and apt to cause trouble for the upper-level government.[5] Therefore, while protests themselves do not deter local officials from launching controversial projects or programs,[6] local officials do have a strong incentive to prevent protests from escalating, to keep protests unnoticed, and to justify violent suppression when suppression becomes inevitable. This is to avoid being blamed by the upper-level government for provoking protests, while at the same time being unable to contain them. But how to achieve all of these goals? Local governments use different strategies, and a lot of them involve firms.

LOCAL GOVERNMENT STRATEGIES AGAINST PROTESTS AND FIRMS' ROLES

To make sure public unrest does not escalate into high-profile incidents, local officials use various strategies to defuse them. Common

[3] Starting in 2018, local governments below the provincial level are no longer allowed to mobilize the PAP. They must get approval from the provincial government.

[4] Interview 20170314.

[5] Cai (2008) similarly identified casualties of protesters and media exposure as factors that might trigger national government intervention in a local protest.

[6] This echoes the findings of Cai (2008) who found that public protests against economic policies do not deter local governments from adopting them.

strategies can be categorized as appeasement and suppression. Appeasement prevents protests from escalating, and suppression ends a high-profile protest. Appeasement includes persuasion and concessions. An example of persuasion includes dialogues with the public and promises to enhance monitoring and regulation of controversial projects. Common examples of concessions include temporary suspension of a controversial project, ordering factories to upgrade safety measures, and providing financial compensations or jobs to protesters. If these measures are not effective in preventing protests from escalating, then local governments use suppression to silence the public. Suppression often involves arresting and detaining leading activists, and harassment of protesters and their families. Echoing what other scholars observed (Cai 2008; Chen 2012; Heurlin 2016; Li 2019), suppression is typically not the first choice for local governments, because it can lead to greater societal dissatisfaction and consequently draw negative attention from the Party-state.

Both strategies, appeasement and suppression, are well documented in different contexts of protests (O'Brien and Li 2006; Cai 2008; Chen 2012; Li 2019; Ong 2022); however, the role of firms in these strategies has largely escaped scholarly attention so far. When protests are directed toward projects or programs that involve firms, local officials often ask these firms to provide political services in societal control. This is often done to deflect from or reduce blame of the government and thereby preserve the state's legitimacy, and sometimes to complement the government's lack of financial resources to use appeasement strategies.

Firms are not the only nonstate actors in China to help the state with societal control. Ong (2022) observed that the Chinese government outsourced violent repression to "thugs-for-hire" in land expropriation during China's rapid urbanization process, and utilized brokers, including those in civil society, to persuade the public to accept unpopular policies. Mattingly (2019) similarly observed that in rural China, civil society groups such as temples and lineage groups, play roles in coopting the public to advance controversial policies. Using firms for societal control is along the same lines as the state using these nonstate actors to deflect blame.

Both private firms and SOEs assist with societal control but do so in different ways. Private firms are good for appeasement strategies, and SOEs, especially large and powerful ones, are particularly helpful when suppression becomes necessary. The difference between the firms lies in their different levels of political capital.

SOEs versus Private Firms in Political Capital

The *political capital* of a firm can be loosely defined as the level of government support available to a firm. In the literature, political capital is often operationalized as political connections of a firm, measured by the firm owner's political positions, the number of board members with a political background, or a firm's expenditure on government relations. While these measurements are a great way to measure an intangible concept, they only reflect the amount of political capital of a firm at a certain point of time, and are less useful in capturing the reliability and stability of the firm's political capital, which depends not only on the number of political connections, but also a few other factors.

The reliability and stability of a firm's political capital are related to the firm's sector, size, and ownership types. Firms in sectors strategic to national and domestic security naturally enjoy higher levels of political capital, because the success of these sectors, such as energy, natural resources, and telecommunications, are tied to a country's stability, sovereignty, economic independence, or economic success. Firms of unusually large size, be they large in employment or assets that span a large section of society, also naturally enjoy higher levels of political capital. These unusually large firms, such as the recently bailed-out state-owned insurance companies and the Evergrande Group in real estate, have an outsized influence on economic stability, and their success and failure is tied to the country's systemic risk. They therefore tend to receive more government support in the forms of preferential treatment or bailouts during times of liquidity crisis.

Political capital also directly comes from firms' ownership types,[7] which is the focus of this book. In China, both SOEs and private firms try to build a vast network of political connections. These connections can come from individual firm executive or board members' personal ties to government officials, their formal political affiliations, or their past political experiences (e.g. Li et al. 2008; Peng, Zhang, and Zhu 2017). These individually based political connections are built through exchange of interests between a firm and government officials. The weakness of this source of political capital lies in its volatility. Political connections appear and disappear based on individual-level changes in the firm and in the government. If the board member with the most valuable political connection leaves the company, or if the government officials connected to

7 A meta-analysis of the literature on political connections of firms indirectly supports this view. It shows that state ownership has independent effects from political connections on firms' business strategies (Tihanyi et al. 2019).

the company are reposted to a different locality, then these political connections risk disappearing.

Private firms have a rather unidimensional source of political capital in most sectors: political connections with a specific set of individuals. This makes their political capital quite volatile in nature. SOEs, extensions of the state's economic function, have ties not only with individual state officials, but also with the state as a whole. SOEs are almost always connected to a set of politicians in power, and therefore their political capital does not depend on individual politicians to the same degree and consequently does not fluctuate as much as that of private firms. Private firms, except for those in strategic sectors and those that are too big to fail, tend to have individual-centered, lower level of political capital than SOEs. SOEs, in general, have a more stable and higher level of institutionally based political capital. In the eyes of the state, then, private firms are better scapegoats when using appeasement strategies, and SOEs are better allies when using suppression in response to social protests.

Private Firms Are Better Scapegoats, and SOEs Better Allies

Scapegoat is a role almost exclusive to private firms. The lower political capital of private firms makes them especially dependent on good relations with local governments for business success, and that gives the local governments power to control private firms. When protests happen, and if the target projects are funded or carried out by private firms, local governments can have the private firms shoulder the blame for protests. Specifically, local governments can punish private firms with fines or suspend operations, have the private firms pay for online censorship services to prevent the spread of information about the protest, and provide monetary benefits or employment opportunities to protesters. By having private firms execute these strategies, the local governments can distance themselves from the source of protests, deflect blame from both the public and the upper-level government officials to private firms, establish an image of an impartial regulator, and not bear responsibility for any negative social consequences.

Local governments cannot easily use SOEs as scapegoats for two reasons. First, SOEs, particularly local SOEs, are commonly considered by the public to be a branch of the government. Blaming protests on them, therefore, cannot effectively isolate local officials from the responsibility for protests. While in theory local governments can achieve blame deflection with nonlocal SOEs, it would be risky to do so because these SOEs are backed by other, and often higher-level, governments. To blame an SOE owned by a different and often higher-level government could introduce conflicts between governments, which might aggravate the situation and attract negative attention from higher-level officials. Second, local governments have difficulties getting SOEs to agree to be scapegoats for local governments. With their higher political capital and less dependence on any single local government, it is much harder for local governments to coerce SOEs against their will. Some powerful SOEs, particularly those directly controlled by China's central government, can even exhibit an equal, if not dominating, position in dealing with local governments.

A business dinner I observed illustrates the power balance between central SOEs and city government officials in China.[8] The dinner was arranged by a central SOE representative to host local government officials to discuss a public infrastructure deal of 10 billion yuan. The SOE had been cultivating this deal in the city for a year. The SOE representative said to a city official over dinner:

> A deal this big matters. We have invested in it and given your top men [city leaders] the fair amount [of bribes]. If our top men [SOE leaders] get disappointed ... you never know, you see these car accidents happen all the time. Some deals are just so big, that we need to take them seriously.

This scenario of course does not imply this SOE would necessarily proceed with some unspeakable plan, nor does it suggest this is how all SOEs routinely conduct business in China, but the fact that this representative did not mind using threatening language to local government officials in front of others says a lot about the power balance between central SOEs and local governments. It would be hard to imagine a private firm or a weaker SOE doing the same.

But the same reasons that make SOEs unsuitable as scapegoats make them ideal allies for local governments. SOEs possess high political capital, which, despite making them harder to control, also makes them valuable during high-profile protests. SOEs, particularly those controlled by higher-level governments, can bring in extra support from higher-level governments if a protest escalates into a high-profile one. And better yet, it is easier to justify suppression when it involves an SOE. Using force to suppress public unrest, particularly unrest against a project built or operated by private firms, could make local governments look as if they are "protecting" business interests, which could invite corruption

[8] Observation 20157631108.

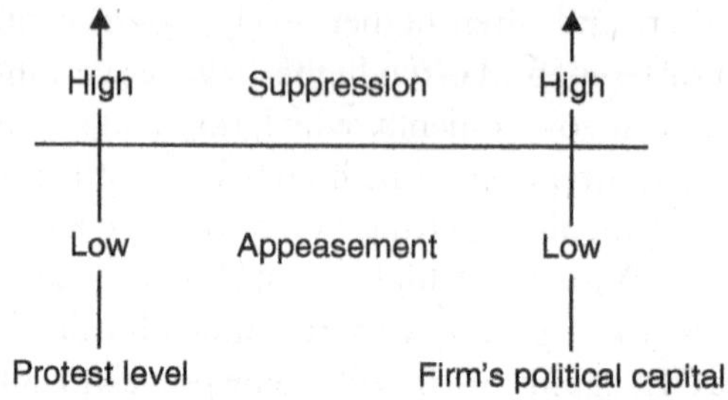

FIGURE 3.1 Government strategy against protests and preferred firm type

investigations from above. This risk is much smaller if a local government is working with SOEs to suppress protests against SOE projects. A city official explained: "Both of them [private firms and SOEs] pay up [bribes] to local officials. But if any investigation happens, bribes from SOEs seldom get mentioned."[9]

This political logic affects how local governments select partners in launching projects. Sometimes, local leaders anticipate high-profile protests around controversial projects, but they still want to launch the projects for various reasons. In situations like this, SOEs can help local governments better justify the decision to launch controversial projects, especially if these decisions might later be questioned owing to the occurrence of high-profile protests. SOEs help pave the way for these projects from the very beginning, including siting decisions, feasibility reports, and getting environmental evaluation approvals. And later, if suppression is needed, SOEs can help local governments influence investigation outcomes and exempt local officials from responsibility. All of these functions come from SOEs' stable and institutionally rooted political capital, and it is very difficult for private firms to compete on these dimensions, which involve negotiation with and cooperation from various levels of government and various government agencies. I describe these dynamics in detail in Chapters 6 and 7.

Figure 3.1 shows the comparative advantage of private firms and SOEs in assisting state officials with societal control. With lower political capital that largely derives from political connections with individual government officials, private firms are more likely to agree to shoulder the blame for unpopular or failed projects, pay for appeasement strategies, and be publicly shamed and punished. In the eyes of the government, therefore, they are better at defusing a protest before it escalates into a high-profile one.

[9] Interview 201903220443.

SOEs, particularly large and powerful SOEs owned by China's provincial or central governments, are better political allies when controversial projects invite large-scale public opposition. With higher levels of political capital that are not only individual-based but also institutionally-based, SOEs can bring in extra political resources to help local officials avoid blame from the upper-level government. However, by selecting a more powerful political ally, local governments must give up more control over the project and the firm.

This difference in firms' political capital creates another playing field for SOEs and private firms to compete in China, particularly over projects that might invite high-profile protests. The effect of protests on business mostly manifests in the long run. If a business operation that invites protests belongs to private companies, then it is more likely for the government to use the private companies as a scapegoat and impose both reputational and economic losses on these companies. But if the business belongs to SOEs, then local governments are more likely to align with the SOEs and impose less punishment on the SOEs. In the long run, this differential treatment could lead private firms to either exit the sector or merge with SOEs to better protect themselves.

In some sectors, high-profile protests might even lead to business "competition" at the stage of business entry into a sector. This is particularly true for sectors that require special government approval beyond regular business licenses to start a business, such as Paraxylene chemical plants and nuclear power plants, or sectors that depend on government contracts such as waste treatment and wastewater treatment. In these sectors, local governments need to consider the potential impact of high-profile protests before a business even starts, and approval or selection of firms becomes a complicated decision that goes beyond the business competitiveness of firms. Local governments could favor a certain ownership type over others depending on the estimated chance of high-profile protests. If local officials do not think high-profile protests are likely or if they are confident that they can prevent protests from escalating into high-profile ones, then they may prefer firms with lower political capital that are easier to control and to expropriate. If local officials believe high-profile protests are likely, then they may prefer firms with higher political capital.

While the overall number of protests in China has decreased since the mid 2010s, the use of suppression has nonetheless increased (Chen 2020). This suggests that those who do mobilize protests are more likely to escalate them into high-profile protests. Under these conditions, we should expect that in sectors prone to high-profile protests – such as mining, hazardous manufacturing, nuclear energy, waste incineration, and wastewater treatment – SOEs, especially the large and powerful ones, will have an advantage over private firms.

Using firms for societal control, the second political service described in this book, thus also creates changes in the landscape of firms in a sector. Private firms and SOEs carry different roles in providing this political service. SOEs are better allies of the state in the presence of high-profile protests, and private firms are better scapegoats. When local governments anticipate high-profile protests, they prefer to work with SOEs. When local governments anticipate regular protests, they are more likely to work with private firms. In Chapters 6 and 7, I test this mechanism with the solid waste treatment sector where "not in my backyard" protests tend to happen, particularly against waste incinerators. Because companies in the solid waste treatment sector often work with the government in public–private partnerships and local governments actively select firms for the sector, firm difference in political capital shows clearly from the very beginning of setting up a business. Chapter 6 describes how private firms and SOEs in the solid waste treatment sector contribute to societal control in different ways, as well as the correlation between high-profile protests and firm preferences of the local government. Chapter 7 uses multiple case studies to examine the underlining mechanism and explains how protests gradually changed the landscape of companies in this sector.

4

Visibility Projects and the End of Marketization in China's Urban Bus Sector

National Trend

On a quiet night in May 2009, in the beautiful coastal city Rivertown in a wealthy eastern province, home to less than a million people, a group of men was on the move. They knocked on the door of each name on a list of more than twenty "uncooperative targets." They sat the target down, talked him through how important his cooperation would be for the wellbeing of everyone, and casually mentioned the occupation, work locations, and schools of the target's spouse, siblings, and children. They then listed some problems the target was having: debts, tax evasion, traffic law violations, and sometimes lawsuits. They kindly expressed regrets about how inconvenient it was for everyone to have to meet up at such a late hour, and how much they wished they did not need to show up at the target's house. Eventually they pulled out a contract, and nicely suggested the target should think things over one more time, and not let personal interests trump the greater good. They then left the target's home and moved on to the next name on the list.

In July, two months after this incident, all private bus firms and individual bus owners in Rivertown agreed to sell their bus firms to the city's sole local state-owned bus firm. The group of men was a taskforce set up by the city government. It comprised officials from the city's Traffic Bureau, Police Bureau, Department of Urban Management, and the state-owned bus firm. The targets they visited were owners of private bus firms in the city. It had all begun half a year before, in 2008, when Rivertown's government decided to deprivatize the urban bus sector in preparation for a "public transportation system upgrade." The upgrade plan included introducing new bus models, building the first light rail system in the city, and re-routing and cutting the existing bus lines around this light rail system. None of these changes was negotiated with the private bus firms or specified in their contracts with the city government, and the firms resisted strongly. Most of the private bus owners still had more than eight years left on their contract. Per the government's request, a lot of them had just replaced many old buses with new, air-conditioned buses not long before. They also found the re-routing without negotiation or fair compensation unacceptable. In response, they organized strikes and reported the city government to the provincial Office of Letters and Visits.[1] In March 2009, the city government's patience ran thin. With an executive order to "get things done quickly," the taskforce was set up and sent into action. After twenty-five years of private provision of urban bus services in Rivertown, deprivatization of the entire sector was completed within two months.

When two officials from that taskforce described this process of "persuasion" to me, they meant to emphasize how difficult their job was. They did not like being on the deprivatization taskforce. They had to work at night and risked revenge from the private bus firm owners who were usually well connected in the city – two of the bus firm owners also ran an underground casino business and had "muscles." They had no choice but to adopt the persuasion style of "those land expropriation and house demolition jobs," because private entrepreneurs "just don't care about the big picture" – referring to the city's big plans in the public transportation sector.[2]

And many more private bus owners all over China did not get the big picture. In all the fifteen cities where I conducted interviews, all of them deprivatized the urban bus sector, most using some form of coercion. Nationwide, deprivatization of the bus sector became a trend from the mid 2000s, going against the national government's call for more private participation in the sector. This is because the urban bus sector, a mundane foot soldier of urban life, had quietly become a top choice for visibility projects and selectoral campaigns.

A BRIEF HISTORY OF MARKETIZATION OF CHINA'S URBAN BUSES

Private firms once dominated the urban bus sector in Chinese cities. This was among the first public service sectors opened to private investors in

[1] An independent government office to collect grievances and complaints from people on government officials.
[2] Interview 201578410.

China. As the economy grew rapidly in the 1990s, demand for public transportation in cities quickly increased. However, city governments did not have the fiscal capacity to meet the increasing demand, especially after the tax reform in 1994.[3] In 1995, joining the global new public management movement of deregulation and privatization of public sectors, the Chinese national government allowed marketization in various urban public service sectors, including urban buses. Marketization of urban buses mostly took the form of government franchising, with the government allowing private firms the right to use a public domain (roads) and sell public services (within-city bus transit) to the public.[4] A standard franchise contract between local city governments and private bus firms had a term of twenty years. Under the contract, private bus firms had to obtain approval from the city's Traffic Bureau before opening new bus routes. They also did not have control over bus fares, which were solely decided by the city's Commodity Price Bureau. Private bus firms did not share their income with the city government. City governments were not shareholders in these private bus firms. Instead, the firms paid a fixed fee for the "special franchise right" when signing the contract and yearly taxes on profits.

Quickly, Chinese cities invited domestic and foreign private bus firms into the sector to start new bus firms. My data collection from 288 cities shows 233 cities (81 percent) privatized their urban bus sectors at some point between 1996 and 2016 (Figure 4.1). On average, each city had eight private bus firms and one public bus firm after privatization. Private urban buses became an important component of China's thriving urban life.

Things took a turn in the early 2000s. Going against the national government's continued call for private actors in municipal public service sectors, most Chinese cities started to deprivatize the once dominant private bus firms in the mid 2000s. As shown in Figure 4.1, only 19 percent of cities still had the urban bus sector under private control by the end of 2016, compared with 81 percent in 2006, and 27 percent in 1996. There is also local variation between cities in how long the bus sector was opened to private firms, ranging from a mere two years to twenty years, with an average lifespan of 11.5 years of private ownership.

[3] The 1994 tax sharing reform boosted central revenue by extracting more tax revenue from local governments, and shrank most city governments' revenues greatly. Facing tightened fiscal constraints, local city governments were concerned about their ability to provide public services.

[4] This form of franchise is also called a "concession": see Savas (1999).

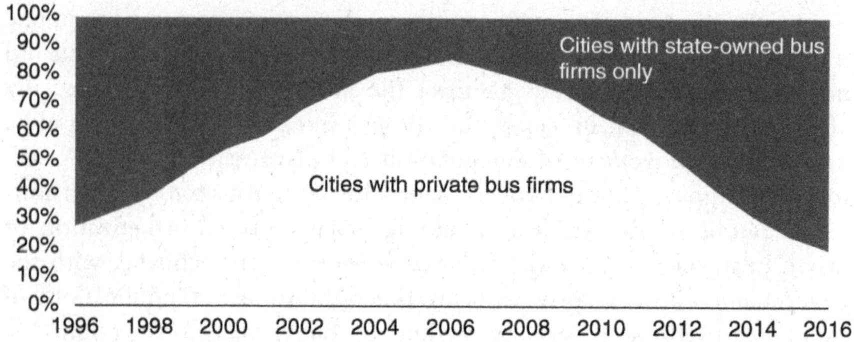

FIGURE 4.1 Ownership change in China's urban bus sector: 288 cities, 1996–2016

A PUZZLING SECTORAL CHOICE FOR DEPRIVATIZATION

The urban bus sector is not a typical choice for systematic state takeover. The phenomenon of deprivatization is still understudied, but scholars have identified sectors vulnerable to state takeover, including utilities, oil, mining, rail, telecommunications, banking, and sometimes media. For monopolistic public service sectors such as water supply, private ownership might provide less efficient and more expensive public goods than under public ownership, prompting the state to take over these sectors to provide cheaper services (Ohemeng and Grant 2008). Sectors that are politically sensitive to the presence of foreign firms, such as banking, rail, telecommunications and natural resources, are likely to be nationalized to avoid foreign dependency (Jodice 1980; Shafer 1983; Kobrin 1984). Sometimes sectors such as oil and mining are expropriated simply because they possess profitable assets that can produce long term returns for the state (Guriev, Kolotilin, and Sonin 2011; Hajzler 2012). An authoritarian state might also deprivatize politically important sectors, such as media, to control the public (Gehlbach and Sonin 2014). However, the urban bus sector does not fit into any of these sectoral profiles. It is not monopolistic in nature and in practice; it is not a politically sensitive sector crucial to national security; its assets – the buses – have high discount rates and usually lose most of their value within six years; and it does not produce high profit margins owing to heavily controlled bus fares. For these reasons, most countries that have privatized their bus services still have this sector in private hands (Finn and Mulley 2011). Even in the case of China, the trend of deprivatization of urban buses is going against the national government's call for more private participation in the sector.

Why do Chinese local governments deprivatize urban buses, a non-monopolistic, thin-profit, and nonstrategic public service sector? By examining local variations and timing variations of deprivatization of the urban bus sector across Chinese cities, this chapter provides a new explanation for deprivatization in the authoritarian context. The end of marketization in the urban bus sector began when the sector became a political playground for visibility projects, part of selectoral campaigns. Deprivatization of the urban bus sector became primarily a political measure whereby local officials removed private bus firms that resisted visibility projects, rather than a policy borne out of economic or social concerns.

VISIBILITY PROJECTS AND THE INCREASINGLY INCONVENIENT PRIVATE FIRMS

The urban bus sector became a popular choice for visibility projects in the mid 2000s along with several other public service sectors, after an earlier generation of visibility projects such as overly grand government buildings and excessive airports fell out of favor with central leaders in 2004.[5] This change, along with the center's policy shift to sustainable development instead of economic growth alone, pushed local government officials to look for new visibility projects in line with the center's new preference. The urban bus sector was chosen against this background.

The urban bus sector was chosen primarily because it is a highly visible sector. Chinese city governments call urban buses "the moving window" of a city. The sector's key facilities – buses and bus stops – are highly exposed, and every change in these facilities is visible, making them a great vehicle for city leaders to showcase their ability in city management. A Bureau of Urban Management official said jealously in an interview that "urban buses are so easily used to show achievement. You change the buses, you add buses, you build lanes, anything you do in this sector makes the city immediately look different. What other sectors can compare to this?"[6] Furthermore, buses provide a quasi-public service. As such, local officials can frame projects in this sector as beneficial to the general public,

[5] In 2004, the national government openly criticized and halted some ludicrous and unnecessary construction projects and punished over 400 local leaders for misuse of public funds related to these projects.

[6] Interview 20158396.

rather than to a select group of beneficiaries. This gives these projects more of an appearance of being genuine efforts to improve social welfare, however ostentatious or unsustainable they might later prove to be.

Justification for launching visibility projects in the urban bus sector became available when the national government launched a series of central environmental initiatives from 2002. As environmental degradation worsened in China, the national government issued four "guidance and suggestions" documents (*zhidao yijian*) in 2002, 2005, 2012, and 2015, calling for further development of the public transportation sector to replace private vehicles so as to reduce exhaust fumes and to alleviate traffic congestion. These central initiatives are not incorporated into the formal cadre evaluation, they do not provide financial support to local governments, and they are open to local interpretation. Basically, these central suggestions are vague and optional, rather than specific and mandatory. Visibility projects in this sector thus present little political risk of inadvertently defying or challenging the authority of higher-level officials.

Therefore, local officials turned their eyes to the urban bus sector following these initiatives. In interviews with government officials and bus firm managers in fifteen cities, when asked about what prompted sectoral upgrades and changes in the urban bus sector, all interviewees mentioned it was in response to these central initiatives. Only a few officials also mentioned local development needs. With justification provided by the national government, and as a highly visible sector, the urban bus sector became a popular choice for visibility projects.

There are three major visibility projects in the urban bus sector, as confirmed by interviews with both government officials and bus firms: (1) bus beautification projects; (2) bus upgrade projects; and (3) construction of Bus Rapid Transit (BRT) systems.

First are bus beautification projects, often associated with a city's effort to apply for national city title awards that have a long tradition under CCP rule. Interviewees identified two important national titles that require cooperation from bus operators to beautify their buses: the "National Civilized City" (*quan guo wenming chengshi*) and "National Public Transportation City" (*gongjiao dushi*).[7] The central government awards these titles to multiple cities at a time based on whether the city is orderly, clean, beautiful, and civilized. Winning a title helps city leaders stand out in urban management, and government interviewees

[7] Before 2011, "National Public Transportation City" was named "National Transportation Model City" (*jiaotong guanli mofan chengshi*).

consistently mentioned that winning a title is "an important line" on city leaders' resumes and work reports, and leaders "care about these titles very much."[8]

Applications for these city titles focus on the looks of the buses, and in the run-up, city officials often embark on a project of cleaning and repainting dirty buses, taking advertisements off them, and replacing old-looking buses. Bus beautification projects do not have any obvious social welfare implications in and of themselves, as they do not bring substantial rewards from the central government. Meanwhile, the improvement in the looks of buses tends to be done in a quick and short-lived style, paid for by the bus operators and enforced by the city government only during the title application period. Neither the titles nor the beautification projects provide any clear long-term benefits to bus companies themselves. They primarily provide reputational benefits to local leaders.

The second visibility project is bus upgrade projects – purchases of extra-contract, new-model buses. Bus firms usually replace their buses every eight to ten years as part of a standard contract. However, since the average tenure for party secretaries and mayors in Chinese cities is less than three and a half years,[9] they sometimes impose extra-contract demands on bus firms to upgrade the entire bus fleet before their terms expire.

There are two major kinds of upgrades: new-energy buses and "aesthetically pleasing" buses. New-energy buses run on fuel such as liquefied petroleum gas (LPG), liquefied natural gas, or electricity, instead of diesel or petrol. "Aesthetically pleasing" buses are those that look nice (or even "cute"), such as double-deckers, retro buses, and trolley buses. Purchase of these models is usually not specified in contracts.

Upgrade projects are often associated with other city level projects such as "beautiful Zunyi" or "clean Guangzhou" to showcase local leaders' vision for tourism development or environmental preservation. The benefits of these upgrades are often unclear to everyone except the local government officials. While clean-energy buses could in theory lead to improvements in air quality, the reality is often less clear-cut. For example, LPG fueled buses became popular in the late 1990s for reducing black smoke, but by the mid 2000s, cities began to discover that LPG was producing more pollutants than diesel because of the

[8] Interviews 20150616, 20150713, 20150816.

[9] Author's data.

prevalent use of cheap and ill-suited bus engines incompatible with LPG. Chinese cities that adopted LPG buses have subsequently abandoned them and moved on to other types of fuel.[10] Another example is the more recent shift to electric buses without the city investing in charging stations, so bus firms have to revert to traditional fuels and let their new electric buses sit idle.[11]

Meanwhile, these upgraded buses are typically at least twice as expensive as regular buses. Without financial assistance from local governments, firms find these extra-contract purchases very difficult to afford. Even state-owned enterprises (SOEs) with soft budget constraints struggle with ad-hoc upgrades. In one conversation I observed between a bus manager at an SOE and a senior official from the local Fiscal Department regarding a required purchase of a batch of "cute" double-deckers, the SOE manager failed to persuade the official to subsidize the purchase, and the manager said to the official that "the city needs an image, fine, we support that, no problem, it's our duty. But leaders must understand it costs money, please understand our difficulties!"[12]

The third type of visibility project is the construction of BRT, a system of enclosed, dedicated bus lanes with priority given to buses at intersections. BRT can "show the vision of leaders in urban planning" and "looks impressive."[13] Establishing a BRT typically involves a switch from standard 8-meter-long buses to 12- to 18-meter buses, to increase capacity. It also involves the creation of dedicated lanes servicing new bus routes in the most populous area of the city, to relieve congestion. Chinese cities that adopted BRT have advocated it as a "citizen life quality project" (*minsheng gongcheng*). BRT construction is entirely a city-level decision that does not require upper-level government approval (unlike subway construction), and is solely financed by the city government.

However, BRTs in Chinese cities are often built quickly within a leader's term without careful planning, with a construction period between eight months and one year, resulting in incomplete BRT lanes, poorly designed intersections between BRT lanes and regular lanes, and BRT lanes in less populated areas. In many cities, BRTs caused more congestion and traffic accidents than before. Besides this, several cities that built

[10] These cities include Beijing, Shanghai, Guangzhou, and Shenzhen.

[11] For example, in Guangzhou, Beijing, Shenzhen, Zhengzhou, Zhuhai between 2013 and 2016, among others. Data come from author's news collection.

[12] Interview 20150713b.

[13] Interview 20150503.

BRTs already had subway systems in place, making the need for BRTs unclear. By June 2017, of the twenty-three cities that had built BRTs, fourteen cities experienced worse congestion, and five cities have subsequently demolished their BRT systems after a few years.[14]

From the bus firms' perspective, BRTs are very expensive undertakings. They overlap with many existing bus routes, sometimes the most profitable ones, yet the firms are required to reroute away from the BRT lines. Bus firms are not involved in the decision-making process to build BRT, so they rarely have a chance to negotiate on routing arrangements. Therefore, out of all the visibility projects in the bus sector, firms resist BRTs the hardest. BRTs not only require firms to invest in new and expensive buses, but also cause them to lose many of their most profitable routes.

All three visibility projects – bus beautification, bus upgrades, and BRT – impose significant costs on bus firms but do not bring them obvious benefits. Particularly because local governments strictly maintain inexpensive bus fares as "people are used to low bus fares, otherwise they will be unhappy,"[15] bus firms cannot recoup their investments through higher fares. These costs imposed on bus firms are, in effect, corporate contributions to visibility projects and selectoral campaigns of local officials, and are often coerced as firms usually strongly resist them. As a result, state–business relations deteriorate in the sector quickly, and in many cities, local governments eventually chose to force out private firms and replace them with local SOEs to more conveniently launch visibility projects. Before I present qualitative evidence of this process, I use a new dataset to examine the frequency of these visibility projects in Chinese cities and their association with firms' outcomes.

EFFECT OF VISIBILITY PROJECTS ON PRIVATE FIRMS' SURVIVAL

To examine the frequency of visibility projects and its relationship to firm outcomes in China's urban bus sector, I construct an original dataset covering 233 Chinese cities that privatized urban buses at some point

[14] The five cities are Kunming, Chongqing, Hefei, Changzhou, and Jinan. Reports on worsened traffic congestion after BRT was built also occurred in Xiamen, Guangzhou, Nanchang, Urumqi, Nanjing, Hangzhou, Linyi, Zhengzhou, and Wuhan. Data from author's news collection.

[15] Interview 20150713a.

before 2016.[16] The dataset contains information about the timing of privatization in any city where it occurred between 1996 to 2016, as well as the timing of the three types of visibility projects. In addition, the dataset records all instances where city governments deprivatized local bus services, the ultimate negative outcome for private firms. Finally, the dataset includes several variables on the characteristics of cities and their public transit systems, as well as leadership tenure. All data are compiled from Chinese newspapers, city government documents, and government yearbooks.

Visibility projects were common. A quarter of cities launched bus beautification projects at least once during the study period, 58 percent launched bus upgrade projects, and 9 percent built BRT. I use a Cox proportional-hazards model to test whether these projects are related to eventual deprivatization. The proportional-hazards model takes the sequencing of annual observations into account and estimates the cumulative probability of deprivatization.

I follow the data setup procedure in Hosmer et al. (2008) to account for left truncation, delayed entry, and right censoring of the outcome variable. Cities enter the analysis when they privatize their bus sector, at which point they become at risk of deprivatization. Cities exit the analysis when they deprivatize. These data are left truncated because forty-one cities became at risk – privatized – before 1996. There is also delayed entry for 169 cities in which the bus sector was privatized after 1996. No city experienced deprivatization prior to 1996, therefore data are not left censored. The data are right censored because forty-four cities had not yet deprivatized their buses at the end of the observation period. The process in Hosmer et al. (2008) ensures that the proportional-hazards model produces unbiased estimates under these conditions.

I model the cumulative probability of deprivatization – the state-initiated procurement of all private bus firms in a city – as a function of the city's history of visibility projects. The dependent variable, "Duration of Private Ownership," is a count of years elapsed between the foundation of the first private bus firm in a city and the start of deprivatization of all private bus firms in a city. Only ownership change that targets all the private bus firms in a city, rather than selecting a number of them, is

[16] There are 333 Chinese cities in total. I was able to confirm that buses were at some point privatized in 233 of these cities and never privatized in 55 cities (288 cities in total). For the remaining 45 cities, I could not confirm whether or not the bus sector had ever been privatized.

coded as deprivatization. If individual private firms chose to leave the sector without government pressure, then it is not coded as deprivatization, which makes this measure conservative. Deprivatization is coded as 0 if it does not happen in a year, and 1 for the year it starts.

I hypothesize that contributions to visibility projects in the urban bus sector will increase the risk of deprivatization of the sector, since they are not in the interests of private firms. To avoid accidentally registering projects that are not visibility projects, I only include projects that are obviously initiated by the city government and involve *all* bus firms in a city.

> H1: Bus beautification projects will raise the hazard rate of deprivatization of the urban bus sector.

Beautification project is a binary variable. A value of 1 indicates an announcement to enter one of the following national city title competitions: National Civilized City, held every three years; and National Public Transportation City, held every year. A value of 0 indicates the city makes no such announcement.

> H2: Bus upgrade projects will raise the hazard rate of deprivatization of the urban bus sector.

Upgrade project is a binary variable. A value of 1 indicates a news report or government announcement of a government-initiated extra-contract purchase of aesthetically pleasing buses or new-energy buses. Absent such an announcement, a value of 0 is recorded.

Regular replacement of aging buses is not included in this measure. For example, if a news story mentions a bus firm is replacing buses at the end of their life, this is coded as 0. If a news story mentions nothing about bus replacement, but simply introduction of new-model buses into the city, it is coded as 1. Only purchases that are obviously state-initiated are included.

> H3: Major infrastructure projects that will impose extra costs on the bus firms will raise the hazard rate of deprivatization of the urban bus sector.

BRT is also a binary variable, with a value of 1 for city/years where BRT construction was announced, and 0 when no such announcement was made. Only announcements of actual BRT construction are coded as 1, while "plans" or "prospects" for BRT is coded 0, since the threat to the bus firms is not yet present or certain.

Any sectoral features affecting the risk of deprivatization (e.g. asset mobility and incomplete contract problems) are automatically controlled for by the single-sector design. However, I do have to condition on factors that potentially affect the government's decision to deprivatize.

Fiscal Health is the ratio of government expenditures to revenues, which provides a measure of the state's fiscal capacity to deprivatize the bus firms. After all, fiscal constraints are what motivated the original push to privatize. A lower ratio signals greater fiscal health and that the city has more resources to carry out deprivatization.

Buses per 1,000 people and *paved roads per capita* capture the fact that larger, denser bus networks present a greater regulatory challenge. Regulatory success is an important factor to the success of privatization (Hart, Shleifer, and Vishny 1997; Gerard 2008), and Chinese local officials in interviews constantly mention how large systems of urban buses are "hard to manage." It is possible that deprivatization was a state attempt to compensate for the difficulty in regulating bus services, and if this were true, we should expect deprivatization to be more likely in cities with larger and denser transit systems. I also measure the *Routine bus replacement* by the annual replacement in number of buses as a percentage of total buses, to take into consideration the regular activity of replacing buses. I include *GDP per capita* to control for the general wealth level of a city.

Political leaders' tenure – the term year of a city's party secretary and mayor – are also included to capture the potential influence of political cycles on local budgeting decisions (Guo 2009) that could affect the decision of deprivatization.

I use the Cox proportional-hazards model to test the hypotheses. All models use robust variance estimators to adjust for potential correlation among outcomes from the same city. Model specification 1 presents analysis with the key independent variables. Models 2 and 3 add different control variables to the model.[17]

As predicted, all visibility projects increase the hazard rate of deprivatization of a city's urban bus sector over time. Compared with cities that never launched these projects, launching BRT increases the probability of deprivatization by 6.7 times, *bus upgrade projects* by 4.2 times, and *bus beautification projects* by 3.8 times (Figure 4.2, model 3).

[17] Also see Appendix 4.A. and 4.B. An analysis of the Schoenfeld residuals for model 3 (the main model) indicates neither the general model nor any individual independent variable violates the proportionality assumption (Appendix 4.C.). A Cox–Snell residual plot also shows the goodness of fit (Appendix 4.D.).

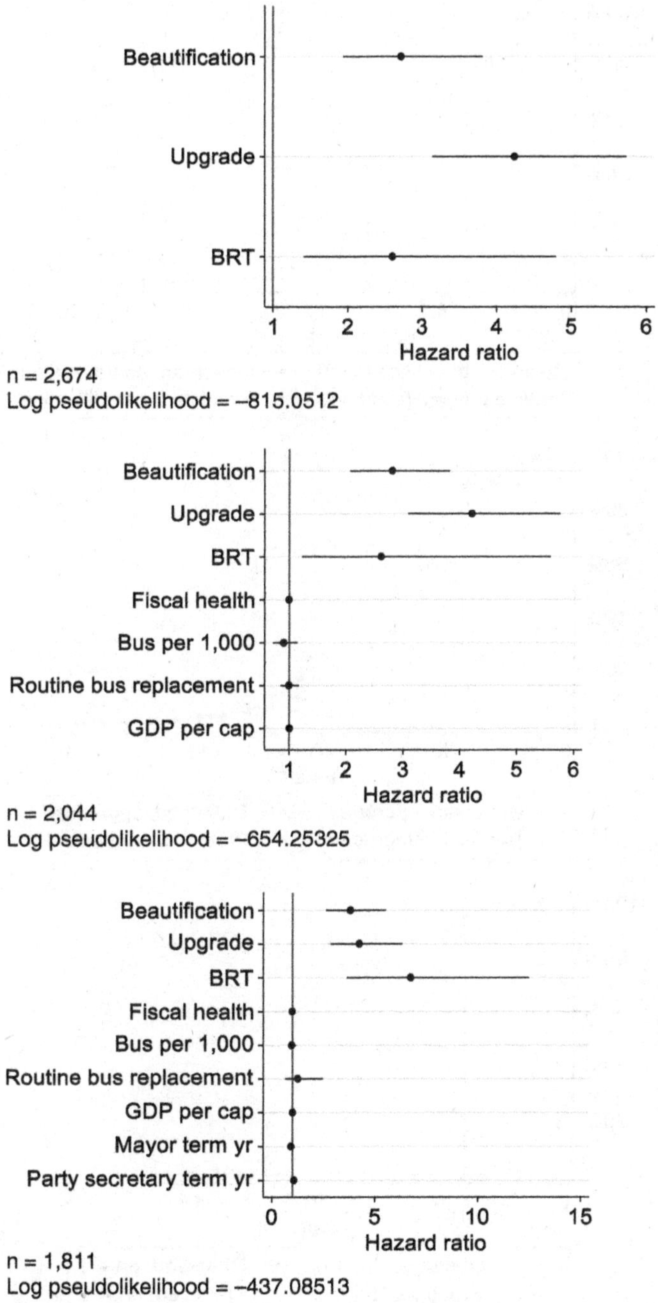

FIGURE 4.2 Coefficient plots, Cox proportional-hazards model

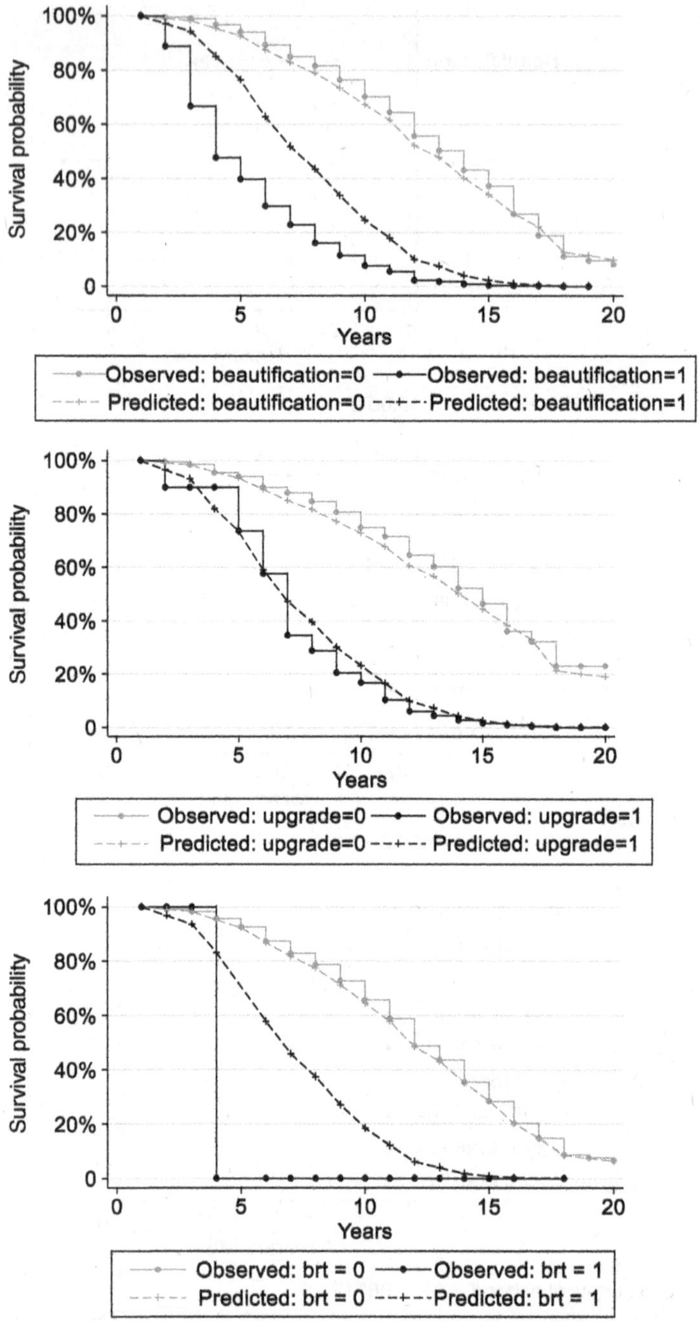

FIGURE 4.3 Effects of visibility projects on deprivatization, Cox predicted versus Kaplan–Meier observed survival probability

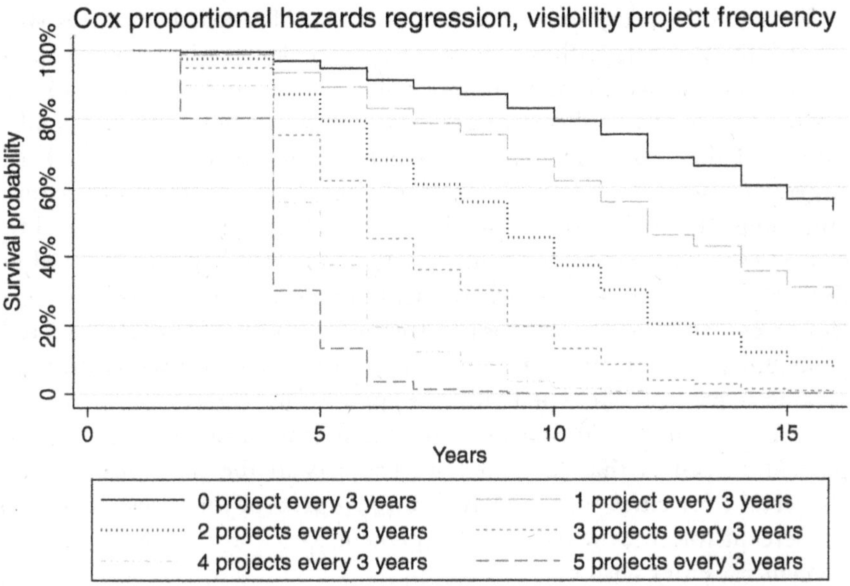

FIGURE 4.4 Predicted survival probability of private firms by visibility project frequency

As Figure 4.3 shows, the predicted probability of private firm survival declines over time after each wave of visibility projects. Holding all other variables at their mean value, the probability of the bus sector remaining private declined much more quickly in cities that launched visibility projects. For example, only 78 percent of cities will still have a private bus sector within five years after a bus beautification project, compared with 94 percent of cities that did not launch the same project. After ten years, the difference increases to 38 percent versus 76 percent, and after fifteen years it increases to 12 percent versus 52 percent. This pattern of increased deprivatization following visibility projects is consistent across the different project types. This association is even stronger for BRT and upgrade projects, where launching BRT will *certainly* lead to deprivatization within five years. This is most likely because of the higher costs associated with these projects. These findings are also robust to the use of the nonparametric Kaplan–Meier estimator.[18]

[18] Cox predicted survival probability is based on the estimates from Model specification 3 (Appendix 4.B.), and, Kaplan – Meier survival probability

$$= \frac{\textit{number of subjects "living" at the start} - \textit{number of subjects who "died"}}{\textit{number of subjects "living" at the start}}.$$

We would expect, moreover, that cities that launched several waves of visibility projects within a short time frame deprivatized sooner than cities that launched the same number of visibility projects over a longer period. Frequent visibility projects mean rapidly accumulating expenditures and debt for private firms, which in turn increases the risk of deprivatization. Here, I remove BRT projects from the analysis because launching BRT will certainly lead to deprivatization, so I only need to test whether increasing frequency in the other two types of visibility projects will increase the risk of deprivatization. Indeed, Figure 4.4 shows evidence for this "dosage frequency" effect.[19] The predicted probability of firm survival declines more rapidly with each additional visibility project launched in the preceding three-year period.[20] The chance that the bus sector remains private after five years is 98 percent for cities that launched no projects in the past three years, 92 percent for cities that launched one, 79 percent for cities with two, 61 percent for cities with three, 39 percent for cities with four, and 18 percent for cities with five.

Clearly, frequent visibility projects lead to faster deprivatization of the sector. This could be because visibility projects increase costs for private firms, which could result in stronger firm resistance to future visibility projects, and eventually to politically expedient deprivatization.

In this chapter, I show the correlation between visibility projects and the survival of private firms across Chinese cities. Once visibility projects are launched, private firms exit the urban bus sector. The more visibility projects are launched and the more frequently they are launched, the quicker private firms exit the sector. But how exactly do visibility projects lead to private firms' exit, and how do these exits happen? In Chapter 5, I use a comparative case study with process tracing and in-depth interviews to show the mechanism of how visibility projects lead to deprivatization of the urban bus sector.

19 See Appendix 4.E for the full result.

20 Other frequency periods were also used (four years and five years), and the results are consistent with using three years as the frequency period. Using three-year frequency loses fewer observations, therefore I report the results using project frequency for every three years.

5

How Visibility Projects Ended Marketization in the Urban Bus Sector

A Tale of Two Cities

How exactly did visibility projects lead to deprivatization of the bus sector? How did deprivatization happen? In this chapter, I adopt a most-similar case comparison method to showcase the causal mechanism linking visibility projects to the private bus companies' forced exit from the sector. I show that deprivatization occurred as a direct result of visibility projects, not as a result of government capacity or the locality's general investment environment. From my 233-city sample of bus sectors, I select Guangzhou and Nanning to construct the most-similar case comparison. Guangzhou deprivatized its bus sector and Nanning did not. These two cities experienced different levels of government engagement in visibility projects in the bus sector, but are similar in other aspects that could potentially explain deprivatization, such as the city government's regulatory capacity and the general investment environment in the city.

AN OPPOSITE MARKETIZATION OUTCOME IN GUANGZHOU AND NANNING

Guangzhou is the capital city of Guangdong province in south China and Nanning is the capital city of neighboring Guangxi province. As provincial capitals, they both receive the most political attention and fiscal subsidies from their respective provincial governments. Guangzhou deprivatized its bus sector in 2007 and Nanning still has a privately controlled bus sector. Guangzhou launched multiple visibility projects in the urban bus sector and Nanning only launched a few.

Guangzhou and Nanning are ideal cases to tease out the effect of visibility projects because they allow me to exclude two other potential explanations for deprivatization of the bus sector.[1] First, it is possible that deprivatization of the bus sector takes place because of different government capacities in regulation. Maybe Guangzhou deprivatized its bus sector because the Guangzhou city government does not have enough government capacity to regulate private bus firms. But because Guangzhou and Nanning do not vary in the dimension of regulatory capacity, as will be discussed at the end of this chapter, we can exclude this explanation.

Another possible explanation is that Guangzhou city has a worse investment environment and the Guangzhou government treats private investors worse than in Nanning. And while these two cities do differ on investment environment, the difference in fact creates a bias *against* finding the effects I expect, making this comparative case study an even stronger empirical test. Guangzhou has a better investment environment than Nanning. It has been consistently rated as one of the top cities in China for investment environment, property rights protection, and contract enforcement. In the 2006 World Bank investment climate survey of firms in 120 Chinese cities, Guangzhou ranked fourth on general investment environment, while Nanning only ranked sixty-seventh. Of all the private firm respondents, 61 percent were confident their contracts would be protected in Guangzhou and only 36 percent were confident their contracts would be protected in Nanning (World Bank 2006).[2] This should make deprivatization less likely in Guangzhou than in Nanning, contrary to what happened. Therefore, investment environment also cannot explain the different outcomes for the private bus companies in these two cities.

Instead, the politicization of business in this sector, specifically through government requests for firms to contribute to visibility projects, led to the deprivatization of private bus firms. But let me start from the beginning, when the two cities privatized their urban bus sectors.

[1] I only control for the control variables included in statistical analysis in Chapter 4 that are tested to be significant. Variables included in the statistical analysis but that are not statistically significant are not discussed in this chapter.

[2] "Government Management, Investment Environment and Harmonious Society: Improvement in Competitiveness of 120 Cities in China," World Bank Group, 2006-10-09, http://documents.worldbank.org/curated/en/403061468214209753/China-Governance-investment-climate-and-harmonious-society-competitiveness-enhancement-for-120-cities-in-China.

PRIVATIZATION OF URBAN BUSES IN GUANGZHOU AND NANNING

Guangzhou and Nanning had experiences with privatization in the bus sector typical to most Chinese cities. In 1994, Guangzhou became one of the earliest cities in China to open its urban bus sector to private firms. By the end of 2006, nine out of fourteen bus firms in Guangzhou were privately owned, including three Hong Kong bus firms and one Macau firm. Wholly private firms ran 37 percent of all buses in Guangzhou. Even the five bus state-owned enterprises (SOEs) all had private investors. The number of urban buses in Guangzhou had increased by 188 percent since 1994, and buses became the primary public transportation mode in Guangzhou in the 2000s. All bus firms signed twenty-year renewable franchise contracts with the Guangzhou government for bus service provision. Bus firms agreed to provide more buses and bus lines, and more frequent buses. They also agreed to replace buses every ten years. Bus firms did not have the right to decide bus fares and plan bus routes, which were solely controlled by the city's Traffic Bureau.

Nanning had a nearly identical experience in privatizing the bus sector, albeit a few years later. In 2001, Nanning opened its urban bus sector up to private investors. Nanning now has a total of six bus firms: Five are privately owned and the remaining one is a state–private joint venture. Like Guangzhou, wholly-private bus firms in Nanning operated 38 percent of all urban buses in the city. By 2013, thirteen years after privatization, the number of buses in Nanning had increased by 217 percent and the number of bus lines increased from 37 to more than 200. Following the standard procedures in Chinese cities, private bus firms signed twenty-year renewable franchise contracts with the Nanning city government. All bus firms agreed to replace buses every ten years, and bus fares could not be raised without agreement from the city government. Bus firms also could not change or open new bus routes, as these decisions were controlled by the Traffic Bureau.

DIFFERENT OUTCOMES: DEPRIVATIZATION IN GUANGZHOU, BUT NOT IN NANNING

In January 2007, a mere thirteen years after Guangzhou's initial privatization of its bus sector, and long before any contract between the private bus firms and the Guangzhou government would end, Guangzhou's city government announced it would put the bus sector back under state control. Deprivatization was fully realized by the end of 2009. All fourteen bus companies were merged into three state-owned bus groups.

The city government formed a deprivatization task force led by the Traffic Bureau to oversee the mergers and acquisitions. There was only limited resistance from private bus firms to deprivatization, partly because of what happened to a Macau bus firm that refused to purchase new energy buses in 2005. The Macau firm resisted the Guangzhou city government's requirement to replace new, functioning buses with new energy buses by organizing strikes and by suing the city government for not following the contract, which stated buses only needed to be replaced every ten years. However, the Macau firm lost the case and was punished by the city government, which mobilized the Bureau of Environment and the Bureau of Commerce to ban the operation of the Macau firm for reasons including excessive exhaust emissions and tax evasion. The Macau firm quickly lost its main source of income. With this precedent, when the Traffic Bureau in Guangzhou announced the plan for deprivatization, other private bus firms followed the order quietly. As a vice president of a former private bus firm said, "If you [firms] do not follow the government's demand, you won't have a good ending, like that Macau firm."[3]

In contrast to Guangzhou, the Nanning government steadily pushed for further privatization in the sector from 2001, with the most recent private firm entering the city's bus sector in 2007. The Nanning government's intervention in the urban bus sector has been limited to regulation and a push for new energy buses. Starting in 2013, Nanning's Traffic Bureau founded a regulation enforcement task force with officials from the Traffic Bureau, the Police Bureau, and representatives from all the bus firms to conduct biannual inspections of bus operations. Task force members ride buses as ordinary passengers, observe bus operation at bus stops, and inspect the condition of the buses.

What explains the different outcomes in the two cities' urban bus sectors? I discuss the roles of visibility projects and city leadership first, and the alternative hypothesis later.

DEPRIVATIZATION FOR VISIBILITY PROJECTS

I find Guangzhou's deprivatization to be primarily a result of long-term tension between the private bus firms and the city government, induced

[3] Interview 20150507.

TABLE 5.1 *Comparison of visibility project history: Guangzhou 1994–2006; Nanning 2001–2013*

	Guangzhou	Nanning
Outcome	Deprivatization in 2007	No deprivatization to date
New type buses	2002, 2005, 2006	2013
City title application	1998, 2001, 2004, 2006	2001, 2009
BRT	2006	N/A

by eight waves of visibility projects in the city over the course of nine years. One major visibility project in 2006 – construction of a BRT system – broke the private bus firms' bottom line and triggered widespread grievances from them, which led to the government's decision to deprivatize. Nanning, on the other hand, did not have nearly as many visibility projects by 2013, also thirteen years after the initial privatization of the urban bus sector, and did not experience deprivatization of the bus sector. Guangzhou had an ambitious leadership in charge of the public transportation sector pushing for visibility projects and Nanning did not. See Table 5.1 for visibility projects in the two cities.

GUANGZHOU: VISIBILITY PROJECTS AND THE EVENTUAL DEPRIVATIZATION

The 2007 deprivatization of buses in Guangzhou is an outcome of a long history of visibility projects since 1998 and intensive launches of visibility projects between 2004 and 2006, with three simultaneous visibility projects in 2006 that pushed the private bus firms to the edge. These visibility projects created a high level of tension between Guangzhou's city government and the private firms, and the city government eventually used deprivatization as a measure to keep pushing for visibility projects by removing the resisting private bus firms.

A Peaceful Start to Visibility Projects

From 1998 and 2004, the private urban bus sector and Guangzhou's city government had a friendly relationship. The city launched three waves of city title applications, while also asking Guangzhou's urban bus sector to purchase air-conditioned buses during this period (as shown in Figure 5.1). These requests received full support from the private bus firms. Guangzhou applied for the National Civilization City title three times; for the National

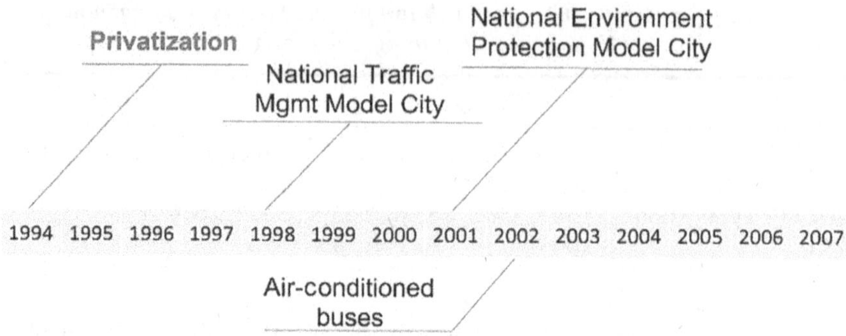

FIGURE 5.1 Phase I of visibility projects, 1994–2002

Traffic Management Model City title in 1998 and 2004; and for the National Environment Protection Model City in 2001. All these applications required the bus firms to clean their buses, replace old ones, and maintain orderly bus operation. Guangzhou won the provincial level Civilization City title and the National Traffic Management Model City title in 2004, and the National Environment Protection Model City in 2001.

At the end of 2001, the Guangzhou Traffic Bureau ordered all bus firms to fully replace the city's 6,000 buses with air-conditioned buses within five years, without government subsidies. A subtropical city that has hot and humid summers, providing air-conditioned buses is not exactly a visibility project but has a real developmental impact. While this demand was costly and not specified in the contracts, the time frame of five years made it possible for bus firms to spread the costs. Moreover, five years means a lot of the air-conditioned buses would replace buses reaching the end of their service life, and so were already included in the budget of the private bus firms. Therefore, the private bus firms did not resist the call for air-conditioned buses, and Guangzhou became a city with 100 percent air-conditioned buses in 2005. The Guangzhou government proudly praised the bus sector, calling them a "beautiful name card" for the city.[4]

Tensions Rise with More Visibility Projects

Between 2003 and 2005, the relation between the city government and the bus firms started to deteriorate with a new requirement from the city

[4] "Wunian nei quanbu genghuan xinchexing, fangbian gongjiao chengwei guangzhou liang mingpian," *Xinhua News*, 2002-9-22, http://news.xinhuanet.com/newscenter/2002-09/22/content_570269.htm.

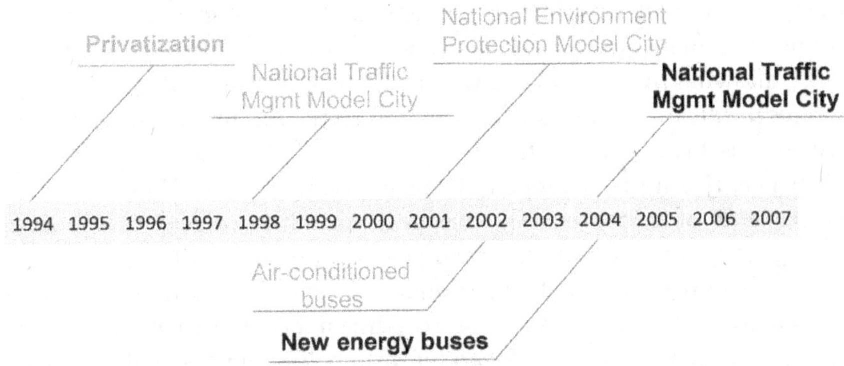

FIGURE 5.2 Phase II of visibility projects, 2003–2005

government (Figure 5.2). Guangzhou's Traffic Bureau announced a plan in 2004 to completely replace all buses using traditional diesel or petrol with buses that used liquefied petroleum gas (LPG) fuel. This plan aimed to reduce exhaust emissions, as LPG was believed to release few visible emissions, and was therefore thought to be much cleaner. Guangzhou's city government announced it would become the first city in the world to use only LPG fueled buses for public transportation.

This time, the government's resolution did not get support from the bus firms. The LPG bus plan was essentially asking the bus firms to replace their almost brand-new, air-conditioned buses that were not even four years old. And a lot of the air-conditioned buses were new models that met the environmental standards for exhaust emissions. Bus firms asked for subsidies from the government or they would not make the purchase, and the Traffic Bureau had to stall the plan for LPG buses for a year.

In 2005, the Traffic Bureau reissued an announcement to replace all current buses with LPG buses within a year, this time with help from other government departments. In an interview with a national newspaper in January 2005, the head of Guangzhou's Traffic Bureau told journalists they would use administrative means to ensure bus replacement. With coordination help from the city government, Guangzhou's Traffic Bureau issued an official notification along with the city's Bureau of Environment and Bureau of Public Security. In the notification, the three departments made it clear that all bus firms had to either replace their current vehicles with LPG ones, or to modify the engines on current vehicles into LPG compatible ones within a year, otherwise their operations would be suspended. The Traffic Bureau also promised bus firms a symbolic subsidy of 20,000 yuan for each new LPG bus purchase, which was around a twentieth to a thirtieth of the cost. The Guangzhou government did not designate any specific new energy bus manufacturers to the bus firms, allowing them to choose whichever manufacturers they wished.

This notification sent a strong signal to all the bus firms in Guangzhou. Private bus firms realized the government was determined. "They [the government] want it to happen, then we [private bus firms] must do it."[5] At the end of 2006, exactly one year after the official notification, Guangzhou had successfully turned nearly 90 percent of its urban buses into LPG buses. Only a Hong Kong bus firm and a Macau bus firm refused to replace the remaining 10 percent because their buses were barely three years old. The Macao bus firm collected its own data, which showed no environmental hazards from their buses, and sued Guangzhou's Traffic Bureau. Eventually, they lost the case and their bus operation was suspended, as described earlier in the chapter.

The 2005 LPG bus purchase pushed every bus firm in Guangzhou into a financial abyss, including the bus SOEs. First, LPG as a fuel cost twice as much as traditional fuel. According to an interviewee working for a bus SOE, the cost of the traditional diesel fuel per bus per day was around 400 yuan, but LPG fuel cost more than 1,000 yuan per bus per day. As a result, the SOE firm immediately turned from operating on thin profits to huge losses after six months.[6] Another private bus firm manager described the purchase of LPG buses as a "hemorrhage" on the firm's balance sheet.[7] Second, engines compatible with LPG fuel were a new product in China and their quality was unreliable. Some of the engines needed to be repaired or replaced every six months, imposing another high cost on the bus firms. However, the bus firms still went along because, "what else can you do? There are many ways the government can cause trouble for you."[8]

Even More Visibility Projects, and Passive Resistance

With their balance sheet turned upside down with the purchase of LPG buses in 2005, a new visibility project in 2006 dashed the last hope of bus firms to make ends meet. The new project was a grand plan to build a "modern" public transportation system in Guangzhou. The plan affected

[5] Interview 20150507.
[6] Interview 20150320.
[7] Interview 20150507.
[8] Interview 20150317.

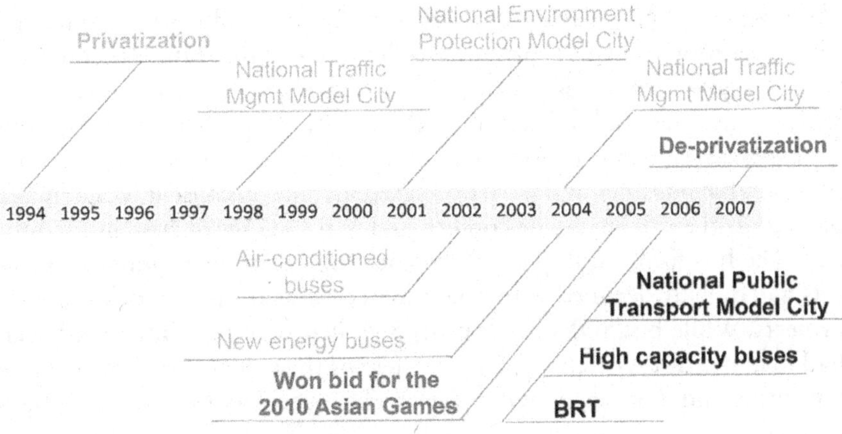

FIGURE 5.3 Phase III of visibility projects, 2005–2007

the bus sector in two ways. First was the construction of a 70-kilometer-long BRT system. The Guangzhou government planned to have this built by 2009, and once it started operating, eighty-seven regular bus lines would cease service, a third of which were privately operated. Secondly, the Guangzhou government required bus firms to provide more than 2,000 new, longer buses (12 meters instead of the regular 8 meters) for the BRT system, and demanded that all the other urban buses were identical in color, which required bus firms to purchase new buses and to repaint the current ones. These projects are shown in Figure 5.3.

Given these requirements, the construction of the BRT system broke the private firms' back. The BRT system not only increased the bus firms' costs by asking them to purchase new buses for the BRT lines, but also decreased the bus firms' income by removing bus lines and demanding income-sharing with the government. BRT would cover two of the busiest districts in the city, meaning the existing bus lines would need to be removed to make room for the BRT, which were also the most profitable lines for the bus firms. Even though the private firms that operated these removed bus lines were given the right to operate the new BRT buses, the generated income was to be shared with the Traffic Bureau.

When the announcement of BRT construction was made in early 2006, the private bus firms affected simply received a notice that bus lines overlapping with the BRT system would be removed, and that their income from operating in the BRT system must be shared with the government after the BRT was put in place. Private bus firms were angry as they had not been consulted beforehand, and there was no arrangement about what happened after these most profitable bus lines were removed from operation. When the private bus firms signed the franchise contracts with the government, they had paid for ten years of exclusive rights to specific bus lines, and the contracts still had seven years until expiration.

It was also a bad time for the private bus firms to lose a large number of profitable bus lines and have decreased income, because it would make paying off their debts on air-conditioned and LPG buses even more difficult. The bus firms' ability to afford constant government-initiated projects had quickly declined with accumulated debts from previous visibility projects. While bus SOEs could postpone their debt repayment and even had loan interest written off with the help of the city government, private bus firms did not have that luxury. They decided to resist the BRT project.

Only a few firms used aggressive means such as strikes and lawsuits. Having observed the fate of the Macau firm that aggressively resisted the purchase of LPG, other private firms decided that "extreme measures are no use, they are bad for you."[9] Instead, most private bus firms used what James Scott described as "weapons of the weak" (Scott 1987). Their passive resistance was observed in the fall of 2006, when Guangzhou became one of the finalists in a competition for "National Public Transportation Model City."

To prepare for this, buses in a city needed to look clean and new, arrive on time, not produce visible exhaust, and operate in an "orderly" fashion, with no hard braking, no sudden lane shifts, and so on. The evaluation was done in October and November by a national government task force, which visited all the candidate cities and graded them. In the past, Guangzhou had always won this title through the cooperation of bus firms. In 2006, the private bus firms decided to do a bad job. They sent out fewer buses during the time of competition, making buses look more crowded than usual.[10] The drivers also deliberately drove badly, causing chaotic scenes by forcing lane changes, "lane hogging" to block other traffic, and racing other buses to get to the bus stop first and take the most passengers on board.[11] There were also reports of buses stopping in the middle of the road to let passengers off instead of stopping at bus stops, and parking on the roadside right outside an empty bus parking

[9] Interview 20150507.

[10] Interview 20151209.

[11] "Guangzhou jiaojing tongchen liang zhiluan yuanyin, gongjiao zhixu keyong shikong xingrong," *Information Times* (*Xinxi Shibao*), 2006-12-09, https://news.sohu.com/20061209/n246910689.shtml.

lot to cause slow traffic.[12] Because of the lack of cooperation from private bus firms, Guangzhou did not win the national title for the first time. This alarmed Guangzhou's city government, which started to worry that the bus firms would continue their passive resistance during the upcoming Asian Games.

The Asian Games is the Olympics of Asia, held every four years with athletes from forty-five Asian countries. Guangzhou would be hosting the sixteenth Asian Games in 2010, and had started preparing for it in 2005. Before Guangzhou, the last time a Chinese city hosted the Asian Games was Beijing, in 1990. Hosting the Asian Games is a great opportunity for city leaders. It puts their city under an international spotlight, attracts political attention from the top, and brings in fiscal subsidies from both the central and provincial government. If a city leader succeeds in organizing the games, their opportunity for further promotion increases.

Both BRT and new energy buses were visibility projects, as the Asian Games guarantees the highest level of publicity and attention from upper-level governments. The city government would not allow any type of resistance to these visibility projects. To make sure they went well, the city government decided to deprivatize the bus sector to get rid of the private bus firms.

Deprivatization to Continue Visibility Projects

In a 2009 internal document to the city government summarizing the deprivatization process, Guangzhou's Traffic Bureau listed four reasons for deprivatization: (1) It wanted to make sure no black exhaust was released from buses during the Asian Games, but private bus firms were not cooperative. (2) The BRT system construction was planned to finish by the end of 2009. Deprivatization would prevent any possible protests and strikes by the private bus firms opposing the BRT's operation. (3) More subway lines would be in operation from 2010, and more bus lines would be adjusted in response to that. Deprivatization made it easier to get cooperation from only bus SOEs. (4) Bus services require safety and service quality. The profit-driven nature of private firms makes them unsuitable in providing public services.

12 "Guangzhou gongjiao hengchong zhizhuang weizhang pinfa," *Information Times* (*Xinxi Shibao*), 2006-12-12, https://news.sina.cn/sa/2006-12-12/detail-ikftpnny3786723.d.html.

Deprivatization was essentially a measure to guarantee the smooth implementation of the visibility project of upgrading the city's transportation system, as described by the second and third reasons listed in the statement. The first listed concern was already taken care of by the replacement with LPG buses. The fourth reason, if it were true, would have been a constant factor since privatization and does not explain the timing of deprivatization. As a former private firm bus manager commented when asked about his opinion on the aforementioned document, "BRT was the direct reason, and purchase of new buses was the indirect reason [for deprivatization]."[13]

The potential conflict between private bus firms and the upgrading of Guangzhou's urban bus system lies in the costs and speed of the upgrading process. Guangzhou's city leaders needed the implementation of the BRT, the replacement of more than 2,000 buses, and the removal or merger of more than eighty-seven bus lines to be done within three years. Resistance from the private bus firms through strikes and refusal to renew buses or merge bus routes had occurred, and the city government expected more resistance in the course of implementing the changes. If the city government chose to negotiate with the multiple private bus firms, then the process might take too long, especially considering what had happened with the previous LPG upgrade plan, in which the city government spent two years just to have bus firms change buses or engine type. Furthermore, the concern that some private bus firms might start protests and even lawsuits against the city government was real. What had happened with the Macau bus firm during the LPG upgrade plan showed this was a genuine risk.

Therefore, deprivatization of the sector became the optimal choice, as it removed the opposition standing in the way of the sectoral upgrade, rather than requiring negotiation and compromise. This is not to say deprivatization would not lead to protests or lawsuits, as it often does. But these protests and lawsuits would happen after the bus firms were stripped of their operation, and therefore no longer posed a threat to the visibility projects themselves.

Ambitious Leadership behind Visibility Projects

The multiple waves of frequent visibility projects were a result of ambitious leadership in the public transportation sector. In the thirteen years

[13] Interview 20150507.

between privatization and deprivatization of the urban bus sector in Guangzhou, a small number of government officials overseeing Guangzhou's public transportation sector were promoted step by step with each visibility project in the sector, who in turn were incentivized to promote more visibility projects. The vice mayor, Guangning Zhang, who oversaw public transportation development in Guangzhou city in 1998 was promoted to be mayor in 2003, after two applications to national city titles, promotion of air-conditioned buses in the city, and the first two lines of subway construction. After pushing for a second wave of bus replacement – the LPG buses in 2005 – and the launch of BRT in 2006, Zhang was further promoted to be the party secretary of Guangzhou in 2010 after the Asian Games. The head of the Traffic Bureau in 1998, Bingchang Ou, who enforced the visibility projects in the public transportation sector with Zhang, was offered a lucrative job as the chairman of one of Guangzhou's largest real estate SOEs in 2003. The head of Guangzhou's Bureau of Development and Reform in 2002, Xin Gan, who pushed for the air-conditioned buses and the LPG buses, was promoted to be the vice mayor of the city in 2006, and he pushed for the BRT project as vice mayor. After the Asian Games and BRT construction in 2010, he was further promoted to be a CCP committee member of the municipal committee, among the highest level of leaders of the city. The head of Traffic Bureau in 2002, Weixiong Xian, who enforced the projects for LPG bus purchase, BRT, and deprivatization was granted the extra position of CEO of Guangzhou's new airport in 2005, and further became the chairman of Guangzhou's Political Consultative Committee. He stayed in these positions until 2015.

In 2006, right before deprivatization, Guangzhou had a new and ambitious party secretary, Xiaodan Zhu. Becoming the party secretary of Guangzhou, the top leader of one of the richest provincial capitals in China, is a huge step up in a Chinese official's career. The party secretary took on big plans to transform the city, including more trees, cleaner rivers, new stadiums for the Asian Games, and the construction of an "Asian Games Village" to accommodate athletes. BRT construction was one of the plans suggested to and adopted by Zhu. To ensure this went smoothly, Zhu promoted the Bureau of Development and Reform head, Gan, to be the vice mayor, after Gan had suggested this, and had Gan oversee the BRT construction and deal with the bus firms affected by the plan. Knowing the bus firms and their past resistance to visibility projects very well, Gan and the Traffic Bureau officials suggested deprivatization to guarantee the smooth construction of the BRT system, and the fate of the private bus firms was sealed. After the 2010 Asian Games, Zhu was promoted to be the vice governor of Guangdong province.

Therefore, deprivatization in Guangzhou was the outcome of several factors. First and foremost, there was a long history of visibility projects in the sector, which negatively affected the relationship between the bus firms and the city government. By the last visibility project, construction of a BRT system, the private bus firms were running at a loss owing to the large investments required by previous visibility projects, and they started to resist yet another new demand on them. This resistance met a leadership who faced a great opportunity – the Asian Games – to increase their political visibility and show off their capability in city management. The leadership was determined to build the BRT before the Asian Games, and the time frame made the leadership unwilling to negotiate with private firms. Deprivatization became the most effective way to overcome resistance by private firms.

NANNING: LACK OF VISIBILITY PROJECTS AND A STABLE BUS MARKET

Nanning, unlike Guangzhou, did not have any of the conditions just described by 2013, thirteen years after their privatization of the urban bus sector. The bus sector in Nanning did not have to respond to nearly as many visibility projects as in Guangzhou (Figure 5.4). While the bus sector participated in two waves of national city title competitions in 2001 and 2009, the costs associated with these title competitions were affordable to the firms, and the two applications were far enough from each other to give the bus sector time to breathe in between.

FIGURE 5.4 Visibility projects in the bus sector, Nanning City

Nanning also had the bus firms purchase new energy buses, but only once. In 2013, clean energy buses were introduced for the first time. The city government promoted two newer types of fuel, compressed natural gas and liquefied natural gas, which were believed to be much cleaner than traditional diesel or petrol. The 2013 plan was to deliver 1,500 new energy buses by 2018, replacing half of the operating buses in the city. Nanning's city government did not provide any direct subsidies to the bus firms as Guangzhou provided. Instead, they helped the firms obtain loans from state-owned banks. A few private firms tried to resist at first, and Nanning's government responded with administrative measures similar to those seen in Guangzhou. Nanning's Traffic Bureau and Bureau of Environment cooperated, issuing "suggestions" to bus firms who resisted purchasing new energy buses, warning them of suspension of operations if they would not replace their buses on time.

With this warning from the government, all bus firms quickly cooperated. The goal to replace half of the buses with new energy vehicles was reached two years early in 2016. In this process, Nanning's city government also did not specify bus manufacturers. The six bus firms in Nanning purchased buses from Shanghai, Beijing, and two smaller bus manufacturers in Guangxi province.

The push for new energy buses in Nanning in 2013 was a one-time project in the thirteen years since privatization, and it was not a quick and hard demand from the government as was the case in Guangzhou, even though the city government also had to use some form of coercion. Nanning's bus firms had five years to replace only a part of their bus fleet, instead of replacing all the buses within one year as in Guangzhou. Nanning's private bus firms could afford the costs, and they quickly abandoned resistance, providing the city government with no incentive to deprivatize.

Furthermore, Nanning did not have ambitious city leaders at the time it hosted a major event that could have justified visibility projects. In 2003, Nanning became the permanent host of the annual China–ASEAN Exposition, a trade fair for businesspeople from China and the ASEAN countries. However, Nanning's top leaders did not have enough incentives for large urban planning projects for this event for an unusual reason. In 2002, the whole province of Guangxi, including Nanning city, was in political turmoil. Back in 2000, a Central Committee member of the Chinese Communist Party and Vice Chairman of the National People's Congress, Kejie Cheng,[14] had been executed for corruption.

[14] These positions made Cheng a deputy state level (*fu guo ji*) official in China, among the top eighty national leaders.

Cheng was the governor of Guangxi province in the early 1990s. After he was arrested, his political network in Guangxi was also investigated, including top provincial and city leaders. In 2002, Nanning's regional chief party secretary was arrested;[15] a top city leader in Nanning's neighboring city, Guigang, was executed; two vice provincial governors were arrested and sentenced; and many other lower level officials all over the province were arrested.[16]

With this unusual political atmosphere in Guangxi province, local politicians were attention-averse rather than attention-seeking. Though lacking direct information on how the anti-corruption campaign in Guangxi province affected the then city leaders of Nanning, my interviews with other officials can shed some light. One city leader talked about how he and his fellow politicians viewed the current anti-corruption campaign: "With [the] anti-corruption [campaign] in place, why would you do anything? Whatever you do will draw attention and could make you look suspicious [of being corrupt], even if you didn't actually do anything. Why take the risk? Might as well not do anything and stay in peace."[17] Another official said: "Anti-corruption makes no one dare to do anything. One more project is one more trouble. It's better to do less."[18] City leaders in Nanning in 2003 likely shared the same mentality when their colleagues all over the province were being investigated. As a result, they did not take advantage of the 2003 China–ASEAN Exposition to launch any visibility projects. Therefore, this international event did not have an effect as was the case for the Asian Games in Guangzhou.

Nanning did have an ambitious city leader in 2013 who launched visibility projects, and the bus sector was a part of them. The ambitious city party secretary, Yuanhui Yu, launched a campaign called "Beautiful Nanning" in 2013. A key component of this campaign was to make the city look attractive, so Yu ordered strings of lights to be hung on the trees along the river banks of the city's main river, remove street vendors from

[15] Before 2003, Nanning city was part of a larger Nanning region, which had a regional chief party secretary with more power than Nanning's city party secretary.

[16] Jun Mo, the chief party secretary of Nanning region, was sentenced for corruption in 2002. Chenglong Li, then vice mayor of Guigang city, a city neighboring Nanning, was executed in 2002. Bingsong Xu, the then vice governor of Guangxi province, was sentenced to life in prison in 1999. Zhibing Liu, the other vice governor of Guangxi province, was sentenced to 15 years in 2002. Both Xu and Liu were vice governors of Guangxi province. All four were involved in Kejie Cheng's corruption case and were sentenced by Nanning city court.

[17] Interview 20150307.

[18] Interview 20150816.

sidewalks, and repaint the walls of old residential buildings. In the public transportation sector, bus firms were required to purchase new energy buses as described earlier, but the time frame was lenient. Other requirements from the local government were limited to establishing order on the streets, with specific goals such as reduced traffic congestion, orderly and safe bus operation, and refurbished, clean buses.

None of these extra requirements was particularly costly for the bus firms, and therefore there was not much resistance from them. The city government formed a regulation enforcement task force to monitor the urban buses for this campaign instead of deprivatizing the sector because they had no incentive to deprivatize – resistance was minimal and there were no large events or new central policies to provide a legitimate reason for deprivatization. No justification meant no support from higher-level government, and a fundamental change without any legitimate reason could easily have led to suspicion of misuse of public funds, much like the old-style achievement projects that came to be so heavily criticized. To deprivatize the whole sector, leaders need legitimate reasons and must be able to benefit from it politically. Unlike in Guangzhou, where both factors were present, Nanning did not have solid justification. Therefore, the urban bus sector has so far remained stable.

ALTERNATIVE EXPLANATION: LACK OF CAPACITY TO REGULATE THE PRIVATE BUS FIRMS

In this section, I address an alternative hypothesis from the literature, which was not tested in the statistical analysis owing to data unavailability. City governments might have an incentive to deprivatize if they cannot effectively regulate private buses, which would make the government unable to address lower service quality in the urban bus sector.

A key finding from the literature of privatization is that regulation capacity is crucial to ensure effective private provision of public services. With weak regulatory capacity, private providers of public services will be incentivized to reduce costs by providing lower-quality services (Hart, Shleifer, and Vishny 1997; Gerard 2008). Low-quality bus services in Chinese cities is a phenomenon commonly reported in the media. Guangzhou and Nanning both had various media reports of low-quality private bus operations, including speeding, passing other cars illegally, not stopping at every bus stop, and other safety and operational problems. Both cities also had fatal traffic accidents involving private urban buses. In April 2006, an urban bus owned by Nanning's largest private bus firm had an accident involving eleven deaths, with the bus driver being held responsible. In February 2007, when deprivatization was already under way, a private bus in Guangzhou struck and killed a biker. While there is no publicly available data to systematically examine the difference in service quality between private buses and publicly owned buses, this chapter assumes the private bus services were more problematic than public ones in both Nanning and Guangzhou, as depicted in media.

With this assumption, an alternative explanation for deprivatization in Guangzhou but not in Nanning is that Guangzhou had weaker regulatory capacity than Nanning, and therefore had to deprivatize to improve service quality. According to the literature on China's policy enforcement, a major obstacle to regulation enforcement is widespread bureaucratic fragmentation, where government departments have no incentives to cooperate with each other (e.g. Lieberthal and Lampton 1992; Pearson 2007; Mertha 2009). It is possible that the Nanning city government was more capable of bringing its bureaucracy together to rein in the private bus firms, and therefore did not need to deprivatize the sector. The Guangzhou city government may have had fragmented bureaucracy so could not bring together all the necessary bureaucratic departments to regulate the private bus firms, and therefore had to take the drastic step of deprivatizing them. Following this logic, we should expect deprivatization to be a bureaucratically easier solution than regulation. Empirically, however, I find this is not true.

Deprivatization in Guangzhou took a total of ten different government departments and twenty-four months to complete. As one official who went through the process said, "it was so very hard to cooperate with so many departments, truly annoying."[19] First, the Guangzhou Development and Reform Commission and the Guangzhou Traffic Bureau made plans for deprivatization. Then eight more government departments were involved in implementation: the Bureau of Transportation Management, Bureau of Public Security, Bureau of Finance, Bureau of Commerce, Bureau of Environment, Department of Publicity, Tax Bureau, and Bureau of Labor and Social Security. All ten departments created a task force led by the Traffic Bureau to negotiate with the private bus firms, reassign bus routes belonging to the private firms, work on mergers of assets and liabilities, and downsize and reorganize the labor force. The process was extremely complicated, and each step required multiple departments to cooperate with each other. For example, to assess the monetary value

[19] Interview 20150414.

of one privately owned bus involved the Traffic Bureau, the Bureau of Environment, and the Tax Bureau.

Regulation in Nanning took only two government departments to implement: the Traffic Bureau and the Public Security Bureau. Traffic Bureau staff took buses as regular passengers and graded the performance of bus services, then fined the bus firms or suspended their operations if they found serious violations of safety codes. Traffic police checked on the buses' condition and could suspend a bus that was deemed unsafe or environmentally harmful. Starting in 2013, Nanning's Traffic Bureau set up an extra task force to monitor bus operation in the city twice a year. This task force included representatives from each bus firm. It took only two months for Nanning's Traffic Bureau, the Bureau of Public Security, and the city's six bus firms to agree on specific codes for regulation and to start enforcement operations.

Obviously, deprivatization is much costlier and involves many more bureaucratic agencies to carry out than regulation. If a city government has the capacity to deprivatize, it will also have the capacity to regulate the bus sector. Deprivatization is thus not a measure to improve service quality, because city governments could achieve that goal with much less extreme and costly measures. This is further supported by several studies that show deprivatization is not related to service improvement. Dalian and Urumqi, for example, both deprivatized their bus services. But after deprivatization, these cities continued to face bus service problems by SOEs, and had to set up a city-level task force to oversee the enforcement of regulations in the already deprivatized bus sector (Mu and Jong 2012, 2016). Therefore, through comparing the fate of private bus companies in Guangzhou and Nanning, deprivatization of the urban bus sector is a direct outcome of visibility projects imposed on firms.

In this chapter and Chapter 4, I show that visibility projects sponsored by firms, a form of politicization of business, is the direct reason for deprivatization of China's urban bus sector. The urban bus sector became a popular sector for visibility projects, which is a distortion of the central government's call for clean air. Local government officials rightfully translated this central government agenda into more public transportation to disincentive the use of private cars. However, in the process of execution, they focused on the visible components of this policy endeavor. Throughout China, local governments launched visibility projects in the urban bus sector, applied for national city titles, demanded purchases of aesthetically pleasing buses and new energy buses without providing adequate supporting infrastructure, and built BRT systems hastily, often without proper planning.

Bus firms were asked to contribute to these visibility projects, but the sector-wide nature of these visibility projects means that no single bus firm could claim credit for them, making these visibility projects more like regulation than bribes. As a result, when the costs of visibility projects become exceedingly high and threaten a firm's survival, private firms with hard budget constraints are the first to resist sponsoring more of the local governments' visibility projects. Such resistance threatens the progress of visibility projects and thus the political future of ambitious local government officials, especially when local leaders have a limited time frame to push for these visibility projects. And the most effective measure to remove resistance is to force out private firms and replace them with SOEs. Visibility projects in the urban bus sector, therefore, ended the marketization process of the sector.

6

Protests, Societal Control, and Firms in the Solid Waste Treatment Sector

National Landscape

We are now entering the empirical chapters on the second political role of firms, societal control. I use the solid waste treatment sector as the context for this part of the book. A young sector that took off in the mid 1990s, solid waste treatment has been a sector that invites public opposition and protest. If not operated up to standard, landfills can cause soil and water pollution, and waste incinerators can produce various air pollutants. In this chapter and Chapter 7, I will focus on the waste incineration sector to examine the relationship between protests, the political service of societal control provided by firms, and the changing landscape of firms of different ownership types. The waste incineration sector started off with a mix of private firms and state-owned enterprises (SOEs), but protests had gradually changed the relationship between local governments and businesses that build and operate waste treatment plants. In the thirty years of rapid expansion of waste incinerators, cities in areas that experience high-profile protests began to see more large, powerful SOEs and less private firms in this sector. In this chapter, I use an original dataset on Chinese cities' incineration plants to show how high-profile protests are strongly associated with the gradual retreat of private firms in the incineration sector. I will then use comparative case studies and process tracing to show the mechanism of this shift in Chapter 7.

SOLID WASTE TREATMENT, A NEW SECTOR IN CHINA

Modern sanitary solid waste treatment has a short history in China. Before the 1990s, Chinese cities simply disposed of their municipal solid waste in unregulated dump sites in city suburbs or burnt the waste in the open. Problems from these primitive garbage disposal methods gradually emerged in the late 1990s, as untreated solid waste and leachate (hazardous liquid that drains from solid waste) posed major threats to soil and groundwater, allowing toxins and pollutants into farm products and the environment in general. They also created public health issues as they harbored mosquitos and flies that transmitted epidemic diseases. The Chinese national government started to pay attention to solid waste treatment and designated certain cities as experimental sites for sanitary solid waste treatment.

In 1988, the first modern waste incinerator in the country was built in Shenzhen. In 1991, the first sanitary landfill in the country was built in Hangzhou. In 1995, the Chinese national government included urban solid waste treatment into the ninth five-year-plan, encouraging city governments to treat municipal waste in a sanitary way. Nonetheless, the speed of building solid waste treatment facilities remained slow until the 2000s.

In the 2000s, the Chinese national government issued a series of national environmental initiatives promoting solid waste treatment. In 2002, the Chinese national government issued a notification to accelerate the development of wastewater and solid waste treatment, setting specific goals for the amount of solid waste to be treated.[1] The same document also encouraged more private firms and nonstate capital to invest in this sector to relieve some of the fiscal stress on local governments, something the state often does when pushing for sectoral development. In 2008, the Chinese national government officially established a Ministry of Ecology and Environment. Soil and water pollution joined air pollution to become the focus of a series of environment preservation initiatives put out by this new ministry in 2008, 2011, 2012, 2015, and 2017. In general, these initiatives called for waste-to-energy (WtE) projects, including waste sorting and recycling systems, incineration projects, anaerobic digestion projects,[2] and gasification in landfills.[3] The purpose of these WtE projects is to turn sorted and recycled solid waste into energy, such as electricity or heat. WtE proj-

[1] "Guanyu tuijin chengshi wushui, laji chuli chanyehua fazhan de yijian," Ministry of Housing and Urban-Rural Development of the People's Republic of China, Document [2002]-1591.

[2] Incineration plants can use an anaerobic decomposition process on the sludge left after burning to produce methane. This methane can then be used instead of fossil fuels to fire the incinerator's burners, ideally making the plants closer to carbon neutral. However, most of China's incinerators do not use this technology.

[3] Landfills naturally produce methane, which can be collected and used to generate electricity. This is preferable to keeping it in the ground or allowing it to leak into the air, as methane is a major greenhouse gas.

ects are essentially intended to be clean and sustainable ways to treat solid waste; turning useless garbage into a valuable resource. In 2012, the national government also started to offer a preferential price of 0.65 yuan per kwh for electricity generated from WtE projects, much higher than the approximately 0.4 yuan per kwh for electricity generated by coal.[4]

The heavy focus on solid waste treatment in these national initiatives drew local governments' attention to the solid waste sector, which had been largely ignored until then. Among all the WtE projects proposed by the national government, incineration plants received the most attention from local governments. In densely populated areas where land is scarce, incineration plants are a more economic policy solution to the waste problem as they take up less land. In areas that are less densely populated, incineration plants could become visibility projects, which still make them more popular than other WtE projects. Compared with landfills, which are gaping holes in the ground, or recycling systems that are scattered around the city without much visual effect, incineration plants can occupy acres of land and include large buildings that display an impressive scale. Combined with striking architectural designs and landscaping, incineration plants are easy to show off to the upper-level government.[5] Most of the fifteen cities where I did fieldwork have modern, park-like incineration plants. Other scholars also find that aesthetically pleasing incineration plants are particularly common in less populated areas (Lu et al. 2019).

For these reasons, waste incineration plants quickly became a trend in China's solid waste treatment sector. As Figure 6.1 shows, in the twenty-five years from 1993 to 2017, the number of incineration plants in China grew from 8 to 351 (author's data), with an accelerated increase of more than 6 percent in annual growth rate since 2002. China has seen the fastest growth in building incineration plants and in 2016 it was the country with the most incinerators in the world.[6] The number

[4] However, many incineration plants find that this policy discourages them from improving incineration efficiency. Only the first 280 kwh of electricity generated from each ton of solid waste receives this preferential price. Any extra electricity generated beyond 280 kwh per ton will be bought by the state at the same or a lower price as that generated by coal. "Guojia fazhan gaige weiyuan hui guanyu wanshan laji fenshao fadian jiage zhengce de tongzhi," National Energy Administration, Document [2012]-801.

[5] Of course, an incinerator plant does not need to have striking architecture and landscaping, but many of them in Chinese cities do have such designs.

[6] "World Energy Resources Report 2016," World Energy Council, 2016-10-03, www.worldenergy.org/assets/images/imported/2016/10/World-Energy-Resources-Full-report-2016.10.03.pdf.

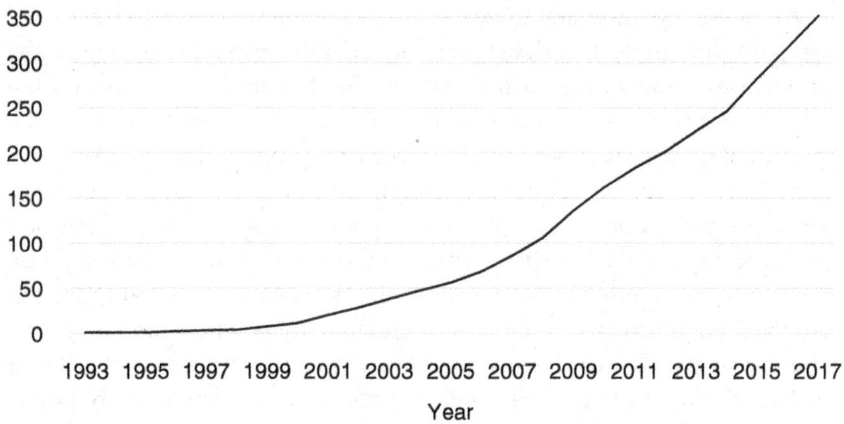

FIGURE 6.1 Number of incineration plants in Chinese cities by year

of incineration plants has grown much faster than that of any other WtE projects. WtE landfills, primarily gasification projects in landfills only increased from two to twelve in the same time period,[7] and only five anaerobic digestion plants were built by 2016.[8]

The solid waste sector welcomed private firms from the beginning of this sectoral development. As in the urban bus sector, marketization in the solid waste sector mostly took the form of government franchising. In this sector, most government franchising occurs through open bidding for a Build–Operate–Transfer contract with the local government. The winning company designs, constructs, and operates the incineration plant for twenty to thirty years, after which the contract can be renewed. The local government collects waste treatment fees from residents and businesses to pay the company for its services at a pre-agreed price by weight. This fee is subject to change over time. The incineration plant also receives government payment for the electricity generated by burning solid waste.

The sector is not highly profitable and only generates a relatively small amount of employment, so the Chinese central government continues to encourage private firms to enter it. For more than twenty years since 1993, the sector was evenly split between private firms and SOEs across Chinese cities. But since 2012, more SOEs, particularly large ones, have begun to enter this sector. There are now more state-owned than private

[7] *Clean Development Mechanism in China Database*, Department of Climate Change, National Development and Reform Commission, http://cdm.ccchina.org.cn.

[8] *China Urban-Rural Construction Statistical Yearbook*, 2016.

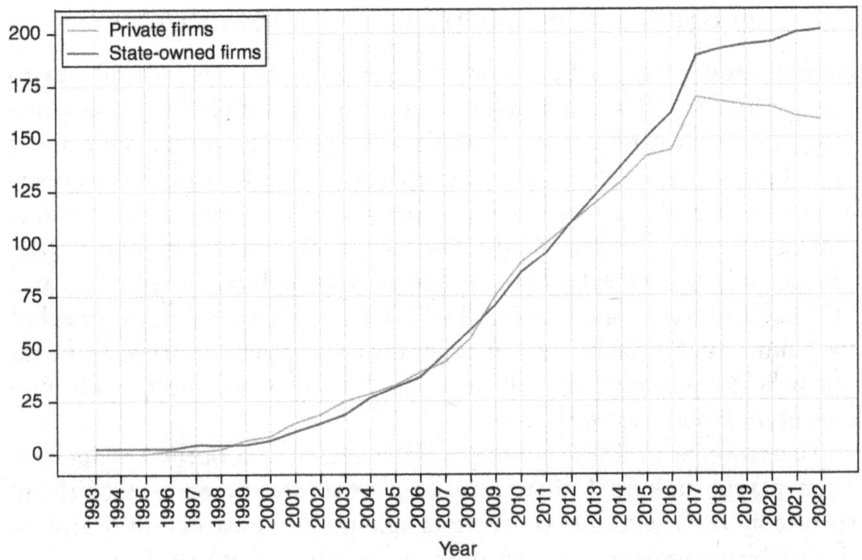

FIGURE 6.2 Number of incineration plants by firm type in Chinese cities

incineration plants. Figure 6.2 shows this trend. But unlike in the urban bus sector, where many city governments forced out the private firms, very few private firms exited this sector involuntarily. Some private firms even actively seek joint ventures with SOEs. In this sector, there are twice as many central and provincial SOEs than small, local SOEs.

On average, each Chinese city has 1.9 incineration plants and two landfills (author's data). On average, each incineration plant has an initial investment of 250 million yuan, and furnaces and other key incineration facilities have a lifespan of no more than twenty-five years. Entry into this sector is relatively easy. There is little proprietary technology in building and operating an incineration plant. The most technology intensive part, the furnace, is usually imported.[9] Similarly, solid waste sorting facilities are also imported, if a solid waste firm decides to use one. Therefore, firms in this sector come from various backgrounds. For example, an incineration plant built in 2009 in Suzhou, Jiangsu, was built and maintained by a local silk firm that specialized in garments.[10]

[9] Germany, Japan, and Belgium are the top exporters of furnaces to China. Source: "Jiakuai laji fadian shichang fazhan de zhengce he baozhang jizhi yanjiu," report by the China Electric Power Promotion Council, 2014-10.

[10] The Wujiang Silk Corporation.

PROTEST-PRONE PROJECTS AND FIRM CHOICES

An important feature of the waste incineration sector is its tendency to attract NIMBY (not in my back yard) protests. Unlike air-conditioned buses and clean-energy buses, building a waste incineration plant can stir up the public's fear of worsened air quality and health risks. If not operated up to standard, waste incinerators produce various air pollutants, among which are notorious dioxins, chemical compounds that induce cancer and birth defects. Dioxins can only be reduced by burning at a high combustion temperature of 800°C for a certain amount of time, but the Chinese public lacks trust in either the government or firms, and does not believe the operators will bear the costs of maintaining such high incineration temperatures.[11]

Therefore, protests are common in this sector. Out of the 351 incineration plants built in China, forty-five, or about 13 percent of them, reportedly experienced mass protests against the construction or operation of the plants between 1999 and 2016 (author's data), see Figure 6.3.[12] This number is unsurprisingly underreported. In my fifteen interview cities, ten experienced protests against their incineration plants, but only the largest four were reported and therefore included in my quantitative dataset. The majority of protests against incineration plants were not high profile and contained locally owing to successful government control of civil society and the news media.

The protest-prone feature of incineration plants is what incentivizes local officials to politicize firms in this sector. When launching an incineration plant invites high-profile protests 13 percent of the time, local leaders need to carefully calculate how to balance between claiming credit for following central policy guidance in building these projects and avoiding blame for the potential high-profile protests. The decision about which firms to work with therefore becomes important. Unlike most public projects in a city, the decision on firm choice for incineration plants is made by the top city leaders rather than the head of the Urban Administrative and Law Enforcement Bureau that manages a city's incineration plants. And for the top leaders, their decision is often based on

[11] See Johnson (2013) for a detailed description of how residents in two cities protested against incinerators because they did not trust the incineration plants or regulation enforcement.

[12] Data on protests and social unrest are collected from author's Chinese news collection, the Global Database of Events, Language, and Tone, and the Social Unrest Database of the Chinese Academy of Social Sciences.

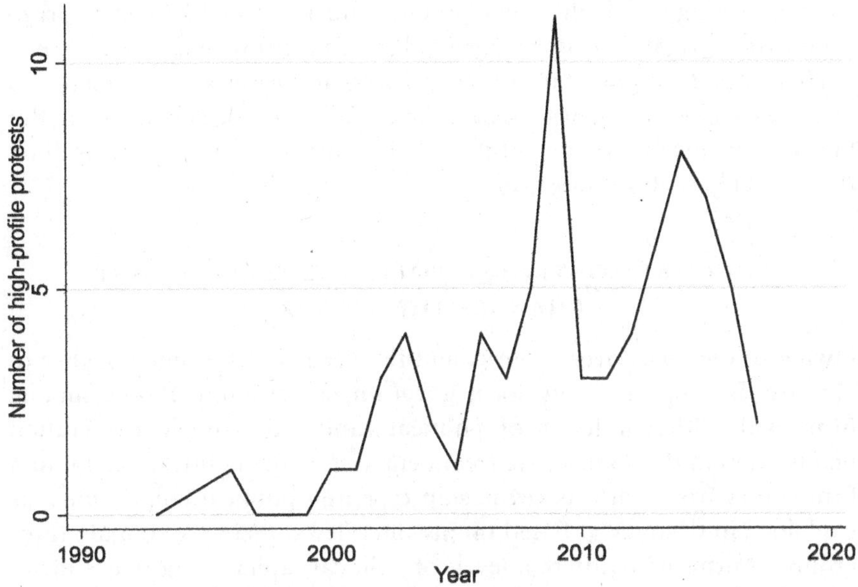

FIGURE 6.3 Number of high-profile protests against incineration plants

the calculation of whether the government can preempt protests, and whether it might need to resort to suppression should high-profile protests break out.

Over time, in the waste incineration sector, we see since 2012 a gradual dominance of SOEs, particularly strong ones. This timeline coincides with the peak year of high-profile protests in 2009, when eleven out of the country's thirty new incineration plants, or 40 percent of them, experienced protests that went out of control and escalated into high-profile events. After this, fewer private firms entered the sector, and some established private firms decided to form joint ventures with SOEs, even when the Chinese national government continued to call for private investment in this sector.

This turn is largely driven by the changing method of societal control, a political service demanded of firms, in the waste incineration sector. With growing awareness of incineration and its environmental and public health impacts, citizens in China are increasingly opposed to incineration plants and less likely to be swayed by appeasement strategies such as persuasion and financial compensation. The increasing public opposition to incineration plants clearly did not deter Chinese local governments from launching incineration plants. However, it does indicate that local governments are finding it increasingly challenging to prevent opposition from escalating into high-profile protests and are more likely to resort to suppression. Against this background, private firms, who have a relatively low level of political capital and who are better as scapegoats and at appeasement strategies, become less useful in societal control. But SOEs, particularly the powerful ones, become more important as allies that can help with suppression.

SOCIETAL CONTROL, A POLITICAL SERVICE THAT CHANGES THE SECTOR

Owing to concerns over protests and the need to determine whether to appease or suppress them, local governments carefully choose among firms with different levels of political capital to launch incineration plants. Within the solid waste treatment sector, the political capital of a firm comes from both its ownership type and political connections, as explained in Chapter 3. Based on my interviews, there are roughly three groups of firms with different levels of political capital in the waste incineration sector: private firms, weak SOEs, and strong SOEs.

Private firms are firms of wholly private ownership, which could be domestic or foreign. They usually have strong political connections, but that is their only source of political capital in most sectors. Weak SOEs are SOEs established by provincial governments beyond the incineration plant's immediate location or by city governments. They have more political capital than private firms because as economic arms of a local government, their political capital comes from both their ownership type and individual political connections. Strong SOEs are SOEs established by the national government or the provincial government of the province where the incineration plant is located. Strong SOEs have the highest level of political capital of all firms. They not only have individual political connections but also the support of the highest level of government or the most important provincial government to city officials. I elaborate next on their political capital and the different political roles they play when protests break out against an incineration plant.

Strong SOEs: Powerful Political Allies at Critical Times

In the presence of high-profile protests against incineration plants, city governments often use suppression to end protests and continue the projects. At such critical moments, firms with high levels of political capital, in this case strong SOEs, can bring a local government the much-needed political support, and can help the local government justify suppression. As a central SOE manager said, "This sector has many protests. Local governments choose us [the central SOE] to do it [launch an incineration plant] in order to shed any responsibility [for protests]. This is the best choice."[13]

Specifically, strong SOEs become allies of local governments in suppressing high-profile protests by doing two things. First and most important, when a protest against an incineration plant escalates, the city government can no longer hide it from the provincial government and will need to suppress it quickly and justify suppression with force. In such instances, having a strong SOE to build and operate the incineration plant helps to justify the government's use of force. The local government is no longer suppressing the public because of the interests of a private firm or the city government's own interests, but is protecting the interests of a strong SOE, the economic arm of upper-level governments. Suppression in this case is more likely to get support from the upper-level government instead of instigating investigations into corruption and nepotism.

When I was doing fieldwork in a city that had accumulated an astonishing level of government debt, equaling fourteen years of total fiscal income that year, I asked about the government's rationale of using a strong SOE for their newly launched and third incineration plant in the city. By then, the city had experienced two protests against the two existing incineration plants, one owned by a private firm and the other by a local SOE. The official in charge of waste management explained the rationale for using a provincial SOE for the third incineration plant: "Using an SOE with a strong background will give us peace of mind. These SOEs have the [provincial] government to back them up. If anything [protests] happens, having the [provincial] government along is better."[14] Another city leader explained the difference between provincial SOEs and private firms: "The most important reason that we favor it [SOE] is the low political risks. We never know what will come out of a project like this. If we give it to a [provincial] SOE, no one will blame us later."[15] Having a strong SOE means the city government has a powerful political ally when facing potential investigations by the upper-level government, particularly when violent suppression becomes necessary.

Second and related, powerful SOEs have the political power to support the local government in justifying the need for an incineration plant

[13] Interview 20180226.
[14] Interview 20151019a.
[15] Interview 20151021.

in the first place. Most of the time, local governments do not need to explain their launch of a municipal waste treatment project. However, when high-profile protests break out against an incineration plant, they might face questioning from the upper-level government. This is particularly challenging considering many incineration plants were not launched properly in China.

Like many other projects in China, incineration plants must pass an environmental impact assessment (EIA) by the Ministry of Ecology and Environment before construction. These EIAs are often manipulated by the evaluating agencies. In 2012, for example, the Chinese central government found that 17.56 percent of EIA contractors who conducted these assessments fabricated facts and data.[16] In 2015, the Ministry of Ecology and Environment criticized the widespread corruption in EIA evaluating agencies and the collusion between these agencies and the businesses being evaluated.[17] When it comes to incineration plants, various types of data showing their safety and public consent can be forged. Examples include the distance between the incineration plant and the nearest residential area, population density in the area, percentage of arable land in the area, and signatures from residents in the area agreeing to an incineration plant in their neighborhood.[18]

Data fabrication is hard to detect and is usually not a problem until a high-profile protest breaks out. High-profile protests can invite upper-level government investigation into the incineration plant, and occasionally evidence of data fabrication is seized upon by the public and exposed to news media. Once this fabrication is exposed, both the city government and the waste treatment firm could be punished by the Ministry of Ecology and Environment for fraud. Receiving a punishment from a national ministry would defeat any credit such projects might bring a local leader.

Therefore, when data fabrication and other illegal acts in launching an incineration plant have a higher risk of exposure owing to potential high-profile protests, strong SOEs are the best partner in crime to help local

16 "Huanping lv zaojia beihou," *People's Daily*, 2013-02-01, https://news.sciencenet.cn/htmlnews/2013/2/274536.shtm.

17 "Huanbaobu: dui yiqie huanping zaojia xingwei douyao yanli chufa," *People's Daily*, 2017-09-27, http://env.people.com.cn/n1/2017/0927/c1010-29563263.html.

18 See, for example, the case of an incineration plant in Tianjin city, where all these data were later found to be fabricated. "Jixian laji fenshao fadianchang huanping zaojia," *China Youth Newspaper*, 2016-12-02, www.chinanews.com/sh/2016/12-02/8081143.shtml.

officials avoid punishment. Strong SOEs can utilize their political support from the upper-level government to influence investigation results and exempt local officials from responsibility. While there is no systematic information on this sensitive subject, I collected eleven cases where the public exposed how incineration firms and local governments illegally forged data, including signatures of nearby residents in support of the environmental impact evaluation.[19] In these cases, six firms were central and provincial level (strong) SOEs, four were private firms, and the last was a local SOE. Among the six strong SOEs, none received any punishment (four investigations were dropped), and only one received minor criticism for unintended mistakes in applying for environmental impact approvals. In the case of the local SOE, the government officials received criticism and the firm was punished with a minor fine. Among the four cases involving a private firm, all firms were punished with fines or suspension of operation. Moreover, in two of these cases the government officials involved received a warning.

In sum, strong SOEs are favored as an ally during a crisis. When local officials anticipate protests will escalate into high-profile ones, and therefore expect the need to use suppression that could negatively affect the government's image and legitimacy, as well as individual officials' careers, they prefer to partner with strong SOEs to avoid blame from the upper-level government later. The high level of political capital of strong SOEs makes them valuable allies in a state–society crisis, directly bringing local governments extra political support to engage in drastic measures such as suppression. Weak SOEs and private firms cannot lend this support as easily.

Private Firms: Compliant Scapegoats

Despite high-profile protests making it more attractive to work with a strong SOE, local officials do not wait for a protest to escalate and then hope for no punishment from the upper-level government. They first try to preempt protests with appeasement strategies, including persuasion and offering concessions, to prevent them from escalating in the first place. While having a powerful firm ally with high levels of political capital helps at difficult times, it also comes at a high cost – it is much harder for the city government to control a strong SOE that is supported by a

19 These eleven cases were respectively in the cities of Huanggang, Nanchang, Wuhan, Xiangyin, Qinhuangdao, Tianjin, Changsha, Hangzhou, Beijing, Heze, and Wuxi.

higher level of government. Interviews with city officials show a dominantly negative experience with strong SOEs. One city official said:

> Honestly, dealing with these [central] SOEs is so much trouble. They are as difficult to work with as us [the local government], if not more! If we ask them to do something, any small thing like purchasing another facility, they will have endless meetings that come to nothing. And they are so slow, and they don't listen. If we ask a private firm to do something, they do it the next day![20]

This compliance by private firms comes from their lower level of political capital and therefore higher dependence on local governments for business success. Private firms' political capital mostly comes from their political connections developed through exchange of interests with individual government officials. Sustaining political connections requires private firms to be acquiescent to officials' personal preferences. When the situation calls for it, private firms have little choice but to act as the local government's "running dog" or scapegoat. This feature provides them with several advantages over strong SOEs from the local government's perspective.

First, private firms are easier to use as political scapegoats. As scholars have noted, intermediaries used to avoid blame are often the powerless ones (Oexl and Grossman 2013). When the public starts to organize protests over an incineration plant, local governments usually appease the public with persuasion. The key message of persuasion is that the incineration plant in question will not produce pollution. To make this message convincing, local governments need to signal to the public that they are on the side of the people and are impartial regulators committed to keeping the firms under close watch and under control. The local government might increase the number of inspections of the plant, punish and fine the firm for substandard operations, and order the upgrade of facilities necessary for clean incineration. It is easier for local governments to adopt these measures for privately run incineration plants, because they do not have enough political capital to resist the government's tougher measures. From data collected on inspection of incineration plants by governments and NGOs, shown in Table 6.1, we can see an obvious bias in the reporting of violations based on firm ownership.

These data show a significant difference in how the government and nongovernmental organizations (NGOs) report violations. Starting in 2015, city governments were required to have inspection teams that

[20] Interview 20151029.

TABLE 6.1 *Reported environmental violations by firm type, 2016–2018*

Firm type	Percentage of firms with violations in the provinces of Anhui, Shandong, Yunnan, Jilin, Heilongjiang, and Guangdong, reported by governments	Percentage of firms with violations, reported by NGOs
Private	64	26
Weak SOEs	31	20
Strong SOEs	17	31

Notes: Only six provincial governments conducted inspections by January 2018.
Source: Compiled by the author from data from websites of NGOs including the Wuhu Environmental Protection Volunteers Association, www.waste-cwin.org/, and Shanghai Qingyue, https://data.epmap.org/page/index.

regularly inspect the operations of incinerators.[21] Inspection results are announced to the public as evidence of strict government regulation. If they find violations, then local governments order firms to improve their operations, impose fines, and sometimes threaten firms with temporary shutdowns. By comparing government inspection reports and NGO inspection reports in the same time period, local governments seem to overreport violations by private firms and underreport violations by strong SOEs.

It is possible that SOEs are more law abiding and operate to a stricter standard than private firms, and that NGOs are biasing their results against SOEs. But this possibility was denied by government officials. When asking an official in a city's Bureau of Environmental Protection about whether some firm ownership types proved better at quality control and were more law-abiding than other firm types, the official said:

> There is really no difference in violations. SOEs and private firms all violate environmental laws and engage in illegal emissions [of exhaust gas and wastewater] and other things. Central SOEs are the worst! They know they have backing and have nothing to fear. And it's bad for us [the city's Bureau of Environmental Protection] to offend them. If we try to inspect and regulate their operations, the next day we ourselves [the bureau] will be inspected by the Party Discipline Commission, asking us why we are suddenly interested in this firm but did not care, say, three years ago, and what we are getting [monetarily and politically] out of inspecting it [the SOE]? Therefore, we are not motivated to do it [inspection and regulation], and they [SOEs] know that.[22]

[21] Inspection teams are usually organized by the Bureau of Environmental Protection and the Bureau of Quality Control in a city.
[22] Interview 20150922.

In another interview with a manager of a city's incineration plant, the manager mentioned that he received requests from a strong SOE in the neighboring city to help treat extra solid waste because the requesting SOE's burners broke down. The manager's firm refused the request, and "they [the other SOE] then [illegally] dumped solid waste in places they shouldn't be dumping it."[23]

Therefore, a more plausible explanation for the difference between reported violations by local governments and NGOs is that local governments are biased either in regulation or reporting against private firms. Violations by private firms are less protected by the local government and are used so the local government can claim credit for regulation enforcement. After all, it is politically less risky to punish private firms than SOEs, especially strong SOEs. In return for the private firms' "service" of letting themselves be exposed and punished, local governments often do not actually enforce the punishment.[24]

Similarly, it is easier to use private firms for the concession strategy. When a protest against an incineration plant is at risk of escalation, one measure to appease the public is to temporarily shut down the incineration plant. It is much easier to suspend a private firm's business. Suspension in either construction or operation means monetary loss to firms, and consequently all firms strongly resist project suspension. Resistance from private firms is the weakest, as seen in the urban bus sector, because private firms lack strong political backing from higher-level governments, and offending private firms does not easily lead to political retribution from higher-level governments. Strong SOEs, on the other hand, are essentially economic arms of higher-level governments, which makes their resistance to business suspension more effective as their resistance is often backed by higher-level governments. From 2000 to 2018, fourteen incineration plants were halted by city governments as a response to escalating mass protests at some point in their construction or operation. Among these halted projects, ten were operated by private firms, two by weak SOEs, and two by strong SOEs.[25] Halting a project run by powerful SOEs is extremely difficult, as they can leverage their political influence with the upper-level government and force a local government to abandon the concession strategy, which is costly to businesses.

[23] Interview 20150714.
[24] Interviews 20150327, 20150728.
[25] Author's data.

The second advantage of private firms in the eyes of local governments is that they are more likely to agree to contributing to visibility projects, which, in the waste incineration sector, are closer to a bribe than regulation in nature, as only one plant is needed to showcase waste treatment capacity of the city.

A popular visibility project for city government officials since 2015 is to build "environmental education bases" for the public, a creative response to the CCP's general policy directive of environmental protection. The solid waste sector is a popular sector to launch these education bases to showcase a city's "advanced measures" in treating solid waste and the city leaders' resolution in environmental protection and preservation. An education base usually includes an impressive building with exhibition halls and sometimes a stadium. It is used to host free school visits and government visits, and to boost a city's chances of winning various national city titles. As education bases are not included in the contracts and do not generate any income, the party with the least bargaining power usually ends up paying for it, and this is usually a private firm. Between 2015 and 2018, nineteen such education bases have been built at existing incineration plants, out of which eleven were built by private firms, four by central SOEs, and four by local SOEs (author's data). Compared with persuading a central SOE, it is easier to have the private firms take on the local government's extra-contractual demands.

And lastly, private firms are better at serving the personal monetary incentives of local officials. This is not to say that incineration plants are launched primarily based on their potential for corruption. From interviews, the consensus is that solid waste plants do not bring nearly as many corruption opportunities as other large infrastructure projects. Since incineration plants are prone to protests, they have a higher risk of being audited and investigated, and therefore are not preferred by local officials for corruption purposes. As a local official in the bureau of urban management said, "Incineration plants are not roads or bridges, they are risky [in provoking protests] and therefore not worth the trouble [to build one for rents]."[26]

But local officials do not mind extra monetary gains from any infrastructure projects. One subtle strategy of corruption is to force construction teams onto the solid waste firm. My interviews in this sector in fifteen cities covered four strong SOEs (two central SOEs and two provincial SOEs), one local SOE, and six private firms. A common complaint from the private firms is that once they win the bid to build and operate

[26] Interview 20180226.

an incineration plant, they will have to accept construction teams "introduced" by the local government leaders.[27] But among the SOEs I talked to, only the one local SOE used local construction teams. All four strong SOEs admitted that they received the same request from the city government, but they did not feel obliged to accept it. A provincial-level SOE even said, "We are doing them [the city government] a favor [by building the incineration plant]. We ask the local government to use our own construction teams on their other projects as payback to us."[28]

Therefore, compared with strong SOEs, private firms have much less bargaining power when dealing with city governments, making them attractive partners for the local government. The bargaining power of strong SOEs often make them less likely to cooperate with a city government's extra-contract demands. As one provincial SOE manager explained, "If they [the local government] want to renege on things we agreed upon, or change their mind, we will play the provincial governor card. That's how we do business in our province."[29] From the perspectives of local officials, this shifts their preference to private firms, the easiest type of firm to control. Only when local governments anticipate high-profile, potentially uncontrollable protests against an incineration plant, do they relinquish control over the firm in exchange for a powerful political ally – the strong SOEs.

Weak SOEs: An In-Between Choice

Weak SOEs share the advantages and disadvantages of both strong SOEs and private firms, but only to a limited extent. These are either local city SOEs or SOEs owned by a government situated in a different province from the incineration plant. With the backing of government, weak SOEs have more political capital than private firms. However, their political capital is lower than that of strong SOEs, owned by either the national government or directly from the same provincial government under which the city's incineration plant is built. This puts weak SOEs in an awkward position between strong SOEs and private firms in the eyes of the local government. They are easier to control than the strong SOEs, but not as easy to control as private firms. It takes much longer for weak SOEs to make decisions on extra spending, and such decisions are not

[27] Interviews 20150618, 20150921.
[28] Interview 20150301.
[29] Interview 20150327.

always approved. They could lend more political support to the local government for suppression than the private firms. But when compared with what strong SOEs could bring, this support is limited because weak SOEs belong to weaker local governments. When a high-profile protest happens, the city government would prefer support from the national government or from its very own provincial government.

This dilemma thus makes it harder for weak SOEs to compete with the other firms. When asked about their experience doing "outbound" business in other provinces, a vice executive of a provincial SOE said, "It is the most difficult for us to get a project. We do not have as much political background [*zhengzhi beijing*] as the central SOEs, but then we are not as flexible as the private firms. We are more like the central SOEs but our [political] background is weaker."[30] The dilemma thus puts weak SOEs at a most disadvantaged position in the waste incineration sector.

To sum up, the decision on which firm to partner with on a protest-prone project is a trade-off between getting extra political support and having more control over the firm. This decision depends on the local government's calculation of the risk of high-profile protests and the likelihood to resort to suppression. I test this mechanism with an original dataset on protests and firm choice for waste incineration plants in the next section.

A QUANTITATIVE ANALYSIS OF FIRM CHOICE AND PROTESTS

When a city government decides on the type of firms to use for waste incineration plants, the decision is largely based on local officials' expectation of high-profile protests. If they think high-profile protests are likely, they are more likely to use firms with a high level of political capital, which would be strong SOEs in this sector. If city officials believe they can prevent protests from escalating into high-profile protests, they are more likely to select a firm with lower political capital to have the firm serve as scapegoats in appeasement strategies. To test this mechanism, I use a multinomial logit model to estimate the relation between a city government's choice of firms for incineration plants and their estimated risk of high-profile protests.

The hypothesis is that the more likely it is that high-profile protests will break out against an incineration plant, the more likely it is that the

30 Interview 20150503.

city government will choose a firm with high political capital. The dependent variable is firm choice, coded into three categories of firms that have increasing levels of political capital: 1 for private firms, 2 for weak SOEs, and 3 for strong SOEs.[31] Private firms include foreign owned firms. Weak SOEs are SOEs owned by city governments or provincial governments outside the incineration plant's province. Strong SOEs are SOEs owned by the national government or the provincial government of the incineration plant's province. Data for this information come from the company's website and government announcements of a project.

The key variable of interest is *protest history*. This is a continuous variable measured as the total number of high-profile protests that ever happened against incineration plants in the city and its immediate neighboring cities between 1993 and the year of construction of a new incineration plant. This variable only captures high-profile protests as only these are reported in the media. Since local governments are mostly concerned about high-profile protests, selection bias in media reports is less of a concern. *Protest history* indicates the potential for another high-profile protest against a new incineration plant. The more high-profile protests there were in the past and in neighboring cities, the more likely local officials will include the risk of high-profile protests in their decision-making process of firm choice. A history of high-profile protests could either signal that the region has a more vibrant civil society or that the local governments in the region are less capable in containing mass protests and preventing them from escalating. Including past protests in the immediate neighboring cities allows this variable to account for information diffusion between local governments.

I also include a group of control variables. One is the size of the incineration plant, measured as *plant capacity*. An alternative explanation for firm preference is local protectionism (Wedeman 2003; Zhou 2004). Larger plants mean more investment, larger business operations, and greater employment opportunities, and it is possible that the city government will attempt to benefit an SOE by providing it with a larger project. But if local officials are driven by corruption and they are more likely to get bribes from private firms (Shleifer 1998), then large plants,

[31] Some incineration plants have multiple firm investors. In these cases, I code the incineration plant's ownership type by the dominant shareholder who has more than 51 percent of the shares in the plant. The dominant shareholder is usually the one to manage and operate the plant, and the other shareholders are usually investors.

meaning a higher number of bribes, should make local officials favor private firms.

I also include a variable of regulation enforcement of a city, measured by whether the city government has reported and punished violations by the previous incineration plants. Businesspeople have mentioned in multiple interviews that they care about the regulatory environment, even though what they really mean is whether the government is paying too much attention to the sector or is willing to turn a blind eye when business needs to cut corners. As it is difficult to measure the level of enforcement, I measure this variable with government announcements of violations of other solid waste treatment facilities in the city.

I also test the possibility of path dependence by including a variable indicating the type of firms that built the previous incineration plants (if any). This variable is coded the same way as the dependent variable, with 1 indicating a private firm, 2 a weak SOE, and 3 a strong SOE. These indicators control for the likelihood of path dependence on firm choices. While most cities do not use the same firms for different incineration plants, it is worthwhile to test this alternative hypothesis.

I also include several variables measuring the city's economic development level and population size, particularly gross domestic product (GDP) per capita, population density, and the city government's fiscal health. For a government's fiscal health, an ideal measure would be the debts a city government has accumulated. Owing to data unavailability for this measure, I measure city fiscal health instead with the ratio of fiscal expenditure to fiscal income. As city governments often finance public spending with loans from state-owned banks, which is not included in fiscal expenditure, this proxy measure of a city's debt level will overestimate the city's fiscal health. But such overestimation creates bias *against* finding the results I expect, hence enhancing the analysis. The variable *fiscal health* is lagged for one year, as decision-making on infrastructure investment is usually made a year ahead.

Data come from my original data collection of 351 incineration plants in 177 Chinese cities that were already built or were under construction between 1993 and 2018. Data are collected from news articles, government documents, and company reports. Table 6.2 provides a summary description of the data.

A series of multinomial models show a strong relation between firm choices and protest history in a city and its immediate neighboring area: see Table 6.3.

TABLE 6.2 *Descriptive statistics*

Target items	Observations	Mean	S.D.	Min.	Max
Firm choice: total	351				
Private firms	212	1			
Weak SOEs	79	2			
Strong SOEs	60	3			
Fiscal health	331	1.924	1.195	0.857	8.751
Protest history	334	1.207	1.973	0	12
Regulation enforcement	224	0.249	0.433	0	1
GDP per capita (in 10,000 RMB)	330	20.775	22.132	0.426	160.018
Previous firm: none	196				
Private firm	92				
Weak SOE	27				
Strong SOE	96				

A Strong Correlation between Protests and Firm Choice

As predicted, a history of high-profile protests in a city and its immediate neighboring cities has a statistically significant and strong impact on a local government's choice of firms. With each additional protest in the city and its neighboring area, the odds of choosing a strong SOE to build a new plant is 1.43 times higher than choosing a private firm (log odds of −0.358) and 1.71 times higher than choosing a weak SOE (log odds of −0.537), given that all other variables are held at their mean. Weak SOEs and private firms do not exhibit too much difference from each other in local leaders' eyes, but strong SOEs have a clear advantage in areas with a history of high-profile protests. A predictive margins plot illustrates this relationship (Figure 6.4).

Holding other variables at their means, in cities without any high-profile protests in the past and in their immediate neighboring area, the local government favors using private firms to build and operate incineration plants. The predicted chance of using a private firm to build a new incineration plant is 62 percent, much higher than the second-best choice, a weak SOE (23 percent), or a strong SOE (14 percent).

But once the city has experienced or observed high-profile protests against incinerators in its immediate vicinity, the preference starts to change. The likelihood to use a private firm to build and operate incineration plants steadily drops, while the likelihood to use a strong SOE steadily increases. In areas that experienced six high-profile protests

TABLE 6.3 *Firm choice and protests, multinomial logistic regression models*

Base category: Strong SOEs	Model 1		Model 2		Main Model	
	Private firms	Weak SOEs	Private firms	Weak SOEs	Private firms	Weak SOEs
	Coefficients					
Protest history	−0.279**	−0.479***	−0.281**	−0.456***	−0.358***	−0.537***
Fiscal health	(0.119)	(0.164)	(0.122)	(0.161)	(0.134)	(0.018)
	−0.348	0.128	−0.306	−0.301	−0.178	−0.239
	(0.492)	(0.181)	(0.187)	(0.254)	(0.191)	(0.268)
Population density	0	0	0	0	0	0
	(0)	(0)	(0)	(0)	(0)	(0)
Plant capacity	−0.828**	0.067	−0.989**	−0.039	−0.893**	0.068
	(0.375)	(0.455)	(0.400)	(0.464)	(0.419)	(0.498)
GDP per capita	−0.065*	−0.016	−0.014	0.065	−0.014	0.062
	(0.038)	(0.037)	(0.050)	(0.046)	(0.054)	(0.048)
Regulation			−0.492	0.149	0.015	0.650
			(0.345)	(0.313)	(0.417)	(0.533)
Previous firm type:					1.470***	2.316**
Private					(0.556)	(1.026)
Weak SOE					0.431	−0.224
Strong SOE					(1.102)	(0.745)
					0.332	−0.513
					(0.629)	(0.823)
Log likelihood	−200.47		−197.59		−196.19	
N	221		221		221	

Notes: *p≤ 0.10, **p≤ 0.05, ***p≤ 0.01. Standard errors in parentheses. The coefficient for population density is approximately 0.00001, and is therefore reported as 0 in the table.

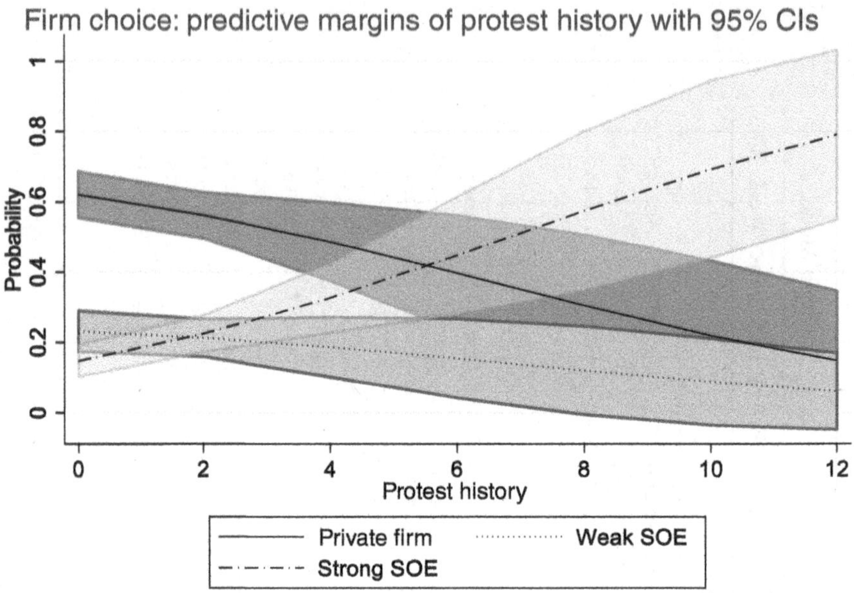

FIGURE 6.4 Protest history and firm choice

against incinerators, holding other variables at their means, the predicted chance for a city in that area to use a private firm drops to 39 percent, and the chance of using a strong SOE increases to 45 percent. Eventually, in areas that experience as high as twelve high-profile protests against incineration plants, the predicted probability of using a private firm is merely 13 percent; while the chance that a city in that area will hire a strong SOE for a new incineration plant increases to 80 percent.

The choice of using a weak SOE seems to be much less affected by protest history, but it is also negatively related to the presence of high-profile protests. This could be because weak SOEs, be they city government SOEs or SOEs owned by other provinces, still lack the political capital of strong SOEs, and therefore are not competitive when a city is expecting high-profile protests.

Other Factors that Play a Role

Of all the control variables, *plant capacity* is statistically significant. When an incineration plant is small, it is much more likely for the local government to use a private firm to build and operate the plant. This is consistent with my interviews, in which a central SOE executive expressed

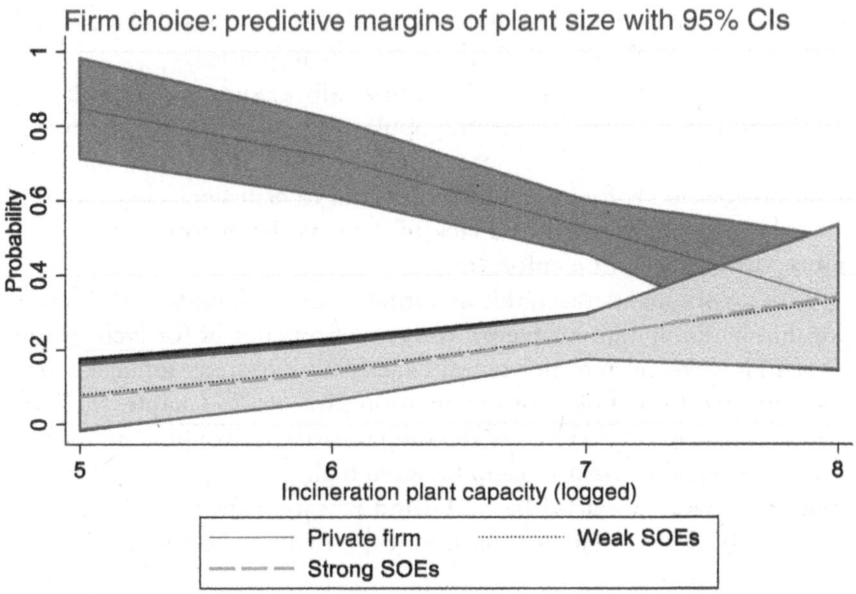

FIGURE 6.5 Plant capacity and firm choice

a lack of interest in smaller plants because "they do not add anything to us. They do not showcase our capacity, and we don't need small projects to survive."[32] But as we can see from Figure 6.5, the larger a plant is to be built, the more likely SOEs, particularly strong SOEs, will be given the job. In other words, competition with SOEs becomes fiercer for large plants, especially the largest ones, where firms of all ownership types have an equal opportunity to win a bid for building and operating incineration plants.

Path dependence also plays a role, particularly if a local government has used a private firm before. If a city has previously used a private firm, then holding other variables at their means, the next project will be ten times (log odds 2.31) more likely to be built by a weak SOE and four times (log odds 1.47) more likely by a private firm, compared with by a strong SOE. But if the local government had used a weak SOE or a strong SOE before, that would decrease the probability of using another SOE for the next project, even though this result is not statistically significant. These results paint a murky picture, but nonetheless indicate that local leaders learn from previous experiences working with different firms.

[32] Interview 20160283.

They seek to strike a balance between their need for control of and political support from firms operating sensitive local projects.

Other control variables are not statistically significant, meaning the fiscal health of a local government, population density, and GDP per capita do not play a role in local leaders' choice of firms for an incineration plant. Regulation enforcement also turns out to be insignificant, but that could have been the result of a lack of data, as the majority of cities do not report on regulation enforcement.

With an original dataset, this quantitative analysis finds a strong relationship between high-profile protests and firm choices for incineration plants. However, it does not reveal exactly how protests influence local governments' firm choice for incineration projects. In Chapter 7, I take a deeper look into two cities with comparative case studies and process tracing to reveal the relationship between high-profile protests, different political services provided by SOEs and private firms for societal control, and how that changes the landscape of firms in the solid waste treatment sector.

7

How Protests Change the Relationship between the State and Firms

Another Tale of Two Cities

How exactly do firms provide the political service of societal control? And how does this political service change the landscape of firms in the waste incineration sector? In this chapter, I answer these questions with in-depth and comparative case studies. First, I use process tracing in a single city, Wuxi, to show how high-profile protests gradually changed the city government's preference for firm types for each new incineration plant. I then use a most-similar comparative case study of two incineration plants in two cities, Wuxi and Qinhuangdao, to highlight the difference between using a firm with high levels of political capital and a firm with low levels of political capital in the presence of high-profile protests.

HIGH-PROFILE PROTESTS AND THE CHOICES OF THREE DIFFERENT FIRMS: WUXI CITY

In the eyes of the government, different levels of protests require different coping strategies, appeasement or suppression, which calls for different types of firms to be partners in societal control. This mechanism is best shown through tracing the waste incineration history in the city of Wuxi, which constructed three different incineration plants using different firms over eight years.

Wuxi is the third richest city in Jiangsu province, one of the richest provinces in China, and a famous tourism town. From 2000 to 2009, its gross domestic product growth rate has been steadily above 13 percent, making it one of the fastest growing cities in terms of economic growth in China. Within merely eight years, Wuxi city launched three incineration plants in 2001, 2004, and 2008. The first plant was built by a local state-owned enterprise (SOE), the second by a joint venture of the same local SOE and private firms, and the third by strong SOEs. A longitudinal comparison of these three cases within the same city controls for all the city level variables that might affect firm choices, such as business environment, regulatory capacity, level of corruption in the government, strength of civil society, and other observable and unobservable variables. Moreover, as the three incineration plants were launched within a short period of eight years, a small group of largely the same city officials was responsible for their establishment. This consistency allows me to control for different individual preferences among city leaders.

The First Incineration Plant: Weak SOE

The first incineration plant in Wuxi was planned in 1999, began construction in 2001, and started operation in 2004. It was built and operated by a local SOE. The launching of this first incineration plant was part of Wuxi city's effort to win the title of National Model City in Civilization (*quanguo wenming dianfan chengshi*) for the second time, and the city's plan to build an "ecologically civilized district" (*shengtai wenming quyu*) as an example to other cities in the province. The leaders of Wuxi's Public Utilities Department and Urban Management Department at the time proposed a waste incineration plant as part of these efforts. This would be the first ever in Jiangsu province and would "put Wuxi way ahead of other cities in the province, especially its long-time competitors of Suzhou and Changzhou cities."[1] With a total investment of 280 million yuan, this plant ranked as the fourth most expensive and the third largest incineration plant (out of eighteen) built in China in 2001, boasting a 1,000-ton daily incineration capacity. The Wuxi government lauded the plant as an important project for improving the people's well-being and as representing a high level of incineration technology.

The decision to have a local SOE build the plant was a simple one. There had not been protests against incineration plants at this time in Wuxi or its neighboring cities, and a local SOE was already running Wuxi's landfills. It would make sense to have the same local SOE build the incineration plant as well. Moreover, there were not many options

[1] Interview 20150922.

in incineration companies back in 1999, as the sector was still taking off in China.

In 2006, when the city's later disgraced party secretary, Weize Yang,[2] launched an industrial park, the Taike Park, right by the incineration plant, problems started to emerge. The industrial park was built to attract high-tech companies to Wuxi to promote clean and knowledge-intensive industrialization, and it was supposed to be, and later became, a signature project of the new party secretary. However, once the high-tech companies settled in the industrial park, they quickly realized there was an incineration plant only 900 feet away, as they saw black smoke and smelled a strong odor every day. The companies started to lose employees who were worried about pollution, and they requested the government relocate the plant. In 2008, the city government promised it would shut down the incineration plant by 2011.[3] But as there were never protests against it, the city government did not proceed with plant shutdown.

In 2014, after years of futile requests to the Wuxi government to either regulate or shut down the incineration plant, companies started to leave the industrial park. This concerned the government. In 2014, a local People's Congress delegate officially proposed the shutdown of the polluting plant.[4] The proposal listed several problems: emission of exhaust, strong odor, leaking leachate, and lack of legally required coverage of the solid waste storage tank. The incineration plant manager admitted that "the plant has not been operating up to environmental standards since before 2011 … the construction quality was low, and the facilities are not functioning correctly … we also have a flawed garbage sorting system, and we can't sort out garbage that shouldn't be burned, causing constant malfunction of the furnace."[5] In 2016, after a mere twelve years of operation, this incineration plant – originally built with a fifty-year lifespan – was closed. The plant was demolished in 2023.

[2] Yang was famous for massive infrastructure building and was eventually sentenced to twelve and a half years for corruption and abuse of power in 2016.

[3] This information was revealed in "Guanyu guanting taike yuan nei Yiduo huanbao redian youxian gongsi de jianyi," Third Conference at the Fifteenth Wuxi People's Congress, 2014-01-17, Proposal 0004.

[4] Ibid.

[5] Ibid.; also "Juzi xingjian de laji fenshao chang weihe xianzhi?," *China Environment News*, 2014-07-03, http://epaper.cenews.com.cn/html/2014-07/03/content_13314.htm.

The Second Incineration Plant: Introducing Private Firms

In 2004, right after the first incineration plant started operations, the Wuxi city government started construction of a second. The total investment was 377 million yuan and it had a treatment capacity of 1,200 tons per day, adding to the city's already large waste treatment capacity of 3,400 tons per day. With the second incineration plant in operation, the city would have an excess treatment capacity of 3,039 tons per day beyond the amount of solid waste it actually produced. This second plant was launched as part of the effort to win a National Civilized City title (*guojia wenming chengshi*) in 2005, hoping to continue Wuxi's success in national title competitions. It was also part of a three-year plan by the party secretary, Weize Yang, to turn Wuxi city into a "Famous City for Mountains and Water (*shan shui ming cheng*)," of which incineration plants were an important element in "making garbage invisible."[6]

The Wuxi city government's fiscal expenditure-to-income ratio increased from 0.97 to a slightly less ideal 1.04 in 2004, but the city's finances remained relatively healthy. The Wuxi government decided to continue using the same local SOE to launch the second incineration plant, but this time it also allowed private firms to enter the industry. Eventually, this plant had a mixed ownership, with the local SOE as the dominant shareholder that controlled its construction and operation.

Given that the second incineration plant was located near a large residential area and the first incineration plant had caused dissatisfaction among nearby companies, the Wuxi government did not publicize the launch of the new one until after it was already built. But after it began operations in 2006, protests quickly followed in 2007. Residents reported the new incineration plant's strong odor and complained that the garbage trucks leaked trash and leachate onto roads while transporting the garbage. At the end of 2007, residents discovered that there was a surge in cancer diagnoses in the neighborhood, and they associated it with dioxin emissions from the incineration plant nearby.[7] Angry residents organized a blockade of the entrance to the incineration plant and demanded the city government either move the incineration plant or compensate the

6 Ibid.; also "2005 nian-2007 nian wuxi shi chengshi jianshe fazhan xingdong gangyao," Wuxi government, https://rd.wuxi.gov.cn/doc/2005/05/10/1670759.shtml.

7 "Guanyu tuijin jiejue Wuxi Huilian laji redian youxian gongsi suo yinfa xiangguan shehui maodun," The Second Conference at the Fifteenth Wuxi Local People's Congress, 2013-01-31, https://rd.wuxi.gov.cn/doc/2013/01/31/1695458.shtml.

residents for moving away.[8] After estimating the amount of compensation at an exorbitant amount of 2.1 billion yuan,[9] almost 1 percent of the city's fiscal income that year, the city government decided not to compensate the residents, and instead announced in 2008 that they would upgrade the new incineration plant to make sure it would not produce more smoke and pollution.[10] However, none of these promises was fulfilled, and complaints and petitions about the second incineration plant continued.

The Third Incineration Plant: Powerful Central SOEs

At the end of 2008, two years after the second incineration plant started operation and amid increasing complaints against the first two plants, the city government decided to launch a third. This was listed as a key government project, and part of the city's application portfolio to the "Most Livable City in the Province (*zui yiju chengshi*)" title. The city government set the goal for the third incineration plant to be the largest in China, the fastest built, and a "garden-like" project.[11] It had a high investment of 1.5 billion yuan and a treatment capacity of 4,000 tons per day, greatly increasing the city's solid waste treatment capacity to 7,200 tons per day, far exceeding the city's daily solid waste production of 2,480 tons per day in 2008.[12]

Yet, when deciding on what firm to use this time, the Wuxi city government made different calculations than before. In 2008, Wuxi had gone through three years of massive infrastructure construction, including highways, roads, industrial parks, wastewater plants and other projects under the party secretary Weize Yang. These projects brought huge debts to Wuxi city. While the exact amount was never publicized, a few reports on the debt problem indicated its severity. One city official said that from 2006 to 2011, Wuxi's fiscal income was "completely depleted" by Yang.[13]

8 "Wuxi shi guti feiqi wu chuzhi zhuanxiang guihua, 2012–2020," Wuxi Government, https://cg.wuxi.gov.cn/doc/2015/06/17/124181.shtml.

9 Ibid.

10 "Juzi xingjian de laji fengshao chang weihe xianzhi?," *China Environment News*, 2014-07-03, https://m.bjx.com.cn/mnews/20140703/524141.shtml.

11 "Zhongguo Enfei Xidong huanbao nengyuan yiqi erqi xiangmu kaishi yunying," China Metallurgical Group Corporation, October 29, 2010, www.mcc.com.cn/mcc/_132154/_132584/jnjpzt/_135345/163184/index.html.

12 Author's data.

13 "Jiangsu Wuxi guanyuan cheng Yang Weize zhuzheng shi jihu taokong Wuxi caizheng," *China Economics Weekly*, 2015-01-13, https://news.sina.com.cn/c/2015-01-13/115231393350.shtml.

A Reuters report showed that the Wuxi government was in such deep debt that in 2012, the city tried to cut civil servants' wages.[14]

In 2008, when the third incineration plant was launched, the city was in the middle of accumulating these debts. Regarding the decision on the third incineration plant, a government official said: "By then [2008] it was a different situation, it was not quite as easy to invest as before. If we can't give money [to the plant], we don't give money."[15] This was also a time when the national government stressed the importance of public–private partnerships to alleviate local governments' fiscal burden on public projects; so the Wuxi government decided to use public bidding and build–operate–transfer (BOT) as the delivery method for this third plant.[16]

At the same time, the city government became aware of potential protests against yet another incineration plant in the city. In 2008, there had been numerous complaints against the first incineration plant, several protests against the second one, and two high-profile protests in the immediately neighboring cities of Changzhou and Huzhou against their waste incineration plants. Now fully aware of the unpopularity of incineration plants among the public, Wuxi local officials took the potential of high-profile protests into consideration when selecting a firm. A local official explained the final decision to use a central SOE: "It is very complicated. We have to consider the social problems [protests] we have. Private firms are also okay ... central SOEs are still better when there are protests."[17] The city government eventually selected Enfi, a newly established subsidiary company of a central SOE, to launch the third incineration plant.

The Wuxi government and Enfi decided to hide the project from the public and committed a series of illegal acts to gain environmental approval from the Ministry of Ecology and Environment. Because there was a lack of justification for another incineration plant, the Wuxi government had a difficult time getting public consent for a third, a required procedure in getting an environmental impact assessment (EIA). In 2007,

[14] "Is China's Debt Nightmare a Province Called Jiangsu?," *Reuters*, 2013-07-24, www.reuters.com/article/china-economy-debt/is-chinas-debt-nightmare-a-province-called-jiangsu-idUSL4N0FQ02820130724.

[15] Interview 20150913.

[16] Build-Operate-Transfer (BOT) is a common contractual arrangement in public–private partnerships, in which a public entity hires a private entity to construct a project, operate it for an agreed period to recoup costs, and then transfer ownership back to the public entity.

[17] Interview 20150924.

the government told the residents they were going to build a temple in the area, not too concerned that a temple would obviously look different from an incineration plant. The government then obtained signatures from residents who believed they were signing to support the building of a temple. This document was later attached to the city government proposal for the incineration plant.[18] In 2008, before construction began, Enfi was also required to submit proof of public consent to construction to the Ministry of Ecology and Environment. Enfi simply forged 200 signatures and submitted them.[19] Construction then started in October 2008, with residents still believing that a temple was to be built.

In 2010, the first part of the incineration plant was completed and started trial operations, which created considerable smoke and a strong odor. Residents finally realized this could not be the smell of sandalwood incense from a temple but was the odor from a solid waste incineration plant. Angry residents petitioned the government to stop construction, and the government appeased them by promising they would urge the incineration plant to pause operation until the company could guarantee no exhaust fumes and odor. However, the residents soon discovered this was an empty promise and the incineration plant was still in operation.[20] Moreover, they also discovered that the incineration plant had dug a trench to directly drain leachate into a local river, which was clearly illegal and caused water pollution. Residents then organized a series of acts of civil disobedience. They printed flyers about the harm of incineration and distributed them nearby, made frequent petition trips to the city government,[21] and guarded the river from which the incineration plant retrieved water.[22]

The government and Enfi at first responded with a strategy of continued appeasement. In March 2011, the government decided to arrange "educational trips" for resisting residents to see other incineration plants. Such trips are common among incineration plants facing protests. Usually, the firm pays for the trip so the protesting residents can visit an

18 "Gongzhong yu laji fenshao de boyi," *Yangcheng Evening News*, 2014-03-31, www.chinacace.org/news/view?id=277.

19 Ibid.; and "Jiangsu Wuxi Taigong miao biancheng laji fenshao chang," *Wohua News*, 2011-05-31, https://news.qq.com/a/20110531/000478.htm.

20 Ibid.

21 "Huanjing zaihai yu shehui sunshi," a special report by Narada Foundation, 2014-10-24, www.naradafoundation.org/Uploads/file/20141024/5449d2febb5eb.pdf.

22 "Zhongguo Enfi Xidong fadian chang kaishi yunying," *China Enfi Report*, 2010-12-29, www.mcc.com.cn/mcc/_132154/_132584/jnjpzt/_135345/163184/index.html.

incineration plant, often a beautiful one, to relieve the concern about health hazards from solid waste incineration. The trip also includes one or two days of "free activities," basically a paid vacation for the protesters. In the case of Wuxi, the government, instead of the firm, arranged for the protesters to visit one incineration plant in Shanghai and another in Jiangyin city. However, instead of taking a vacation, the Wuxi residents used the "free activity" time to secretly visit local residents living near these incineration plants, and heard entirely different and negative accounts about the incineration plants. Therefore, these two paid trips produced the opposite effect of what was intended, and instead increased Wuxi residents' resolve to resist the incineration plant.[23]

The residents escalated their resistance after returning from the "educational trips." Starting in mid-March 2011, they set up tents in front of the entrance to the incineration plant to prevent garbage trucks from delivering solid waste. Retired residents stayed in the tents during the day and working residents stayed in them at night, with local entrepreneurs providing free beds and food. Residents invited media from outside the city to report on this event, though none responded at this point. They also organized protests in front of the city government and sought help from environmental and legal aid nongovernmental organizations (NGOs) in order to sue the Wuxi government.

These developments toward a high-profile protest aggravated the city government and the central SOE, which then changed their strategy from appeasement to suppression. The Wuxi government hired "security guards" for the firm, who cleared the tents and dispersed the crowd. The city government also arrested two residents who had printed flyers. The suppression strategy aggravated the residents, who decided to organize a protest march from the incineration plant to the city government on May 27, 2011. Halfway through the march, the residents encountered local police and the People's Armed Police waiting for them. Violence ensued with more than forty residents arrested, more than a hundred injured, and one paralyzed permanently from brain damage.[24]

The violent ending and the scale of this protest finally drew some media attention, and NGOs started to help residents to prepare for a lawsuit against the Wuxi government at the Jiangsu Provincial Court.

[23] A detailed account of the trips can be seen in "Huanjing zaihai yu shehui sunshi," a special report by Narada Foundation, 2014-10-24, www.naradafoundation.org/Uploads/file/20141024/5449d2febb5eb.pdf.

[24] Ibid. And "Jiangsu Wuxi Taigong miao biancheng laji fenshao chang," *Wohua News*, 2011-5-31, https://news.qq.com/a/20110531/000478.htm.

Observing that this protest had now escalated into a high-profile one, and concerned that more protests and a lawsuit would negatively affect the city leaders, the Wuxi government announced it would temporarily suspend operation of the third incineration plant. This suspension lasted six years, during which Enfi continued to press the Jiangsu provincial government to relaunch the project in Wuxi city.

In 2016, the Wuxi government invited another central SOE, the China Everbright Group, to invest in the incineration plant and restarted its operation. Speaking of the decision to add one more central SOE, a local official simply said that "we invited the China Everbright Group in case there are more protests. One more [central SOE] is better. We told people that Enfi is no longer operating the plant, but they are still behind the scene."[25] Some residents resisted the reopening of the incineration plant by appealing to the National Public Complaints and Proposals Administration, but this office, commonly known as the national office of letters and visits, did not get involved and instead referred the issue back to the Wuxi city government, who simply responded that the reopening of the incineration plant was necessary.[26] In the Wuxi case, even after high-profile protests, the city government and central SOEs successfully launched a highly controversial project, and no official was held responsible for fraud or for provoking high-profile protests.

DIFFERENT LEVELS OF POLITICAL CAPITAL DO MATTER: WUXI AND QINHUANGDAO

Do firms with different types of ownership really serve local governments differently when high-profile protests break out? To show that variation in ownership and political capital of firms makes a difference in the outcomes of high-profile protests, I complement the Wuxi case with a most similar case comparison between two incineration plants in Wuxi, Jiangsu province; and Qinhuangdao city, Hebei province. The Wuxi plant is the third constructed in the city and the Qinhuangdao plant is the second.

Both incineration plants were launched between 2008 and 2009, and they encountered high-profile protests respectively in 2010 and 2011. The Wuxi plant was suspended and reopened after six years, while the Qinhuangdao plant was shut down and never reopened. The Wuxi

[25] Interview 20150923a.

[26] "Jiejue xinfang shixiang," Wuxi Office of Letters and Visits, 2016-8-3, www.wuxi.gov.cn/doc/2016/08/03/1113876.shtml.

incineration plant was built and operated by a central SOE with high levels of political capital and the Qinhuangdao plant was built by a private firm with relatively low political capital. I also show that other possible explanations, such as differences in the local legal environments and the capacity of cities to suppress protests, do not fully explain the variation we see in the state–society and state–business relations in these two cases.

In 2008, Qinhuangdao decided to build a second incineration plant with a treatment capacity of 1,000 tons per day and an investment of 220 million yuan. The new incineration plant was launched as part of the city's application to the 2009 National Civilized City title. Qinhuangdao city had four operating landfills and one incineration plant already under construction in 2008, giving the city an excess treatment capacity of 720 tons per day beyond the amount of solid waste the city actually produced. Responding to the national call for more private investments in this sector, and with a fiscal expenditure to income ratio of 1.74, the city decided to use a BOT contract to build the second incineration plant – a private firm from Zhejiang province called Weiming. There were never protests against incineration plants in the city or in its immediate neighboring cities up to this point.

An Illegal Launch of an Incineration Plant – Similar to Wuxi

Just as in Wuxi, the Qinhuangdao city government and the private firm, Weiming, colluded to illegally forge signatures from nearby residents to pass an EIA. In early 2009, before construction began, Qinhuangdao government and the private firm together forged 100 signatures, many of which were of deceased or incarcerated residents.[27] The firm also claimed that it had hosted two environmental impact hearings for the residents as required in the EIA, and showed a list of attendees, which was later found to be forged as well.[28] With these forged documents, the new incineration plant was approved by China's Ministry of Ecology and Environment and contruction started in April 2009.

[27] "Qinhuangdao laji fenshao xiangmu zao dizhi: huanping baogao zaojia," *Caijing News*, 2012-07-02, http://finance.sina.com.cn/china/dfjj/20120702/101112453572.shtml.

[28] Ibid.

In August 2009, Beijing hosted the international conference Dioxin 2009.[29] China's national TV channel, CCTV, broadcast the conference, which educated the public on the health hazards of dioxins. This broadcast drew considerable attention from the residents in Qinhuangdao. Realizing that solid waste incineration can be a major source of dioxin pollution, more than 1,500 residents near the new incineration plant signed a petition demanding the government stop the plant's construction. Residents also organized protests in front of the construction site. However, the city government ignored their complaints, and construction continued. Angry petitioners then started to send multiple complaints to the Hebei provincial Bureau of Public Complaints and Proposals about the firm and the city government.[30]

No longer able to overlook the complaints, the Qinhuangdao government responded first with appeasement strategies. In September 2009, they ordered the private firm to suspend construction and assured the residents that the government would always be on their side and would not allow dioxin emissions from the plant. Meanwhile, managers and executives of the private firm paid visits to the residents, offered them jobs, and bought them dinner and gifts. However, residents were not swayed and continued to resist the incineration plant. Six months later, the Qinhuangdao government lost patience, and invited the residents' representatives to attend an unrelated meeting on local administrative affairs. During that meeting, the government told them that they would receive reimbursement for attending. The representatives were then asked to write their names on a blank piece of paper as documentation of the reimbursement. The government later attached these signatures to a document that falsely stated the public had agreed to stop resisting and now welcomed the incineration plant.[31]

In May 2010, with this newly forged document showing the approval of residents, construction restarted. This development greatly upset local

[29] The full name of the conference is International Symposium on Halogenated Persistent Organic Pollutants.

[30] See a detailed account of these events in "Mao Da: Qinhuangdao nongmin de fanfen laji yundong," Sohu Green Forum, 2013-05-20, http://green.sohu.com/20130520/n376486520.shtml. The article made a mistake in reporting the month of the Dioxin 2009 conference.

[31] See a detailed account of this development in "Qinhuangdao laji fenshao xiangmu zao dizhi: huanping baogao zaojia," Caijing News, 2012-07-02, http://finance.sina.com.cn/china/dfjj/20120702/101112453572.shtml.; and "Mao Da: Qinhuangdao nongmin de fanfen laji yundong," Sohu Green Forum, 2013-05-20, http://green.sohu.com/20130520/n376486520.shtml.

people, who gathered once again to block the entrance to the construction site, but their protest was suppressed by the police, though without casualties. The residents also petitioned to the Ministry of Ecology and Environment to revoke the approved EIA, only to be rejected.

Left with few other options, the residents sued the Hebei provincial Bureau of Environment for allowing a project to start based on forged documents. This action changed the outcome of the protest. Unlike in the Wuxi case, where the court did not hear the case, the Hebei provincial court decided to press ahead with it. Because lawsuits against a government department could negatively affect government officials' career prospects, the Qinhuangdao city government did not want the case to proceed. Therefore, they offered to revoke the EIA approval and suspend the incineration plant if the residents would drop the lawsuit. The residents accepted this offer, and the city government indefinitely stopped the project.[32]

Different Political Capital of Firms, Different Outcomes of Projects

The Wuxi and Qinhuangdao cases serve as a most similar case comparison. They differ in their outcomes and they differ in the key variable of interests – political capital of the firms they use. But they are similar in other aspects. In both cities, protests started at the construction stage. The scale of protests in both cities was between 1,000 and 1,500 residents. Both protests took the form of peaceful marches and road blockades. Residents in both cities adopted the strategy of "rightful resistance" that does not challenge the regime (O'Brien and Li 2006), and in both cases they resorted to the legal system at some point. Both city governments first used appeasement and later suppression to manage protesters.

Nonetheless, the Wuxi incineration plant restarted six years later, and neither the Wuxi government nor the central SOE was held responsible for the protest. The Qinhuangdao incineration plant, on the other hand, never restarted, and the private firm received a warning from the provincial Bureau of Environment.[33] What explains these different outcomes? I first explore two alternative explanations, and then explain the different

[32] Ibid.

[33] "Qinhuangdao xibu laji fenshaochang xiangmu huanping shishi, huanping jigou jing zheyang zaojia," *People's Daily*, 2013-01-29, http://politics.people.com.cn/n/2013/0129/c1001-20356407.html.

outcomes in relation to the political capital of the firms used to launch the incineration plants.

An alternative explanation for different outcomes of high-profile protests is local variation in the rule of law. If the legal system in Hebei province or Qinhuangdao city was more responsive to the public than that in Jiangsu province or Wuxi city, it could explain why the Jiangsu provincial court did not hear the case from Wuxi residents, but the Hebei provincial court proceeded with it, which led to the Qinhuangdao government's suspension of the project to avoid a lawsuit. While there is little information on the quality and strength of local legal systems in China, we can gain some insight from rankings by China's national government. In 2015, the transparency and quality of the legal system for eighty-one provincial and city level courts was ranked. In this ranking, the Jiangsu provincial court was placed nineteenth, and Hebei's only thirty-fifth.[34] In another 2023 index of the rule of law commissioned by China's central government and compiled from a survey of legal professionals in China, the Wuxi city government ranked tenth out of all Chinese cities, while the Qinhuangdao city government did not even get into the top fifty.[35] If these government rankings reflect the local variation, then Qinhuangdao city and Hebei province actually have weaker legal systems than Wuxi city and Jiangsu province, and we should expect the opposite outcomes in the two cities. Therefore, the difference in rule of law does not explain the different outcomes in the two cities.

Another alternative explanation for the different outcomes is the difference in state capacity to suppress high-profile protests. While it is hard to believe there can be much variation in Chinese local governments' ability to suppress protests, it is possible that Qinhuangdao city is less capable of doing so, and therefore caved in to the residents by never restarting the plant. If this were true, then we should see a consistent pattern of a weak local state in Qinhuangdao when encountering other environmental protests, but this is not the case. As the city whose Beidaihe district is the location of the annual two-month-long summer work retreat for China's top leaders to escape the heat of Beijing and conduct so-called horse trading, Qinhuangdao city has a large presence of the People's Armed Police, and it has had no trouble suppressing other similar protests. For example, in 2014, four years after the first protest against

34 *Blue Book of Rule of Law, Annual Report of China's Rule of Law*, No. 14, 2016.
35 *Assessment Report of Government by Law in China*, 2023.

this incineration plant and under the same city leadership, Qinhuangdao city experienced another high-profile protest against the city's other incineration plant, which was operated by a central SOE. For three days, residents blocked several streets leading to the incineration plant in protest against exhaust and odor emissions, causing tons of garbage to pile up on the streets and traffic congestion. Nonetheless, the city government managed to suppress the protest and the incineration plant suffered no consequences.[36]

Therefore, the different outcomes of the two incineration plants are not due to city level differences in state capacity or legal environment. Instead, the outcomes are directly related to the type of firms used for the incineration project. In Wuxi, the firm building and operating the incineration plant is a central SOE. Central SOEs receive support from the national government when their business faces public opposition. In 2012, not long after the protest happened, Enfi, the central SOE in Wuxi, managed to win several important awards in the industry, including the "Most Trustworthy Solid Waste Incineration Entity," "Best Choice of Bidder," and "Award of Excellent Contribution to Solid Waste Incineration" granted by Bidding in China, a website owned by the Chinese national government.[37] Considering the Wuxi plant was Enfi's first ever plant and it was not even in operation, and that Enfi admitted to a "lack of experience and therefore was not able to operate up to environmental standards" in the trial operations,[38] it is surprising to see these awards amid a major scandal involving the company. Nonetheless, these awards provided the Wuxi city government with much-needed justification to suppress the protest and restart the plant later. The narrative was that a trustworthy central SOE could not have provided bad service; rather, it was that the "ignorant people just wanted to create trouble ... and now they can see [the project is good]."[39]

Furthermore, as a central SOE with high levels of political capital, Enfi had political backing from the very top to push Wuxi city to resume the project. From 2012 to 2016, Enfi sent more than ten formal requests to the Wuxi city government to restart this incineration plant, because the

[36] "Hebei Qinhuangdao jumin baowei laji fenshao chang, lumian biancheng laji chang," *Qinhuangdao Evening News*, 2014-9-18.

[37] "Zhongguo shida zui ju toubiao shili laji fadian danwei jiexiao," *Xibu Shang Bao*, 2012-12-04, https://m.bjx.com.cn/mnews/20121204/405714.shtml.

[38] "Zhongguo Enfi Xidong laji fadian chang kaishi yunying," *China Enfi Report*, 2010-12-29.

[39] Interview 20180430.

firm was incurring losses from it.[40] In 2014, the city had a leadership change, making revival of the plant seem even less likely. New leaders should have no incentive to revive a controversial project started by their predecessor, especially one that could induce more protests, because they cannot necessarily gain credit from the previous leader's project but can definitely be blamed for protests. Residents in Wuxi certainly did not believe that the firm could convince the local government to revive the project. As one resident said, "We have a new party secretary now, it's impossible for the plant to restart operation!"[41] However, the new city leaders could not resist the pressure from the central SOE, and the incineration plant resumed operation in late 2016, to everyone's surprise. An official in the city said, "It [Enfi] is a central SOE, it's backed by the State Council! What can we do?"[42] In December 2017, after the Wuxi incineration plant restarted operation, the then city party secretary attended the opening ceremony and expressed his faith in the highest quality of services provided by central SOEs.[43]

Compared with Enfi's influence in Wuxi city, the private firm Weiming lacked the political capital to distance itself from the protests in Qinhuangdao. In 2010, Weiming was applying to have an initial public offering (IPO) right before the protest broke out. But because the protest exposed Weiming's illegal activities in obtaining an EIA, the firm was inspected by China's Securities Regulatory Commission, and eventually the IPO was not approved.[44] As a private firm, Weiming had only weak political capital that did not bring in high-level government support when its interests clashed with the public. In city government officials' eyes, it was not wise to align with a firm that cannot bring in political support in a public crisis, and it was better to distance itself from the private firm. Therefore, despite Weiming making multiple requests to the Qinhuangdao government to restart the incineration plant, these requests were not heeded, especially after Qinhuangdao city experienced a leadership change. The new leader had no incentive to continue a project initiated

40 "Juzi xingjian de laji fengshaochang weihe xianzhi?," *China Environment News*, 2014-07-03, https://m.bjx.com.cn/mnews/20140703/524141.shtml.

41 "Huanjing zaihai yu shehui sunshi," Narada Foundation, 2014-10-24, www.naradafoundation.org/Uploads/file/20141024/5449d2febb5eb.pdf.

42 Interview 20150922.

43 "Li Xiaomin fu xidong dianchang xianchang jiancha zhidao shi yunxing gongzuo," *Jiangsu News*, https://jsnews.jschina.com.cn/wx/a/201711/t20171125_1218189.shtml/.

44 "Weiming huanbao IPO: er-e-ying chaobiao yu gaoe fuzhai zao zhiyi," *Zhongguo wang caijing*, 2014-07-11, http://finance.people.com.cn/stock/n/2014/0711/c67815-25269740.html.

by the previous leadership. A central SOE manager indirectly summarized this dynamic: "If there are issues [social unrest], using a private firm, the officials cannot distance themselves from it. To keep their 'official hat' [their official position], it is best to choose a big SOE that will not bring trouble."[45]

But why did the Qinhuangdao government use a private firm in the first place? For one thing, they did not foresee the high-profile protests. Additionally, private firms cover more monetary costs during the appeasement stage, as they are more likely to agree to shoulder extra-contract costs when local governments ask, given their lack of political capital. We can gain some insights from the different costs shouldered by Wuxi's central SOE and by Qinhuangdao's private firm when facing protests.

During the appeasement stage, it is much easier to have a private firm bear the costs incurred, and it is harder to get a central SOE to cover similar costs. For example, in Wuxi, the appeasement strategy was to take residents on "educational trips" to other cities, and it was the Wuxi city government that paid for these trips, not the central SOE. In Qinhuangdao, the appeasement strategy included meals, gifts, and job offers, but it was the private firm rather than the city government that paid for these inducements.

Once the incineration plant had to be suspended after protests escalated into high-profile status, again, in Wuxi, it was the city government rather than the central SOE that paid for all the costs incurred from suspension, including salaries for engineers and security guards staying at the suspended plant, and maintenance fees.[46] But in Qinhuangdao, the private firm, rather than the city government, paid for all costs incurred from the suspension. As in the urban bus sector, private firms "are the most obedient,"[47] and such obedience is valued by local governments, which prefer to use private firms when they are confident the appeasement strategy can prevent public opposition from escalating into high-profile protests.

Through the case studies comparing Wuxi and Qinhuangdao in this chapter, I show how firms carry out the political service of societal control for local governments in China. In the eyes of local governments, private firms are better scapegoats to appease the public and SOEs are

45 Interview 20180226.

46 "Huanjing zaihai yu shehui sunshi," Narada Foundation, 2014-10-24, www.naradafoundation.org/Uploads/file/20141024/5449d2febb5eb.pdf.

47 Interview 20150617.

better allies to suppress the public. While the type of firm used does not necessarily change the course or the outcome of protests themselves, firm ownership type plays an important role in the post-protest outcomes for the local government and for the projects in question.

Working with a firm that has high political capital, both the city government and the firm can avoid punishment for suppression of protesters, and the project has a higher chance of continuation or revival. Working with a firm that has low political capital, the firm will help the local government pay for appeasement strategies that could potentially prevent high-profile protests and serve as a scapegoat, but it does not bring political support for suppression, exposing local officials to risks of lawsuits, criticism, and even demotion for failing to maintain social order. Therefore, even though firms with low political capital are easier to control, the city government is more likely to use firms with high political capital when they expect high-profile protests. But because local governments can usually prevent protests from escalating, firms with low political capital are still widely preferred for their ease of control. As one government official described:

> Let's put it this way. When it comes to which [types of firms] is safer politically, the consideration is like what to do with your extra money. Using private firms is like investing in the stock market, you might earn more but it's riskier. Using central SOEs is like putting money in a savings account, you earn less but nothing [bad] will happen. And that decision depends on the local government. It depends on how much risk they can take on.[48]

The political service of societal control in the waste treatment sector, unlike that in the urban bus sector, created a different kind of state–business relations. Facing a mutual threat of public opposition, the state and business in this sector often develop a reciprocal relationship around a controversial project, particularly between local governments and strong SOEs that bring in the much-needed political support for local leaders. Local officials therefore often tacitly consent to firms' cost-saving measures and protect the firm's interests. From interviews and news collections, I identify four specific forms of reciprocation for firms' political services in the solid waste treatment sector.

First, local governments are more likely to actually give waste incineration plants subsidies. Unlike in the bus sector, where bus firms constantly complained about not getting the subsidies promised to them,

[48] Interview 20190317.

in the solid waste sector, local governments are more willing to pay firms what they promised, even though payments are often delayed. Secondly, local governments go out of their way to make sure waste incineration plants get their income. In several cities, local governments coordinate among various departments to ensure waste treatment firms receive their fees from the public. This is done by including garbage treatment fees in personal income tax or by making the payment of these fees a prerequisite for obtaining business licenses. Thirdly, local governments often allow waste incineration plants to engage in cost-saving measures, many of which are illegal, such as the untreated disposal of fly and bottom ash, and allowing waste treatment firms to blend coal into solid waste to generate more electricity at a lower cost.[49] And finally, local governments often go out of their way to shield investigation into incineration plants. For example, a city official told me that when one of the local incineration plants, run by a private company, received a sudden inspection and fine from a Ministry of Ecology and Environment inspection team, the city government stood up for the plant and assured the team that they would ensure the plant changed its practices. The local government later forged documents to show the inspection team that the plant had indeed improved its services, even though it had not.[50]

Ironically, such state–business collusion could further increase the risk of high-profile protests against incineration plants that are not operating up to standards. This, in turn, pushes local governments to rely more on SOEs, which in the eyes of local governments are better allies in high-profile protests, creating a vicious cycle of protests, state–business collusion, and more protests.

These dynamics around the firms' second political services, societal control, is what makes the waste incineration sector less attractive to private firms over time, as shown in the trend of firms operating in this sector in Chapter 6. Unlike in the urban bus sector, private firms in this sector did not resist the political service of societal control and were not forced out of the sector. Their gradual exit from the waste incineration sector was more a result of the rising number of high-profile protests against incineration plants. With the Chinese public increasingly aware of environmental issues and the potential public health hazards of incineration, appeasement strategies to prevent public opposition from

[49] Coal has a lower combustion temperature than solid waste.
[50] Interview 20150922.

escalating lose their effectiveness slowly but gradually, and local Chinese governments increasingly have to resort to suppression, which skews their preference toward large SOEs. Private firms, which are better scapegoats and better at providing appeasement strategies, thus slowly lose their competitiveness in the eyes of local governments, and consequently are more likely to exit the sector or form joint ventures with large SOEs.

8

Reflections on China's Political Economy Model and Sustainable Development

China is arguably the most successful authoritarian state in terms of economic growth in the twenty-first century, but the stability and sustainability of the Chinese model of political economy is questionable. Through a study of state–business relations in China, this book uncovers the politicization of business as a deeply rooted challenge to the Chinese state's efforts to attract and retain private investment and its commitment to sustainable development.

While it is an authoritarian state, the Chinese government has developed high governance capacity, but it has neither solved the inconsistency problem in incentive management for its officials nor advanced its political institutions sufficiently to guarantee autonomy for its economic actors. These unresolved issues create substantial obstacles for China to provide a stable investment environment and to break from a model of economic growth at all costs to one of sustainable development. Moreover, because these issues are deeply embedded in authoritarianism, they will be difficult to resolve. In this concluding chapter, I reflect on how authoritarianism leads to politicization of business, which distorts and discounts the country's efforts in investment attraction and sustainable development.

AUTHORITARIANISM, "SOMEWHAT CREDIBLE" COMMITMENT, AND PRIVATE INVESTMENT

Politicization of business, as described in this book, is the outcome of two conflicting goals of the authoritarian system in China. The first conflict of goals arises from the classic competence–loyalty trade-off that authoritarian leaders face. The second conflict of goals arises from the need to promote investment and growth without politically empowering capitalists and entrepreneurs.

The first conflict of goals lies in choosing between competent and loyal government officials. Dictators need to have competent subordinates to better run the country. However, these competent individuals also pose a greater risk of being able to replace or overthrow the dictator, or they may be more likely to receive invitations to work for the dictator's opponents and potential successors. As a result, dictators often have to choose between the competent and the loyal (Egorov and Sonin 2011; Zakharov 2016). In China, the CCP faces the same trade-off and endeavors to strike a balance by assessing local officials based on both loyalty and competence. The demand for competence brought about a comprehensive and rigid quantitative evaluation system based on objective standards, and the demand for loyalty created a vague and flexible top-down evaluation system based on subjective standards. But this attempt to evaluate both qualities does not mean the CCP has resolved the competence-loyalty trade-off. Instead, as explained in Chapter 2, these two systems end up reflecting the trade-off and producing often contradictory recommendations on promotion, undermining the effectiveness of the evaluation system and causing anxiety among evaluated government officials.

This anxiety of being evaluated by two conflicting qualities – competence and loyalty – thus creates the sufficient condition for Chinese government officials to politicize firms. Those government officials eager for promotion, for example, seek opportunities to demonstrate both competence and loyalty, often creating visibility projects for this purpose. Competence is demonstrated through the large scale and impressive appearance of these "innovative" projects. Loyalty is demonstrated by initiating visibility projects in response to the CCP's latest policy directions and funding them in a prudent manner. Often, this involves engaging companies in the process rather than relying solely on the government's fiscal budget to avoid misusing public funds. This produces the first political service of firms described in the book – to bear the costs of individual officials' self-promotion for the benefit of their political careers. Similarly, when dealing with social conflicts, officials need to show loyalty to the CCP by not giving in to societal actors' challenge to the Party's rule, but also to show competence by carefully containing conflicts without sabotaging the legitimacy of the Party-state. This need creates the second political service of firms depicted in this book – to be allies of or scapegoats for the state, thus distancing societal grievances from the Party-state.

The second conflict of goals in China's authoritarian system provides the necessary condition for politicizing business. This conflict arises from the necessity to promote investment and growth but not to empower capitalists and entrepreneurs. The Party-state needs private investment to achieve its economic goals and to obtain performance legitimacy by fostering growth. However, the Party-state also needs to prevent resourceful economic actors, such as entrepreneurs or private investors, from coalescing into an organized opposition that could challenge the CCP's rule. On one hand, encouraging private investment requires the Party-state to rein in its officials from abusing power and exploiting business. On the other hand, not empowering private entrepreneurs requires the Party-state to grant local officials the power to monitor and control businesspeople when deemed necessary. These goals, once again, are conflicting in nature. They lead the Chinese state to tie its own hands to a certain degree to reduce government expropriation of business, but not to the degree that would prevent the government from controlling business when deemed politically necessary. This leaves open the possibility for government officials to conscript firms for political services.

Authoritarianism, therefore, directly contributes to the sufficient and necessary conditions for the politicization of business. The nature of authoritarianism dictates that unless the rulers – in China's case, the Party-state – feel perfectly secure about their rule, they cannot fully trust their own government officials or resourceful economic actors to have autonomy. And we know that authoritarian rulers do not feel perfectly secure. In his seminal work on authoritarianism, Ronald Wintrobe (1998) framed the dictator's dilemma as follows: "The leader's dilemma is that, given that he or she has such power over the regime's subjects, how can he or she know whether they really support the regime or are merely pretending to do so while secretly plotting his or her downfall?" (1998: 16). Because the dictator does not and cannot know the answer, they will always need to maintain control over political, economic, and societal actors. China's Party-state faces this same dilemma and therefore cannot evaluate its officials based solely on competence or grant economic actors full autonomy in their economic activities. In other words, China's Party-state cannot and will not completely tie its own hands.

This observation aligns with seminal works on authoritarianism and democracy, which establish a consensus that some defining features of authoritarianism include a lack of political equality (Dahl 1991), independent judiciary, and the ruler's flexibility in interpreting laws (Linz 2000). Even when limited institutionalization occurred in authoritarian states, these fundamental features of authoritarianism effectively hinder societal actors from achieving real autonomy from the state. No matter how much these institutions may improve, authoritarian rulers always need to reserve the right to undermine them if they perceive these institutions as empowering dissenting societal actors too much, which would threaten to weaken authoritarian rule. This incompleteness of institutionalization is what makes the investment environment less stable in authoritarian states than in democracies. In other words, the Chinese authoritarian state, like other authoritarian states, does not provide fully credible commitment to capital. It only provides *somewhat* credible commitment to capital through deliberately incomplete institutionalization efforts in order to achieve the goal of economic development.

Politicization of business, as this book describes, is therefore a constant feature of China's political economy model that undermines its potential to attract and retain private investment. It is an independent risk factor in China's political economy model, separate from other better-known problems such as corruption and the dominance of state-owned enterprises (SOEs), and it creates instability in China's investment environment. The Chinese government's policies might look as if they are consistently pro-business, but the Party-state leaves open the possibility to politicize business and introduces political risks into China's economy.

But how do we reconcile this observation with the fact that China managed to attract so much investment throughout its years of rapid economic growth? To begin with, China has an extraordinary market size that makes it attractive. Equally importantly, as described in Chapter 1, China did *some* things right and the government gave *somewhat* credible commitment to capital, which is still better than no credible commitment at all. Economic liberalization to a certain degree, limited institutionalization, rule by law (albeit not rule of law), and controlled policy experiments for a period of time all contributed to China's success in attracting investment and promoting economic growth to the extent that it did. Moreover, private investment exists in practically any market environment, including those with much less protection of property rights and fewer investment-promoting policies than China. It should not be surprising that China, a large country with institutionalization efforts (though limited) would attract capital.

More importantly, we cannot assume that *because* China had an extraordinary record of growth and investment attraction, the Chinese state must have come up with a stable political economy model and overcome every major problem that could have damaged China's economic growth. Instead, so far, the rapid economic growth has obscured many problems deeply embedded in China's political economy model, such as politicization of business. When a sector is experiencing robust growth, then the additional costs imposed on business may erode profit margins but not necessarily jeopardize the viability of the business. Businesses can recoup these costs relatively quickly when the sector is doing well and are more likely to sustain the financial burden over an extended period. However, if a sector is experiencing a slowdown, these additional costs might not only erode profit margins but could eventually erase them entirely.

The urban bus sector described in Chapter 4 and 5 illustrates this dynamic. The bus sector faced intense politicization at a time when China's economy was still growing at a relatively high rate and the population decline had already begun. These two factors combined meant that fewer people were using bus services. Many members of the eventually shrinking populace, particularly from the middle class, replaced bus services with their own cars or emerging subway systems. This shift left private bus companies with few options but to resist the draining political services, particularly the visibility projects that are in nature closer to "regulation" in this sector, which were threatening their survival. Their resistance to the state led to the most drastic form of state encroachment, deprivatization.

Politicization of business is thus a key challenge to China's efforts in maintaining the confidence of private investors. Unlike corruption, which, ironically, is a more predictable and stable risk factor for business, politicization of business has the feature of unpredictability in both its occurrence and its costs, as described in Chapter 1. As politicization stems from some of the fundamental authoritarian logics, it is also less likely for the state to address the issue of politicization. Consequently, it is more difficult to reassure investors and entrepreneurs that politicization will not occur.

Both the government and business realize this, and both worry about the future of attracting investment in China. In a conversation at the end of 2018, a provincial level official told me about all the efforts by the provincial government to calm private investors, whose confidence had dropped after a series of state–business conflicts, including the national government taking over the Anbang Group, one of the largest insurance and finance companies in China, and Jack Ma announcing his retirement from Alibaba's board. This government official said:

"Secretary Xi said we would always support private entrepreneurs, and so our provincial government had several panel discussions with the largest private companies [in the province]. We told them [the entrepreneurs] that we care about them, and we will always support them."

"How did they receive that?"

"They completely freaked out."

"Why is that?"

"Well, it's like the wife that just got beat up by the husband. And then the husband knelt on the ground asking for forgiveness and tried to take care of the wife. Do you think the wife would feel happy or more scared?"[1]

This concern is resonated by private entrepreneurs. A private bus company owner who was forced out of the sector lamented after a series of visibility projects in his sector led to deprivatization of private bus companies,

They [the city government] now want us [private bus companies] back, once they realized how much it costs to maintain a bus system in the city. I told them, "If you think you can lead me by the nose again, you've got another think coming."[2]

Another private entrepreneur in the medical appliance sector said:

We [private firms] are like hens. It all depends on if the local government wants to keep getting eggs from us or also wants to have us for chicken soup. I worry every day about what they might do to us the next day. It would be fine if I just wanted to make some quick money, but my industry is not one for quick money. All I can depend on is the protection from my business partner's dad [a high-level official in the locality], but he is retiring soon.[3]

A Chinese machinery company who supplied equipment to European companies in China's water sector expressed the same concern,

They [the European partner companies] asked us, "Why is it that every time there is a new leader in the city, policies have to change?" We told them this is the way it works, but they didn't want to deal with that anymore, they left with a grudge.[4]

To private entrepreneurs, politicization of business exposes a fundamental disadvantage of theirs: They are more subject to hard budget

[1] Interview 2018110939492.
[2] Interview 20160306203.
[3] Interview 201903a87.
[4] Interview 20160413b.

constraints and they have less political capital compared to SOEs, who can therefore withstand politicization better. As explained in Chapter 3, the political capital of private business is volatile, constantly changing, and individual-based. This disadvantage is particularly obvious when private firms have to compete with SOEs not only in the economic realm but also in providing political services. Unless China can restrict government officials from politicizing firms and level the playing field for companies of different ownership types and therefore different levels of political capital, the process of building a market economy will unavoidably be distorted. These necessary changes would mean fundamental institutional reforms, which will be difficult to achieve. Therefore, politicization of business will most likely persist in China's current political economy model, reducing the credibility of the Chinese government's promises to private investors.

THE INSTITUTIONAL CHALLENGE TO SUSTAINABLE DEVELOPMENT

This book also generates implications for China's prospects for sustainable development. By studying infrastructure and projects that aim to alleviate environmental degradation, this book highlights a mismatch between China's goal of sustainable development and its means. This mismatch goes beyond the information problem and corruption that plague authoritarian countries, as well as the common bureaucratic coordination issues that affect large nations.

To have sustainable development, China needs long-term investments that are often not attractive to local officials. Take the goal of having clean water, for example. Some key infrastructure includes in-ground stormwater collection systems, networks of sewage pipes, infiltration basins, and canals to restore groundwater. Most of these long-term projects are invisible, not economically profitable, and require a large sum of up-front investment, with returns accrued over a long time-horizon and often only in the form of reduced negative externalities. Therefore, compared with many other government projects, sustainability-oriented projects are not inherently appealing undertakings for local government officials.

Knowing the tendency of local government officials to eschew such projects that do not bring in political or economic benefits within a short time frame, the Chinese Party-state attempted to incentivize local government officials using two strategies from its collection of tools, both of which had been used to facilitate economic growth: aligning incentives for local officials and implementing market reforms in relevant sectors.

Central to the first strategy of aligning the incentives of government officials is payoff management and induced competition among local leaders to outperform each other. The key institution to create these incentives is the cadre evaluation system that ties every local leader's career prospects and bonuses to their performance. By incorporating quantitative policy goals such as gross domestic product (GDP) growth and income per capita into this system, China had successfully motivated local officials to promote their local economies.

Central to the second strategy is to put forth market-friendly policies and invite private investors into the relevant sectors. China has successfully used this strategy to mobilize private capital to provide public goods and services that the state lacks the financial or technological capacity to offer. For example, since the beginning of marketization in the health care sector in 2009, there are now at least twice as many private hospitals as state-owned ones at the end of 2020.[5] Similarly, the number of private retirement homes has quickly grown to exceed state-owned retirement homes since marketization of the sector began in 2016.[6] Private investment became an important contributor to China's development in infrastructure, public transportation, telecommunications, energy, education, and many other sectors that play key roles in the pursuit of broad-based economic development. After observing how private investment allowed these traditionally state-directed sectors to expand quickly, the Chinese state appears to have drawn the conclusion that the same strategies would be equally successful in developing sectors key to environmental sustainability, such as nature preservation, water management, drainage systems, and waste and wastewater treatment.

The Chinese state has thus attempted to use these two strategies to protect the environment and promote sustainable development. To incentivize local officials, the CCP gradually added environmental targets into the target responsibility system from 2013,[7] thereby tying the

5 "2009 Guowuyuan guanyu shenhua yiyao weisheng tizhi gaige de yijian," The State Council, Chinese government, 2020-12-31, www.nhc.gov.cn/mohwsbwstjxxzx/s7967/202012/36cdc5cc143148dd8d61303c6c1d4b35.shtml.

6 "Guowuyuan bangong ting guanyu quanmian fangkai yanglao fuwu shichang tisheng yanglao fuwu zhiliang de ruogan yijian," The State Council, Chinese government, 2016-12-23, www.gov.cn/zhengce/content/2016-12/23/content_5151747.htm.

7 "Guanyu gaijin difang dangzheng lingdao banzi he lingdao ganbu zhengji kaohe gongzuo de tongzhi," *Xinhua News*, 2013-12-09, www.gov.cn/jrzg/2013-12/09/content_2545183.htm.

career outcomes of local leaders to quantifiable environmental outcomes. These targets vary across provinces but often include forest and grassland coverage, wetland protection, waste treatment rate, wastewater treatment rate, water quality, and PM2.5 level.[8] To encourage private investment into these sectors, the CCP continued to issue policy directives to increase incentives and reduce risks for private investors beginning in 2005. These directives cover issues from preferential tax rates and land pricing to access to loans for private firms in a sector, stressing policy stability, and ordering local officials to respect public–private partnership contracts. On top of the 1999 Contract Law, the central government issued new guidance in 2016 to stress that contracts made by previous administrations must be respected, and that local governments should not arbitrarily change contract terms after they come into effect.[9]

At first glance, these two strategies seem to have been working wonders in promoting environmental sustainability. The speed and scale of China's development of sustainability projects are as remarkable as China's economic growth in its early stages. For example, since the central government called for sanitary waste treatment and recycling in 2008, the number of waste incineration plants has increased from 100 to 514 in 2020.[10] After the central government encouraged "sponge city" infrastructure projects in 2014 to alleviate urban flooding plaguing many Chinese cities,[11] thirty cities completed the transformation by 2016, and more than 400 cities and towns are in the process of doing so or planning to become sponge cities.[12] Public projects responding to sustainable development mushroomed everywhere, from urban bus systems and sanitary husbandry farms to forests in the desert and wetland parks in cities. Wherever the central government's attention focused, local officials have been quick to respond, and private firms have

[8] PM2.5 stands for the concentration of particles with a diameter of 2.5 micrometers or less. These particles can be inhaled and cause serious health concerns. It is a common indicator for air pollution. The higher the PM2.5, the worse the air quality.

[9] "Zhonggong zhongyang guowuyuan guanyu wanshan chanquan baohu zhidu yifa baohu chanquan de yijian," *Xinhua News*, 2016-11-04, http://gzw.gd.gov.cn/zcjd/content/post_1336990.html.

[10] Author's data collection from Chinese City Yearbooks.

[11] A sponge city is an urban design concept aimed at preventing urban flooding. Its key features include more open green spaces, water reservoirs and catch basins, and porous road surfaces to allow water to drain away rather than accumulating on the ground.

[12] "Haimian chengshi jianshe ruhe dailai "huihuxi" de shenghuo?," *Xinhua News*, 2021-05-11, www.xinhuanet.com/fortune/2021-05/11/c_1127433503.htm.

promptly entered the sector. Together, they seem to be transforming these sectors at an extraordinary speed.

But that is if we only examine the speed of growth in the early stages of development. Upon closer examination of the quality and efficiency of these projects and observing how these developments evolve over time – from project selection to public–private cooperation – the effectiveness of these strategies becomes questionable. The phenomena depicted in this book spread across these sectors. Instead of developmental projects, visibility projects occur, and local governments permit companies to cut corners and compromise quality, especially when asking them to provide societal control services. The strategies that China used to promote economic growth do not guarantee success in promoting sustainable development, for two reasons.

The Difference in the Chinese State's Role in Promoting Growth and Sustainability

Economic growth and sustainable development require different degrees and nature of state intervention. The success of China's economic growth, reexamined in multiple scholarly works, largely depended on the government, both central and local, clearing the way for the private sector and assuming a more passive role. Some scholars argue that China's successful reform happened not because of government intervention, but because of *reduced* government intervention. The high growth era in China corresponded with economic liberalization that occurred as the planning state retreated (Naughton 1995; Pei 2006; Huang 2008; Kennedy 2010; Wang 2024), and growth mostly occurred where the state was constrained from overreaching, such as imposing predatory taxation or bailing out SOEs (Steinfeld 1998). When the Chinese state did assume more active roles by adopting a statist approach to development, such efforts often backfired. In the 1990s, when the state expanded its role in industrial policies, the growth of income per capita slowed down, household savings stagnated, and inequality between urban and rural areas, as well as between different regions, was exacerbated (Chen and Fleisher 1996; Yao 1999; Huang 2008; 2011). Revisiting the role of local Chinese governments in the 1990s, they appear to resemble more of a clientelist state mired in corruption than a developmental state (Ong 2012), and China's tax reform did not benefit public goods and service provision in rural China (Takeuchi 2014). What's more, after a series of industrial policies that promoted SOEs at the expense of private firms, China's economic growth ended up even more dependent on private companies (Lardy 2014).

Environmental sustainability, to a much greater extent than GDP growth, is a process that requires the state to assume a more active role in planning, funding, and regulation.[13] This is because companies are primarily focused on maximizing their bottom-line profits rather than prioritizing environmental goals, thus leaving the government as a more significant leader in promoting sustainability. But as the observations here suggest, the Chinese state has yet to show its ability to mobilize its government officials to take on active and constructive roles in promoting environmental sustainability.

In other policy areas concerning sustainability, such as strengthening the social safety net and reducing poverty, research indicates that progress was primarily a trickle-down effect of economic growth rather than being a result of active policy choices. Economic growth brought in more government revenues and therefore increased the absolute amount of social spending, and even then, the state's role remained minimal and welfare provision largely depended on informal social networks (Saich 2008). Similarly, poverty alleviation in China largely benefited from economic growth itself, and local governments have seriously underinvested in education and healthcare, creating a large population of structurally unemployable labor, which will eventually hurt China's continued growth (Rozelle and Hell 2020). While this does not suggest that the Party-state has done nothing to improve human capital, it does raise a serious question about the Chinese government's ability to play both an active and constructive role in promoting economic sustainability. China's potential to pursue environmental sustainability will rely to a much larger extent on this yet-to-be-demonstrated ability of the Chinese government.

And as this book shows, when the Chinese government, both central and local, takes on an active role in pursuing environmental sustainability, the process becomes vulnerable to politicization, particularly in the form of visibility projects. This is compounded by the nature of environmental protection and preservation, which, unlike economic growth, makes it more difficult for the central government to detect questionable policy choices, creating a second challenge to pursuing environmental sustainability.

[13] Most researchers and practitioners agree that successful sustainable development requires collaboration between the state, firms, and the public (e.g. Hopwood, Mellor, and O'Brien 2005).

The Challenge of Incentivizing Local Officials to Pursue Long-Term Environmental Sustainability

The second reason that China's economic growth strategies fall short in the domain of environmental sustainability lies in the method of incentive alignment of local officials: to include quantitative targets measuring environmental outcomes in China's cadre evaluation system. This approach might have been effective in promoting economic growth because GDP growth is an immediate, localized outcome that can be attributed to specific policy outputs such as tax breaks, subsidies, and preferential land prices. It also worked because local officials' incentives to promote GDP growth align with the profit motives of private entrepreneurs. However, when it comes to environmental outcomes, the dynamics are not exactly the same.

While it is easy for the CCP to incorporate quantified environmental outcomes such as water quality and air quality into the cadre evaluation system, the Party-state cannot ensure that these quantifiable outcomes will translate into long-term investments and efforts by local officials essential for sustainable development. There are simply too many ways to either achieve or fail to achieve these environmental outcomes. Take water quality, for example. It only improves when all localities along the waterbody work together, and it can improve as a consequence of any number of actions, such as regulating polluting factories, conducting river cleaning projects, building and upgrading sewerage networks, separating sewerage and stormwater systems, and constructing wastewater treatment plants. But to a significant degree, water quality is also influenced by natural variability beyond the control of any official – such as storms, floods, droughts, ecological cycles, and so on.

This creates a disconnect between any official's policy output and policy outcome. It would be easy for local officials to show short-term improvement in quantified water quality measures by improving infrastructure, ordering polluting factories to clean up, or even employing "blunt force regulation" (van der Kamp 2023) to temporarily shut down polluting factories. It would be equally easy for local officials to blame less than ideal environmental quality on the insufficient actions of other involved governments or on natural factors. What this suggests is that local officials often have the opportunity to showcase impressive policy outputs, such as visibility projects, without necessarily delivering long-term environmental outcomes. Indeed, Gilley (2012) insightfully documented how China is more effective in producing policy outputs than outcomes in its efforts to counter climate change. This disconnect between outputs and outcomes incentivizes local officials to engage in the most visible actions that allows them to claim credit for short-term, quantifiable, or visible outcomes regardless of long-term improvement in the environment – thus the creation of visibility projects.

Therefore, China's cadre evaluation system is almost perfectly designed to undermine the kind of hidden, unglamorous actions and long-term efforts essential to sustainable development. This system rewards visibility over sustainability.

For these reasons, the way the Chinese Party-state pursues environmental sustainability encourages government officials to be proactive in their actions but does not and cannot hold them accountable for long-term environmental outcomes. As a result, visible actions become the focus of government officials in environmental protection and preservation, conveniently translating into visibility projects, detailed in Chapter 2, that showcase effort without guaranteeing sustainability. This is shown clearly in the bus sector in Chapters 4 and 5, where clean air initiatives lead to visibility projects that are highly wasteful and come at the costs of sustainable development. Another good example is China's failed recycling movement, where visibility, rather than sustainability, became the focus.

In 2000, China's national government started to promote solid waste recycling and offered full subsidies to cities pursuing such projects. Eight Chinese cities were chosen in 2000 as experimental sites to launch a municipal solid waste sorting and recycling system.[14] These cities all invested in the visible components such as recycling bins, recycled garbage collection sites, and public education programs, but they failed to establish the invisible yet crucial post-collection sorting system to separate solid waste into recyclable and nonrecyclable categories. This eventually upset the public, who realized their efforts to separate household garbage were sabotaged by the lack of sorting systems, and they stopped participating in the recycling movement. An official in Shenzhen's urban management department explained to the media how the effort failed: "They [residents] questioned us [government]: 'we [residents] separated the garbage and threw it into the correct garbage bins as you told us to, and then you guys [the government] mixed them up again in the [garbage] truck!' Indeed, we [the government] need to solve this problem [of

14 These cities were Beijing, Shanghai, Nanjing, Hangzhou, Guilin, Guangzhou, Shenzhen, and Xiamen.

mixing garbage] in the collection process."[15] City governments' focus on the visible features sometimes went to such an extreme that at several of my interview sites, street garbage bins had two sides for recyclable and nonrecyclable trash, but there was no internal partition to actually keep them separate. In 2014, the national government announced that after fifteen years the effort had failed.[16]

Therefore, when promoting environmental sustainability, relying solely on strategies for promoting economic growth might not be sufficient. If the Party-state cannot come up with an incentive system that rewards invisible efforts and long-term outcomes, it will be hard to avoid politicization of the promotion of environmental sustainability. Under the current institutional setup, government officials will be incentivized to exploit the environmental agenda as an opportunity for promotion through visibility projects, which are costly and unsustainable.

ACTORS IN THIS BOOK: "PERPETRATORS" AND "VICTIMS"?

To explain the politicization of business, this book presents two pairs of political relations in China: the one between the national government and local governments, and the one between the state and business. I do not intend to leave readers with the impression that the Chinese national government is a benign reformer and a victim of local governments that distort policy implementation. Nor do I suggest that state–business relations in China are simple, with local governments holding absolute power over private firms, making the latter mere victims of politics. Instead, the actors in this book – the central government and the Party-state's command center, local governments, private firms, and SOEs – are all strategic and sophisticated players with multiple goals. Each pair of these political relations is shaped by all actors involved.

To start with the first political relationship: that between local governments and China's national government, the Party center. Does the highest level of the CCP know what is unfolding on the ground? Are they aware of, for example, wasteful visibility projects? I asked every local official this question, and all of them were certain that yes, the national

15 "Laji fenlei, women weishenme juede nan?" *CCTV News*, 2017-06-18, http://m.news.cctv.com/2017/06/18/ARTIcY689r50yIl3PycobKGR170618.shtml.

16 "Wo guo 8 chengshi shidian laji fenlei 14 nian shouxiao shenwei," *People's Daily*, 2014-06-14, http://politics.people.com.cn/n/2014/0611/c1001-25132656.html.

government eventually knows exactly what is going on. But why, then, is the central government always a step behind the gaming behavior of local officials and unwilling or unable to punish these actions later? One major challenge for the national government is the ineffective institutional arrangements for monitoring government officials. On a day-to-day basis, the Chinese national government monitors low-level officials by having the mid-level officials supervise their subordinates and report on misbehavior. For example, provincial leaders are supposed to supervise and monitor city leaders, and national leaders are supposed to supervise and monitor provincial leaders.

This arrangement is reasonable considering that in an authoritarian country lower-level officials are accountable to higher-level officials. But this is where the monitoring system loses power. Because officials always report one level up, having irresponsible subordinates means the superior officials did not do a good job managing their cadres. Therefore, superiors have little incentive to report lower-level officials' misbehavior. Instead, they might even have incentives to cover for the misbehavior of their subordinates so they do not get punished by their own superiors. Moreover, officials that rise in such a system would worry that if they started to report on their subordinates, they would be setting a precedent for others to report on their own misbehavior. As a result, few in the system have an incentive to proactively monitor and report misbehavior, essentially encouraging lower-level officials to game the system and distort policies to serve their own interests.

The central government understands this political logic. After all, the Party-state designed the system. So the system is complemented with two more strategies to keep local officials in check. One approach involves the national government directly assuming the monitoring role, often through central inspection teams (*xunshi zu*). This method is widely used on issues from corruption to various policy distortions, but it has two limits. First, it is highly constrained by fiscal and human resources. It is simply impossible for the central government to identify and curb all the problems in China's gargantuan governmental structure. Second, widespread nepotism and corruption practices reduce the effectiveness of this system. As described in Chapter 7, even when a central environmental inspection team is scheduled to make unannounced visits to cities, local governments could always learn about the inspection team's schedule through their connections. As a result, local officials can resort to ad-hoc measures to pass inspections rather than investing in long-term changes that this monitoring mechanism is intended to foster.

A second strategy employed by the central government is to establish a bottom-up feedback system whereby citizens can report instances of misbehavior by local governments. The most well-known examples include the Administrative Litigation Law, which allows citizens to sue the local government, and the petitioning system of the letters and visits offices (*xinfang*). These systems seem to be more effective at gathering information than deterring misbehavior by government officials (Thireau and Hua 2003; O'Brien and Li 2004; Heurlin 2016; Dimitrov 2023). Moreover, they could even encourage misbehavior from local governments, as they now have precise information on opposition and can use coercion against petitioners and plaintiffs, as well as bribery of relevant central agencies to have cases against them dismissed (Li, Liu, and O'Brien 2012). Occasionally, the central government also sets up online complaint forums for a very limited range of issues, mostly environmental concerns. For example, a "water watch" website was established in 2016 for citizens to register complaints about pollution of natural water bodies. However, worrying that citizens could organize online around a single issue, the central government rarely launches online complaint forums, and their effects remain unclear. In 2018, the national government initiated research into the possibility of implementing a "life responsibility system," wherein local officials could be held accountable for environmental degradation that occurred during their tenure in previous jurisdictions. But with so many officials holding the same position in the same locality over a relatively short period, it is unclear how the national government can determine which official should be responsible for specific aspects of a long-term issue such as environmental degradation.

These extra strategies by the central government, therefore, still fall short in deterring misbehavior by local government officials because the central government cannot actually have true bottom-up accountability systems that empower citizens too much. These systems, if designed to fully tie the hands of local government officials, would be dangerously close to resembling a democratic institution in which the public can hold the government accountable. Therefore, the central government, or the Party center, seems to have deliberately chosen not to fully deter misbehavior by local officials. The central government is therefore not merely a victim of local officials in policy distortion; rather, it has significantly contributed to these distortions by permitting them to occur in exchange for regime stability.

The other political relationship this book describes is the one between local governments and firms. It is true that private firms generally lag behind SOEs both in terms of budget constraints and political capital, as described in Chapters 2 and 3. But to think of private firms in China as solely "victims" of the government would overlook the broader picture of state–business relations in China. While this book demonstrates how political services impose higher costs for private firms than for SOEs, it should not be lost on readers that private firms actively seek opportunities to establish good relationships with the state. Additionally, they may manipulate the state when they have an information advantage.

In both the urban bus and the solid waste sector, the two cases in this book, private firms do not refuse political services at first, but only when these services surpass their financial capacity. Some companies even enter these sectors intending to provide political services. In the bus sector, for example, I have encountered private bus firms in several cities that are operated by local mafia groups, which control underground casinos and brothels. By providing bus services and visibility projects in the bus sector, these mafia groups in return receive protection for their illegal businesses. As mentioned in Chapter 1, firms in authoritarian states understand the importance of good state–business relations, and within their budget limits, many firms would be happy to provide political services either as a form of reciprocity for favors from local officials or in anticipation of future benefits from the local government.

Furthermore, sometimes the interests of the state and business align in these political services. In the solid waste sector, for example, both the local government and waste incineration companies have an incentive to suppress societal protests against incineration plants, as described in Chapters 6 and 7. Therefore, political services in this sector – namely, societal control – essentially lead to state–business collusion. By becoming the local officials' allies and scapegoats against the public, firms, state-owned and private, receive government protection and tolerance of their cost-saving measures, some of which are illegal and result in excess pollution. Unlike in the urban bus sector, private firms in the solid waste sector do not oppose their political services nearly as much. They only gradually lose favor where public awareness and opposition to waste incineration increases, which prompts local governments to favor SOEs that can provide better political support for suppression.

It is also important to note that the politicization of business not only increases costs for business, but has also reinforced a business environment where success is often determined by a company's adeptness in political strategies. This is similar to a corrupt environment, where success is not necessarily determined by a company's capacity, efficiency, or know-how, but by a company's ability to pay bribes. In the solid waste treatment and wastewater treatment sectors, I have come across new companies established by a silk factory, a coal mine, and a fish hatchery. These companies lack experience in municipal sanitation sectors, but they all have experience in polluting the environment and colluding with local governments to manage public protests against their pollution. Their experience in societal control might have been valued by local governments, which were therefore willing to overlook their lack of experience in waste and wastewater treatment.

This creates two problems in these sectors. First, other firms in the same sector will have to compete in providing political services, which could reduce a firm's investments in the actual business they conduct and limit service quality. Secondly, firms that cannot compete in terms of political services also struggle to effectively form alliances to pressure the local government to cease politicizing business with those that can compete. As a result, once a sector is politicized, firms that cannot afford the costs of politicization exit the sector, leaving a sector dominated by the most competent in providing political services. Moreover, those that are competent in providing political services are less inclined to invest in genuine upgrades and are less concerned about maintaining quality, both because they are investing more in political services and because the state tolerates their lower quality more as a reward for their political services. This essentially manifests as a crowding-out effect of politicization, with politically adept firms thriving and conducting business according to political logic, often at the expense of business and sectoral development.

To sum up, both the relationships between China's central government and local governments, as well between the Chinese state and business, are dynamic. Politicizing business is a result of interaction between all levels of governments, as well as between the government and business.

THE INSTABILITY IN CHINA'S POLITICAL ECONOMY MODEL

Back to the beginning of this chapter and to end this book, a country's regime type is key to its development and sustainability. China has long been the poster child of the potential success of authoritarianism and the irrelevance of regime type in growth and development. By observing the country's past success in economic growth and its recent slowdown, it would be easy to come up with explanations such as that state capacity is more important than regime type in growth and development, and that if Xi Jinping had not risen to power, China would have continued its market reform instead of turning against its private and foreign investors. These explanations certainly have merit, as state capacity, without question, matters for growth and development. Xi Jinping, a more personalistic leader, is also not helping with growth or attracting investment. But the authoritarian foundations of the Chinese political economy model have always provided the sufficient and necessary conditions for reversing trends and preying on private capital, and the Party-state's fluctuating attitude toward entrepreneurs and investors has been evident since the beginning of China's economic reform, as described in Chapter 1.

These fluctuations and reversals of the state's attitude toward the private economy stems from an important but less discussed feature of China's political economy model: The Chinese state constrains capital beyond its legal and regulatory framework. In other words, even when entrepreneurs and investors operate within the legal and regulatory framework in China, they still do not have complete autonomy in their operations. The Chinese state reserves the rights to politicize firms when it deems it necessary, and this is deeply rooted in an authoritarian state's fear of a potential organized opposition with abundant resources.

By taking a deep dive into how state–business relations and sectoral development unfold on the ground, this book reveals that politicization of business is an integral part of China's political economy model, affecting different sectors at different times. Unless the Party-state ties its own hands and gives businesses more autonomy in their economic decisions, politicization will discount China's investment outlook. For the Party-state to refrain from politicizing firms, it must be confident that it has resolved the classic competence–loyalty trade-off and overcome the dictator's dilemma. This would require either regime change or an innovative institutional reform of authoritarianism, both of which are extremely difficult to accomplish. Therefore, the politicization of business is likely to continue as part of China's political economy model, creating instability in China's economy and uncertainty for investors.

Appendix for Chapter 1

In the table below, I summarize the search results in Chinese news and academic journals for the phrase "state advancement and retreat of the private sector" (*guo jin min tui*). I summarize several forms of state advancement from these articles, including:

- Shutdown of the private sector. This means the government uses administrative means or changes laws and policies to suspend or ban only the private companies in a sector.
- Merger and acquisition. This is when a state-owned enterprise (SOE) acquires or merges with a private company, resulting in the private company becoming a branch of the SOE.
- Shareholder sale to SOEs. This is when an SOE purchases shares of a private firm.
- Shareholder sale to local government. This is when a local government purchases shares of a private firm.
- Nationalization. This is when an SOE or a local government acquires 100 percent of a private firm's ownership and thus converts a private firm into an SOE.
- Restrictions on entry of private firms. This occurs when the government changes laws, policies, or bidding requirements in a way that effectively restricts private firms from entering a sector.

All the source articles can be accessed in this online archive: https://drive.google.com/drive/folders/11YHwSh7a_mLVR-QUnKU7tm9OI_AIrxTw?usp=drive_link

Sector	Years	Provinces	Forms of state advancement
Steel	2004–2010	Jiangsu, Xinjiang, Zhejiang, Shandong, Jilin, Hubei, Anhui	Shutdown of the private sector; Merger and acquisition
Airlines	2002, 2009–2010	Nationwide	Merger and acquisition
Real estate	2009, 2021–2022	Nationwide	Shareholder sale to SOEs, Shareholder sale to local government
Coal	2006–2009	Henan, Shanxi, Inner Mongolia	Shareholder sale to SOEs, Shutdown of the private sector
Highways and toll roads	2008–2010	Shanghai, Zhejiang	Nationalization
Publication	2003–2004	Nationwide	Shareholder sale to local government
Online streaming services	2009	Nationwide	Restrictions on entry of private firms; shutdown of the private sector
Online payment systems	2018, 2021	Nationwide	Merger and acquisition
Oil and petroleum	2003, 2005	Shannxi	Nationalization
City gas supply	2010	Gansu, Hunan	Shareholder sale to local government; restrictions on entry of private firms;
Water	2008-	Nationwide	Shareholder sale to SOEs
Wastewater treatment	2016–2020	Guangdong, Henan, Liaoning, Shaanxi, Zhejiang, Shandong, Shanxi, Guangxi	Shareholder sale to SOEs
Seed	2010–2018, 2023	Nationwide	Shareholder sale to SOEs; merger and acquisition
Tourism	2016–2022	Guangdong; Fujian; Henan; Shandong; Jiangxi; Gansu; Xinjiang; Hunan; Hubei, Hainan, Sichuan	Shareholder sale to SOEs; merger and acquisition

Sector	Years	Provinces	Forms of state advancement
Hog farms	2011–2012; 2018–2023	Sichuan, Hubei, Shanxi, Zhejiang	Shareholder sale to SOEs; Shareholder sale to local government
Gas stations	1998–2012	Nationwide	Shutdown of the private sector; merger and acquisition
Waste recycling	2009, 2013	Chongqing, Guangdong	Nationalization; restrictions on entry of private firms
Rare earth minerals	2002–2011	Inner Mongolia, Jiangxi, Sichuan, Guangdong	Shutdown of private companies; nationalization
Battery recycling	2022–2023	Sichuan, Guangdong, Hubei	Shareholder sale to SOEs; merger and acquisition
Private schools	2006	Hubei	Shutdown of the private sector
Private tutoring	2021	Nationwide	Shutdown of the private sector
Trust funds	2004–2005	Nationwide	Shareholder sale to SOEs
Food manufacturing	2005, 2009	Xinjiang, Inner Mongolia	Shareholder sale to SOEs
Pharmaceuticals	2010	Shanghai	Merger and acquisition

Appendix for Chapter 4

APPENDIX 4.A. EFFECTS OF DIFFERENT VISIBILITY PROJECTS ON THE RISK OF DEPRIVATIZATION, URBAN BUS SECTOR, 1996–2016. COX PROPORTIONAL HAZARD MODELS

	(1)	(2)
	Whole Sample	20 Cities with BRT
	Hazard Ratio	Hazard Ratio
BRT construction	6.727***	48.695**
	(2.121)	(85.384)
City title application	3.799***	0.996
	(0.724)	(0.560)
New type bus	4.238***	2.370
	(0.862)	(1.522)
Fiscal health	0.989	8.983
	(0.010)	(15.021)
Bus per capita	0.956	6.343
	(0.093)	(10.452)
Annual bus change	1.255	0.066
	(0.430)	(0.151)
GDP per capita	1.005	1.016
	(0.002)	(0.012)
Log pseudolikelihood	−437.08	−10.564
N	1,811	144

Notes: *p≤ 0.10, **p≤ 0.05, ***p≤ 0.01. Robust standard errors in parentheses.

APPENDIX 4.B. EFFECTS OF DIFFERENT VISIBILITY PROJECTS ON THE RISK OF DEPRIVATIZATION, URBAN BUS SECTOR, 1996–2016. COX PROPORTIONAL HAZARD MODELS

	(1)	(2)	(3)
	Coefficients	Coefficients	Coefficients
City title application	1.080***	1.159***	1.092***
	(0.144)	(0.159)	(0.164)
New type bus	1.610***	1.658***	1.640***
	(0.162)	(0.171)	(0.170)
Fiscal health		−0.009	−0.003
		(0.012)	(0.011)
Bus per capita		0.035	−0.137
		(0.052)	(0.145)
Annual bus change			0.018
			(0.115)
GDP per capita			0.004*
			(0.002)
Log pseudolikelihood	−708.29	−570.62	−561.62
N	2,472	1,987	1,870

Notes: *p≤ 0.10, **p≤ 0.05, ***p≤ 0.01. Robust standard errors in parentheses.

APPENDIX 4.C. TEST OF PROPORTIONAL-HAZARDS ASSUMPTION, MODEL SPECIFICATION 3 IN FIGURE 4.2

As shown here, all of the variables are not significant either collectively or individually, thus supporting the assumption of proportional hazards.

	rho	chi2	Df	Prob>chi2
City title application	−0.03202	0.11	1	0.7380
New type bus	−0.04863	0.34	1	0.5583
Fiscal health	−0.08621	0.22	1	0.6357
Bus per capita	0.18505	2.16	1	0.1414
Annual bus change	−0.10404	0.26	1	0.6128
GDP per capita	−0.15068	2.26	1	0.1327
Global test	n.a.	3.99	6	0.6783

Note: robust variance–covariance matrix used.

APPENDIX 4.D. COX–SNELL RESIDUAL PLOT FOR MODEL SPECIFICATION 3 IN FIGURE 4.2

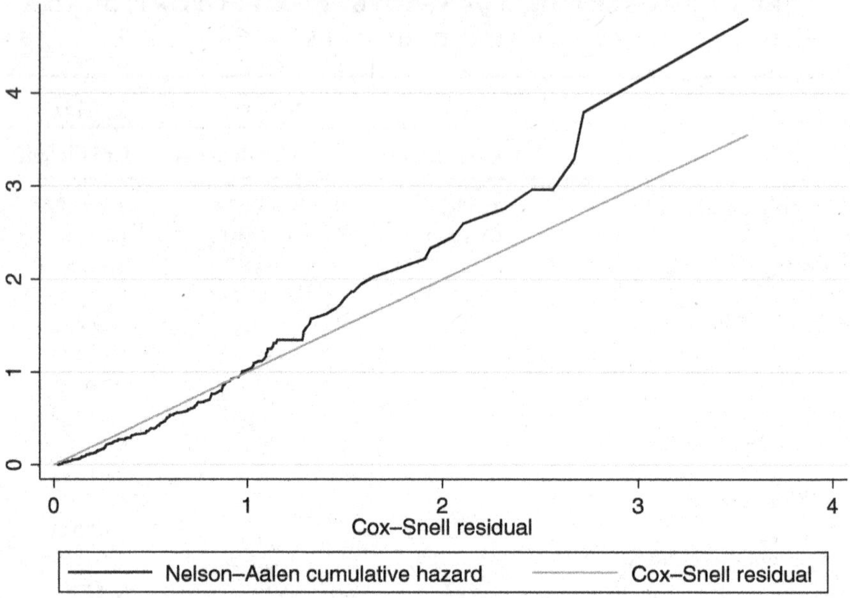

As shown in the figure, I plot the Nelson–Aalen cumulative hazard function against the Cox–Snell residuals to check for general model fit. If the hazard function follows the 45-degree line, then it approximately has an exponential distribution with a hazard rate of 1, meaning the model fits the data well. As shown in the plot, the hazard function follows the 45-degree line closely except for very large values of time. The large values of time are mostly likely due to censored data, a common phenomenon in survival data. Overall, we can conclude that the model has an approximately exponential distribution with a hazard rate of 1 and that the main model fits the data well.

APPENDIX 4.E. COX PROPORTIONAL HAZARD MODEL WITH THREE-YEAR FREQUENCY

	Hazard ratio		Hazard ratio
City title application	2.324***	Fiscal health	0.994
Three-year frequency	(0.268)		(0.012)
New type bus	1.879***	Bus per capita	0.889
Three-year frequency	(0.195)		(0.112)
		Annual bus	1.480
		replacement	(0.636)
		GDP per capita	1.005
			(0.003)
Log pseudolikelihood	−397.96		
N	1,664		

Notes: *p≤ 0.10, **p≤ 0.05, ***p≤ 0.01. Robust standard errors in parentheses.

APPENDIX 4.F. FRAILTY MODEL AND LOGIT MODEL

	Cox frailty model	Logit model, random effects, panel data
	Hazard Ratio	Coefficient
City title application	7.090***	2.018***
	(2.814)	(0.280)
New type bus	3.889***	2.159***
	(1.363)	(0.238)
Fiscal health	0.839	−0.012
	(0.141)	(0.029)
Bus per capita	0.920	−0.174
	(0.162)	(0.229)
Annual bus change	1.102	1.432
	(0.816)	(0.551)
GDP per capita	1.061*	1.005**
	(0.034)	(0.003)
Log pseudolikelihood	−413.62	−387.36
N	2,112	1,667

Notes: *p≤ 0.10, **p≤ 0.05, ***p≤ 0.01. Robust standard errors in parentheses.

APPENDIX 4.G. EFFECTS OF DIFFERENT VISIBILITY PROJECTS ON THE RISK OF DEPRIVATIZATION, URBAN BUS SECTOR, 1996–2016. COX PROPORTIONAL HAZARD MODELS. WITH LEADERSHIP TENURE

	Hazard ratio		Hazard ratio
City title application	4.011***	Fiscal health	0.988
	(0.803)		(0.012)
New type bus	4.667***	Bus per capita	0.906
	(0.994)		(0.098)
Secretary tenure	1.078	Annual bus change	1.431
	(0.201)		(0.055)
Secretary tenure	1.002	GDP per capita	1.005*
Squared term	(0.022)		(0.003)
Mayor tenure	0.873	Log pseudolikelihood	−387.29
	(0.161)	N	1666
Mayor tenure	1.008		
Squared term	(0.025)		

Notes: *p≤ 0.10, **p≤ 0.05, ***p≤ 0.01. Robust standard errors in parentheses.

Appendix: Additional Notes on Data Collection

INTERVIEW SITES

I conducted interviews in fifteen cities in five provinces (including Beijing) from February 2015 to August 2019. Interview sites cover four geographic areas: the capital city, the East, the South, and the Southwest. The selection of interview cities follows the principle of stratified sampling, with the cities varying along the dimensions of population size, economic development level, and industry composition. The East and the South are the two most developed regions in China, with the highest gross domestic product (GDP) level and the highest GDP per capita level, but different industrial organizations. The East has a larger service sector and the South has a larger manufacturing sector. Both have similarly high level of population density. The Southwest is among the poorer regions in China, relying more on agriculture and having a lower population density.

Interviews are organized into multiple waves. The first wave included thirty-four loosely structured interviews to generate hypotheses and develop a question bank, while the follow-up waves consisted of semi-structured interviews across all fifteen cities to test the hypotheses.

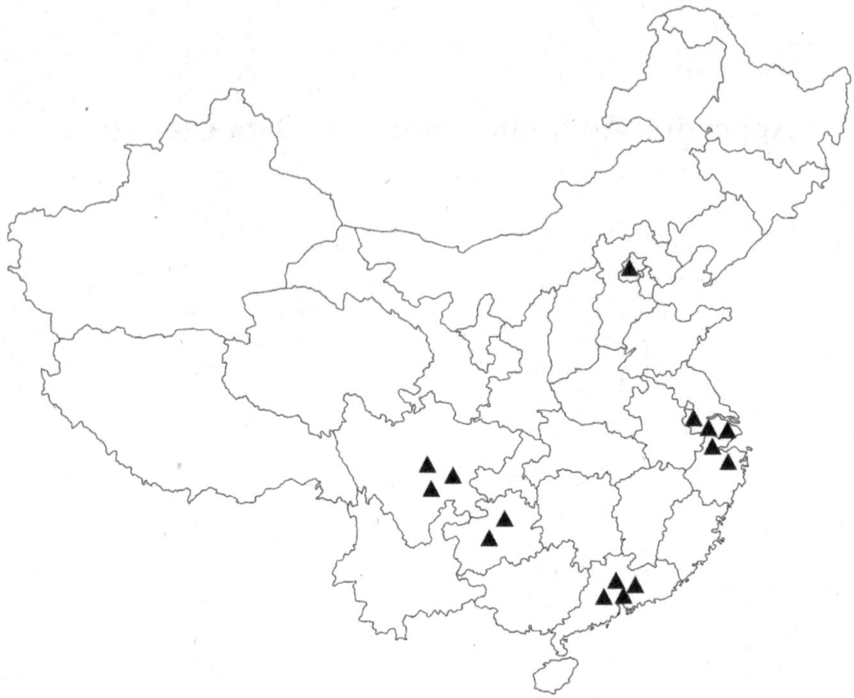

INTERVIEWEES

Of the 256 interviewees, 41 percent are city government officials in charge of a public service sector, 46 percent are business executives and managers of companies providing these public services, and 13 percent are academics, nongovernmental organization managers, and journalists specializing in public services sectors.

QUANTITATIVE DATA COLLECTION FOR KEY VARIABLES

Firm Ownership

Ownership of individual firms is identified through a firm's website, a firm's annual report (if the firm is listed), or the State Administration for Industry and Commerce's firm search engine (gsxt.saic.gov.cn/). A firm is coded as private if the majority shareholder is a private party or a foreign company. A firm is coded as state-owned if the majority shareholder is the city government or the State-owned Assets Supervision and

Administration Commission at any government level. If the firm cannot be identified through all three channels, I categorize them by what news reports identify them as.

Deprivatization

Defined as a state-initiated process to procure the private bus firms in the urban bus sector. Only ownership change that targets all the private firms in a city, rather than selectively, is coded as deprivatization. Data are collected from local news reports, government-issued notifications, and media interviews with government officials. Chinese keywords used include: 国有化，收归国有，回归国有，取消民营，取缔民营，民营退出，公交整合。

Incineration Plants

I identify a total of 351 incineration plants in all Chinese cities, including those already built and those under construction by the end of 2017. This number is higher than the reported 287 incineration plants in the China Construction Yearbooks, because yearbooks only include plants already built by 2016. Incineration plants are identified through Chinese keyword searches by city name and year on Google, Baidu, city government websites, and environmental company websites.

Protest

Protest data are collected from two main sources. The first is the author's Chinese keyword search on Google and Baidu by city, year, and sector (solid waste treatment and public transportation). Keywords indicating protests include 抗议，抗争，集会，聚集. The second source is Wickedonna, a news blog[1] that kept track of mass demonstrations in China via social media, including Twitter, Weibo, Blogspot, and YouTube, until it was censored in 2016.

I also referred to the Global Database of Events, Language, and Tone and the Social Unrest Database of the Chinese Academy of Social Sciences to check for possibly omitted protests. These two databases report fewer protests than my keyword searches in the solid waste sector and the public transportation sector.

[1] This blog is now moved to: https://newsworthknowingcn.blogspot.com/.

Environmental Violations

Data are collected through keyword searches by city name and year on Google, Baidu, and Soubao. Keywords are combined with city, year, and sector in the searches. Chinese keywords indicating "inspection" and "violation" include 检查，检验，视察，违规，违法，不达标，未达标，不合格，未合格。

GOVERNMENT YEARBOOKS

Control variables such as GDP, population size, and fiscal data are collected from government yearbooks, including the China Urban–Rural Construction Statistical Yearbooks, China Construction Yearbooks, China City Yearbooks, China Communications and Traffic Yearbooks, and Yearbooks of Public Transportation.

References

Ang, Yuen Yuen. 2020. *China's Gilded Age: The Paradox of Economic Boom and Vast Corruption*. Cambridge: Cambridge University Press. https://doi.org/10.1017/9781108778350.

Bae, Suho. 2010. "Public versus Private Delivery of Municipal Solid Waste Services: The Case of North Carolina." *Contemporary Economic Policy* 28 (3): 414–28.

Baekkeskov, Erik, and Olivier Rubin. 2016. "Information Dilemmas and Blame-Avoidance Strategies: From Secrecy to Lightning Rods in Chinese Health Crises." *Governance* 30 (3): 425–43. https://doi.org/10.1111/gove.12244.

Baker, George P. 1992. "Incentive Contracts and Performance Measurement." *Journal of Political Economy* 100 (3): 598–614.

Baker, George P., Robert Gibbons, and Kevin J. Murphy. 1994. "Subjective Performance Measures in Optimal Incentive Contracts." *The Quarterly Journal of Economics* 109 (4): 1125–56.

Bartone, Carl R., Luiz Leite, Thelma Triche, and Roland Schertenleib. 1991. "Private Sector Participation in Municipal Solid Waste Service: Experiences in Latin America." *Waste Management & Research* 9 (6): 495–509.

Bel, Germà, and Mildred E. Warner. 2008. "Competition or Monopoly? Comparing Privatization of Local Public Services in the US and Spain." *Public Administration* 86 (3): 723–35.

Bel, Germà, Xavier Fageda, and Mildred E. Warner. 2010. "Is Private Production of Public Services Cheaper than Public Production? A Meta-Regression Analysis of Solid Waste and Water Services." *Journal of Policy Analysis and Management* 29 (3): 553–77.

Boycko, Maxim, Andrei Shleifer, and Robert W. Vishny. 1996. "A Theory of Privatisation." *The Economic Journal* 106 (435): 309–19. https://doi.org/10.2307/2235248.

Cai, Hongbin, Hanming Fang, and Lixin Colin Xu. 2011. "Eat, Drink, Firms, Government: An Investigation of Corruption from the Entertainment and Travel Costs of Chinese Firms." *The Journal of Law and Economics* 54 (1): 55–78. https://doi.org/10.1086/651201.

Cai, Hongbin, and Daniel Treisman. 2006. "Did Government Decentralization Cause China's Economic Miracle?" *World Politics* 58 (4): 505–35. https://doi.org/10.1353/wp.2007.0005.
Cai, Yongshun. 2000. "Between State and Peasant: Local Cadres and Statistical Reporting in Rural China." *The China Quarterly* 163: 783–805.
2004. "Irresponsible State: Local Cadres and Image-Building in China." *Journal of Communist Studies and Transition Politics* 20 (4): 20–41.
2008. "Local Governments and the Suppression of Popular Resistance in China." *The China Quarterly* 193: 24–42.
Chen, Chih-Jou Jay. 2020. "A Protest Society Evaluated: Popular Protests in China, 2000–2019." *Mobilization: An International Quarterly* 25 (SI): 641–60. https://doi.org/10.17813/1086-671X-25-5-641.
Chen, Jian, and Belton M. Fleisher. 1996. "Regional Income Inequality and Economic Growth in China." *Journal of Comparative Economics* 22 (2): 141–64. https://doi.org/10.1006/jcec.1996.0015.
Chen, Jie, and Bruce J. Dickson. 2010. *Allies of the State: China's Private Entrepreneurs and Democratic Change*. Cambridge, MA: Harvard University Press.
Chen, Xi. 2012. *Social Protest and Contentious Authoritarianism in China*. New York: Cambridge University Press.
Choi, Eun Kyong. 2012. "Patronage and Performance: Factors in the Political Mobility of Provincial Leaders in Post-Deng China." *The China Quarterly* 212 (December): 965–81. https://doi.org/10.1017/S030574101200118X.
Choi, Jay Pil, and Marcel Thum. 2004. "The Economics of Repeated Extortion." *The RAND Journal of Economics* 35 (2): 203–23. https://doi.org/10.2307/1593688.
Clarke, Donald C. 2003. "Economic Development and the Rights Hypothesis: The China Problem." *American Journal of Comparative Law* 51 (1): 89–112.
Clarke, Donald C., Peter Murrell, and Susan Whiting. 2008. "The Role of Law in China's Economic Development." In *China's Great Economic Transformation*, Vol. 11, edited by Loren Brandt and Thomas G. Rawski. Cambridge: Cambridge University Press.
Coleman, James S. 1988. "Social Capital in the Creation of Human Capital." *American Journal of Sociology*, 94, January. https://doi.org/10.1086/228943.
Dahl, Robert A. 1991. *Democracy and Its Critics*. Reissue edition. New Haven: Yale University Press.
David-Fox, Michael. 2011. "The Potemkin Village Dilemma." In *Showcasing the Great Experiment: Cultural Diplomacy and Western Visitors to the Soviet Union, 1921–1941*, edited by Michael David-Fox, 98–141. Oxford: Oxford University Press. https://doi.org/10.1093/acprof:oso/9780199794577.003.0004.
De Mesquita, Bruce Bueno, Alastair Smith, Randolph M. Siverson, and James D. Morrow. 2005. *The Logic of Political Survival*. Cambridge, MA: MIT Press.
Deng, Yanhua, Zhenjie Yang, and Xiao Ma. 2022. "Riding on the Power of the Masses? How Different Modes of Mass Mobilization Shape Local Elite Bargaining in China." *Journal of Chinese Governance* 7 (4): 559–82. https://doi.org/10.1080/23812346.2021.1945284.

Dickson, Bruce J. 2003. *Red Capitalists in China: The Party, Private Entrepreneurs, and Prospects for Political Change*. New York: Cambridge University Press.
Dijkgraaf, Elbert, and Raymond Gradus. 2007. "Collusion in the Dutch Waste Collection Market." *Local Government Studies* 33 (4): 573–88.
Dimitrov, Martin K. 2016. "Structural Preconditions for the Rise of the Rule of Law in China." *Journal of Chinese Governance* 1 (3): 470–87. https://doi.org/10.1080/23812346.2016.1213029.
2020. "Chapter 5. The Evolution and Adaptation of Business–Government Relations in Zouping." In *Zouping Revisited*, edited by Jean C. Oi and Steven Goldstein, 113–38. Stanford University Press. https://doi.org/10.1515/9781503604551-007.
2023. *Dictatorship and Information: Authoritarian Regime Resilience in Communist Europe and China*. Oxford and New York: Oxford University Press.
Ding, Iza. 2022. *The Performative State*. Cornell University Press.
Dong, Fureng. 1999. 中华人民共和国经济史. 经济科学出版社.
Du, Julan, Yi Lu, and Zhigang Tao. 2015. "Government Expropriation and Chinese-Style Firm Diversification." *Journal of Comparative Economics* 43 (1): 155–69. https://doi.org/10.1016/j.jce.2014.07.003.
Eaton, Sarah. 2015. *The Advance of the State in Contemporary China: State-Market Relations in the Reform Era*. New York: Cambridge University Press.
Edin, Maria. 2003. "State Capacity and Local Agent Control in China: CCP Cadre Management from a Township Perspective." *The China Quarterly* 173: 35–52.
Egorov, Georgy, and Konstantin Sonin. 2011. "Dictators and Their Viziers: Endogenizing the Loyalty–Competence Trade-Off." *Journal of the European Economic Association* 9 (5): 903–30.
Evans, Peter. 1995. *Embedded Autonomy*. Princeton, NJ: Princeton University Press.
Faccio, Mara. 2006. "Politically Connected Firms." *American Economic Review* 96 (1): 369–86. https://doi.org/10.1257/000282806776157704.
2010. "Differences between Politically Connected and Nonconnected Firms: A Cross-Country Analysis." *Financial Management* 39 (3): 905–28. https://doi.org/10.1111/j.1755-053X.2010.01099.x.
Fewsmith, Joseph. 2013. *The Logic and Limits of Political Reform in China*. Cambridge: Cambridge University Press. https://doi.org/10.1017/CBO9781139381703.
2016. *Dilemmas of Reform in China: Political Conflict and Economic Debate*. New York: Routledge. https://doi.org/10.4324/9781315287171.
Fewsmith, Joseph, and Andrew J. Nathan. 2019. "Authoritarian Resilience Revisited: Joseph Fewsmith with Response from Andrew J. Nathan." *Journal of Contemporary China* 28 (116): 167–79. https://doi.org/10.1080/10670564.2018.1511390.
Finn, Brendan, and Corinne Mulley. 2011. "Urban Bus Services in Developing Countries and Countries in Transition: A Framework for Regulatory and Institutional Developments." *Journal of Public Transportation* 14 (4): 89–107.

Firth, Michael, Chen Lin, Ping Liu, and Sonia ML Wong. 2009. "Inside the Black Box: Bank Credit Allocation in China's Private Sector." *Journal of Banking & Finance* 33 (6): 1144–55.

Fisman, Raymond. 2001. "Estimating the Value of Political Connections." *American Economic Review* 91 (4): 1095–102. https://doi.org/10.1257/aer.91.4.1095.

Frye, Timothy. 2002. "Capture or Exchange? Business Lobbying in Russia." *Europe-Asia Studies* 54 (7): 1017–36.

Fuller, Douglas B. 2016. *Paper Tigers, Hidden Dragons: Firms and the Political Economy of China's Technological Development*. Oxford: Oxford University Press.

Gallagher, Mary Elizabeth. 2011. *Contagious Capitalism: Globalization and the Politics of Labor in China*. Princeton University Press.

Gallagher, Mary E., and Jonathan K. Hanson. 2015. "Power Tool or Dull Blade? Selectorate Theory for Autocracies." *Annual Review of Political Science* 18 (1): 367–85. https://doi.org/10.1146/annurev-polisci-071213-041224.

Gao, Jie. 2009. "Governing by Goals and Numbers: A Case Study in the Use of Performance Measurement to Build State Capacity in China." *Public Administration and Development* 29 (1): 21–31.

2015. "Pernicious Manipulation of Performance Measures in China's Cadre Evaluation System." *The China Quarterly* 223: 618–37.

Gehlbach, Scott, and Konstantin Sonin. 2014. "Government Control of the Media." *Journal of Public Economics* 118: 163–71.

Gerard, Roland, ed. 2008. *Privatization: Successes and Failures*. New York: Columbia University Press.

Gilley, Bruce. 2012. "Authoritarian Environmentalism and China's Response to Climate Change." *Environmental Politics* 21 (2): 287–307.

Goldman, Eitan, Jörg Rocholl, and Jongil So. 2009. "Do Politically Connected Boards Affect Firm Value?" *The Review of Financial Studies* 22 (6): 2331–60. https://doi.org/10.1093/rfs/hhn088.

Gomez-Ibanez, Jose, and John R. Meyer. 1993. *Going Private: The International Experience with Transport Privatization*. Washington, DC: Brookings Institution Press.

Gormley, William T., and David L. Weimer. 1999. *Organizational Report Cards*. Cambridge, MA: Harvard University Press.

Grizzle, Gloria A. 2002. "Performance Measurement and Dysfunction: The Dark Side of Quantifying Work." *Public Performance & Management Review* 25 (4): 363–9.

Guo, Baogang. 2017. "China's Administrative Governance Reform in the Era of 'New Normal.'" *Journal of Chinese Political Science* 22 (3): 357–73. https://doi.org/10.1007/s11366-017-9483-x.

Guo, Gang. 2009. "China's Local Political Budget Cycles." *American Journal of Political Science* 53 (3): 621–32.

Guriev, Sergei, Anton Kolotilin, and Konstantin Sonin. 2011. "Determinants of Nationalization in the Oil Sector: A Theory and Evidence from Panel Data." *The Journal of Law, Economics, and Organization* 27 (2): 301–23.

Hajzler, Christopher. 2012. "Expropriation of Foreign Direct Investments: Sectoral Patterns from 1993 to 2006." *Review of World Economics* 148 (1): 119–49.

Hart, Oliver. 1995. *Firms, Contracts, and Financial Structure*. Oxford: Clarendon Press.
Hart, Oliver. 2003. "Incomplete Contracts and Public Ownership: Remarks, and an Application to Public–Private Partnerships." *The Economic Journal* 113 (486): C69–76.
Hart, Oliver, and John Moore. 1990. "Property Rights and the Nature of the Firm." *Journal of Political Economy* 98 (6): 1119–58.
Hart, Oliver, Andrei Shleifer, and Robert W. Vishny. 1997. "The Proper Scope of Government: Theory and an Application to Prisons." *The Quarterly Journal of Economics* 112 (4): 1127–61.
Heilmann, Sebastian. 2008. "From Local Experiments to National Policy: The Origins of China's Distinctive Policy Process." *The China Journal* 59: 1–30. https://doi.org/10.2307/20066378.
Hellman, Joel S. 1998. "Winners Take All: The Politics of Partial Reform in Postcommunist Transitions." *World Politics* 50 (2): 203–34. https://doi .org/10.1017/S0043887100008091.
Heurlin, Christopher. 2016. *Responsive Authoritarianism in China: Land, Protests, and Policy Making*. New York: Cambridge University Press.
Hirschman, Albert O. 1967. *Development Projects Observed*. Washington, DC: The Brookings Institution.
Holmstrom, Bengt. 1979. "Moral Hazard and Observability." *The Bell Journal of Economics* 10 (1): 74–91.
Holmstrom, Bengt, and Paul Milgrom. 1991. "Multitask Principal-Agent Analyses: Incentive Contracts, Asset Ownership, and Job Design." *Journal of Law, Economics, & Organization* 7: 24–52.
Hood, Christopher. 2006. "Gaming in Targetworld: The Targets Approach to Managing British Public Services." *Public Administration Review* 66 (4): 515–21.
2010. *The Blame Game: Spin, Bureaucracy, and Self-Preservation in Government*. Princeton, NJ: Princeton University Press.
Hopwood, Bill, Mary Mellor, and Geoff O'Brien. 2005. "Sustainable Development: Mapping Different Approaches." *Sustainable Development* 13 (1): 38–52. https://doi.org/10.1002/sd.244.
Hosmer, David W., Stanley Lemeshow, and Susanne May. 2008. *Applied Survival Analysis: Regression Modeling of Time to Event Data*. 2 edition. Hoboken, NJ: Wiley-Interscience.
Hou, Yue. 2019. *The Private Sector in Public Office: Selective Property Rights in China*. Cambridge and New York: Cambridge University Press.
Hsueh, Roselyn. 2011. *China's Regulatory State: A New Strategy for Globalization*. Cornell Studies in Political Economy. Ithaca, NY: Cornell University Press.
Huang, Jingyang, and Kellee S. Tsai. 2022. "Securing Authoritarian Capitalism in the Digital Age: The Political Economy of Surveillance in China." *The China Journal* 88 (July): 2–28. https://doi.org/10.1086/720144.
Huang, Yasheng. 2003. *Selling China: Foreign Direct Investment during the Reform Era*. Cambridge: Cambridge University Press.
2008. *Capitalism with Chinese Characteristics: Entrepreneurship and the State*. New York: Cambridge University Press.
2011. "Rethinking the Beijing Consensus." *Asia Policy* 11, 1–26.

Jia, Ruixue, Masayuki Kudamatsu, and David Seim. 2015. "Political Selection in China: The Complementary Roles of Connections and Performance." *Journal of the European Economic Association* 13 (4): 631–68. https://doi.org/10.1111/jeea.12124.

Jodice, David A. 1980. "Sources of Change in Third World Regimes for Foreign Direct Investment, 1968–1976." International Organization. April 1980. https://doi.org/10.1017/S0020818300018737.

Johnson, Thomas. 2013. "The Health Factor in Anti-Waste Incinerator Campaigns in Beijing and Guangzhou." *The China Quarterly* 214: 356–75.

Kamp, Denise Sienli van der. 2023. *Clean Air at What Cost?: The Rise of Blunt Force Regulation in China*. Cambridge Studies in Law and Society. Cambridge: Cambridge University Press. https://doi.org/10.1017/9781009152655.

Keefer, Philip, and Stephen Knack. 2007. "Boondoggles, Rent-Seeking, and Political Checks and Balances: Public Investment under Unaccountable Governments." *The Review of Economics and Statistics* 89 (3): 566–72. https://doi.org/10.1162/rest.89.3.566.

Keller, Franziska Barbara. 2016. "Moving beyond Factions: Using Social Network Analysis to Uncover Patronage Networks among Chinese Elites." *Journal of East Asian Studies* 16 (1): 17–41.

Kennedy, Scott. 2009. *The Business of Lobbying in China*. Cambridge, MA: Harvard University Press.

2010. "The Myth of the Beijing Consensus." *Journal of Contemporary China*, 19 (65): 461–77. https://doi.org/10.1080/10670561003666087.

King, Dwight Y. 2000. "Corruption in Indonesia: A Curable Cancer?" *Journal of International Affairs* 53 (2): 603–24.

King, Gary, Jennifer Pan, and Margaret E. Roberts. 2013. "How Censorship in China Allows Government Criticism but Silences Collective Expression." *American Political Science Review* 107 (2): 326–43.

Kobrin, Stephen J. 1984. "Expropriation as an Attempt to Control Foreign Firms in LDCs: Trends from 1960 to 1979." *International Studies Quarterly* 28 (3): 329–48.

Kornai, Janos. 1979. "Resource-Constrained versus Demand-Constrained Systems." *Econometrica: Journal of the Econometric Society*, 47 (4): 801–19.

Kornai, Janos, Eric Maskin, and Roland Gerard. 2003. "Understanding the Soft Budget Constraint." *Journal of Economic Literature* 41 (4): 1095–136.

Kostovetsky, Leonard. 2015. "Political Capital and Moral Hazard." *Journal of Financial Economics* 116 (1): 144–59. https://doi.org/10.1016/j.jfineco.2014.12.003.

Landry, Pierre F. 2008. *Decentralized Authoritarianism in China: The Communist Party's Control of Local Elites in the Post-Mao Era*. Vol. 1. New York: Cambridge University Press.

Landry, Pierre F., Xiaobo Lü, and Haiyan Duan. 2018. "Does Performance Matter? Evaluating Political Selection Along the Chinese Administrative Ladder." *Comparative Political Studies* 51 (8): 1074–105. https://doi.org/10.1177/0010414017730078.

Lardy, Nicholas R. 2014. *Markets over Mao: The Rise of Private Business in China*. Washington, DC: Columbia University Press.

Leng, Ning, and Cai (Vera) Zuo. 2021. "Tournament Style Bargaining within Boundaries: Setting Targets in China's Cadre Evaluation System." *Journal of Contemporary China* 31 (133): 116–35. https://doi.org/10.1080/10670564.2021.1926099.

Li, Hongbin, Lingsheng Meng, Qian Wang, and Li-An Zhou. 2008. "Political Connections, Financing and Firm Performance: Evidence from Chinese Private Firms." *Journal of Development Economics* 87 (2): 283–99. https://doi.org/10.1016/j.jdeveco.2007.03.001.

Li, Lianjiang, Mingxing Liu, and Kevin J. O'Brien. 2012. "Petitioning Beijing: The High Tide of 2003–2006*." *The China Quarterly* 210 (June): 313–34. https://doi.org/10.1017/S0305741012000227.

Li, Yao. 2019. *Playing by the Informal Rules: Why the Chinese Regime Remains Stable despite Rising Protests*. Cambridge: Cambridge University Press.

Liang, Jiaqi, and Laura Langbein. 2015. "Performance Management, High-Powered Incentives, and Environmental Policies in China." *International Public Management Journal* 18 (3): 346–85.

Lieberthal, Kenneth G., and David M. Lampton, eds. 1992. *Bureaucracy, Politics, and Decision Making in Post-Mao China*. Berkeley: University of California Press.

Linz, Juan José. 2000. *Totalitarian and Authoritarian Regimes*. Boulder: Lynne Rienner Publishers.

Lipset, Seymour Martin. 1960. *Political Man: The Social Bases of Politics*. Johns Hopkins University Press.

Liu, Adam Y., Jean C. Oi, and Yi Zhang. 2022. "China's Local Government Debt: The Grand Bargain." *The China Journal* 87 (January): 40–71. https://doi.org/10.1086/717256.

Liu, Lizhi. 2024. *From Click to Boom: The Political Economy of E-Commerce in China*. Princeton, NJ: Princeton University Press.

Liu, Yi, Yuanhua Jia, Xuesong Feng, and Jiang Wu. 2018. "Bus Route Design with a Bayesian Network Analysis of Bus Service Revenues." *Mathematical Problems in Engineering* 2018 (January): e5176920. https://doi.org/10.1155/2018/5176920.

Lorentzen, Peter L. 2013. "Regularizing Rioting: Permitting Public Protest in an Authoritarian Regime." *Quarterly Journal of Political Science* 8 (2): 127–58.

Lu, Jia-Wei, Yingshi Xie, Beibei Xu, Yuanqing Huang, Jing Hai, and Jixian Zhang. 2019. "From NIMBY to BIMBY: An Evaluation of Aesthetic Appearance and Social Sustainability of MSW Incineration Plants in China." *Waste Management* 95 (July): 325–33. https://doi.org/10.1016/j.wasman.2019.06.016.

Lu, Xiaoli, and Lan Xue. 2016. "Managing the Unexpected: Sense-Making in the Chinese Emergency Management System." *Public Administration* 94 (2): 414–29. https://doi.org/10.1111/padm.12261.

Lubman, Stanley B. 1999. *Bird in a Cage: Legal Reform in China after Mao*. Stanford: Stanford University Press.

Ma, Liang, Huangfeng Tang, and Bo Yan. 2015. "Public Employees' Perceived Promotion Channels in Local China: Merit-Based or Guanxi-Orientated?." *Australian Journal of Public Administration* 74 (3): 283–97.

Ma, Xiao. 2022. *Localized Bargaining: The Political Economy of China's High-Speed Railway Program*. Oxford: Oxford University Press.

Mahdavi, Paasha. 2020. *Power Grab: Political Survival through Extractive Resource Nationalization*. Business and Public Policy. Cambridge: Cambridge University Press. https://doi.org/10.1017/9781108781350.

Malesky, Edmund, and Jonathan London. 2014. "The Political Economy of Development in China and Vietnam." *Annual Review of Political Science* 17 (1): 395–419. https://doi.org/10.1146/annurev-polisci-041811-150032.

Manion, Melanie. 1985. "The Cadre Management System, Post-Mao: The Appointment, Promotion, Transfer and Removal of Party and State Leaders." *The China Quarterly* 102: 203.

2004. *Corruption by Design: Building Clean Government in Mainland China and Hong Kong*. Cambridge, MA: Harvard University Press.

2016. "Taking China's Anticorruption Campaign Seriously." *Economic and Political Studies* 4 (1): 3–18. https://doi.org/10.1080/20954816.2016.1152094.

Marsh, Robert M. 2014. "Modernization Theory, Then and Now." *Comparative Sociology* 13 (3): 261–83. https://doi.org/10.1163/15691330-12341311.

Mattingly, Daniel C. 2019. *The Art of Political Control in China*. Cambridge Studies in Comparative Politics. Cambridge: Cambridge University Press. https://doi.org/10.1017/9781108662536.

Mertha, Andrew C. 2005. "China's 'Soft' Centralization: Shifting Tiao/Kuai Authority Relations." *The China Quarterly* 184 (December): 791–810. https://doi.org/10.1017/S0305741005000500.

2009. "'Fragmented Authoritarianism 2.0': Political Pluralization in the Chinese Policy Process." *The China Quarterly*, no. 200, 995–1012.

Montinola, Gabriella, Yingyi Qian, and Barry R. Weingast. 1995. "Federalism, Chinese Style: The Political Basis for Economic Success in China." *World Politics* 48 (1): 50–81.

Moore, Barrington. 1966. *Social Origins of Dictatorship and Democracy: Lord and Peasant in the Making of the Modern World*. Reprint edition. Boston: Beacon Press.

Mu, Rui, and Martin de Jong. 2012. "Establishing the Conditions for Effective Transit-Oriented Development in China: The Case of Dalian." *Journal of Transport Geography*, Special Section on Theoretical Perspectives on Climate Change Mitigation in Transport, 24 (September): 234–49.

2016. "A Network Governance Approach to Transit-Oriented Development: Integrating Urban Transport and Land Use Policies in Urumqi, China." *Transport Policy* 52 (November): 55–63.

Nathan, Andrew J. 2003. "Authoritarian Resilience." *Journal of Democracy* 14 (1): 6–17. https://doi.org/10.1353/jod.2003.0019.

Naughton, Barry. 1995. *Growing Out of the Plan: Chinese Economic Reform, 1978–1993*. Cambridge: Cambridge University Press.

2008. "SASAC and Rising Corporate Power in China." *China Leadership Monitor* 24 (2): 1–9.

Nee, Victor. 1992. "Organizational Dynamics of Market Transition: Hybrid Forms, Property Rights, and Mixed Economy in China." *Administrative Science Quarterly* 37 (1): 1–27. https://doi.org/10.2307/2393531.
Nolan, P. 2001. *China and the Global Economy: National Champions, Industrial Policy and the Big Business Revolution*. New York: Palgrave Macmillan.
O'Brien, Kevin J., and Lianjiang Li. 1999. "Selective Policy Implementation in Rural China." *Comparative Politics* 31 (2): 167.
2004. "Suing the Local State: Administrative Litigation in Rural China." *The China Journal* 51 (January): 75–96. https://doi.org/10.2307/3182147.
2006. *Rightful Resistance in Rural China*. New York: Cambridge University Press.
O'Brien, Kevin J., Lianjiang Li, and Mingxing Liu. 2020. "Bureaucrat-Assisted Contention in China." *Mobilization: An International Quarterly* 25 (SI): 661–74. https://doi.org/10.17813/1086-671X-25-5-661.
Oexl, Regine, and Zachary J. Grossman. 2013. "Shifting the Blame to a Powerless Intermediary." *Experimental Economics* 16 (3): 306–12.
Ohemeng, Frank K., and John K. Grant. 2008. "When Markets Fail to Deliver: An Examination of the Privatization and de-Privatization of Water and Wastewater Services Delivery in Hamilton, Canada." *Canadian Public Administration* 51 (3): 475–99.
Oi, Jean C. 1999. *Rural China Takes Off: Institutional Foundations of Economic Reform*. Berkeley: University of California Press.
Olson, Mancur. 1993. "Dictatorship, Democracy, and Development." *American Political Science Review* 87 (3): 567–76.
Ong, Lynette H. 2012. "Between Developmental and Clientelist States: Local State-Business Relationships in China." *Comparative Politics* 44 (2): 191–209.
2022. *Outsourcing Repression: Everyday State Power in Contemporary China*. Oxford and New York: Oxford University Press.
Paterson, Peter. 1967. *The Selectorate: The Case for Primary Elections on Britain*. London: MacGibbon & Kee.
Pearson, Margaret M. 2000. *China's New Business Elite: The Political Consequences of Economic Reform*. 1 edition. Berkeley: University of California Press.
2005. "The Business of Governing Business in China: Institutions and Norms of the Emerging Regulatory State." World Politics. January 2005.
2007. "Governing the Chinese Economy: Regulatory Reform in the Service of the State." *Public Administration Review* 67 (4): 718–30.
Pearson, Margaret, Meg Rithmire, and Kellee S. Tsai. 2021. "Party-State Capitalism in China." *Current History* 120 (827): 207–13. https://doi.org/10.1525/curh.2021.120.827.207.
Peerenboom, Randall. 2002. *China's Long March toward Rule of Law*. Cambridge: Cambridge University Press.
Pei, Minxin. 1997. "Citizens v. Mandarins: Administrative Litigation in China." *The China Quarterly* 152: 832–62.
2006. *China's Trapped Transition: The Limits of Developmental Autocracy*. Cambridge, MA: Harvard University Press.
2016. *China's Crony Capitalism*. Cambridge, MA: Harvard University Press.

Peng, Hongfeng, Xiao Zhang, and Xiaoquan Zhu. 2017. "Political Connections of the Board of Directors and Credit Financing: Evidence from Chinese Private Enterprises." *Accounting & Finance* 57 (5): 1481–516. https://doi.org/10.1111/acfi.12331.

Perry, James L., and Timlynn T. Babitsky. 1986. "Comparative Performance in Urban Bus Transit: Assessing Privatization Strategies." *Public Administration Review* 46 (1): 57–66.

Poncet, Sandra, Walter Steingress, and Hylke Vandenbussche. 2010. "Financial Constraints in China: Firm-Level Evidence." *China Economic Review* 21 (3): 411–22.

Powell, Lynda W. 2012. *The Influence of Campaign Contributions in State Legislatures: The Effects of Institutions and Politics*. Ann Arbor: University of Michigan Press.

Prendergast, Canice. 1999. "The Provision of Incentives in Firms." *Journal of Economic Literature* 37 (1): 7–63.

Przeworski, Adam, and Fernando Limongi. 1997. "Modernization: Theories and Facts." *World Politics* 49 (2): 155–83. https://doi.org/10.1353/wp.1997.0004.

Putnam, Robert D. 2000. *Bowling Alone: The Collapse and Revival of American Community*. Simon and Schuster.

Rithmire, Meg. 2023. *Precarious Ties: Business and the State in Authoritarian Asia*. Oxford and New York: Oxford University Press.

Robinson, James A., and Ragnar Torvik. 2005. "White Elephants." *Journal of Public Economics* 89 (2): 197–210. https://doi.org/10.1016/j.jpubeco.2004.05.004.

Rodrik, Dani. 2000. "Institutions for High-Quality Growth: What They Are and How to Acquire Them." *Studies in Comparative International Development* 35 (3): 3–31.

Rose-Ackerman, Susan, and Bonnie J. Palifka. 2016. *Corruption and Government: Causes, Consequences, and Reform*. New York: Cambridge University Press.

Rozelle, Scott, and Natalie Hell. 2020. *Invisible China*. The University of Chicago Press.

Saich, Tony. 2008. *Providing Public Goods in Transitional China*. New York: Palgrave Macmillan.

Savas, Emanuel S. 1999. *Privatization and Public-Private Partnerships*. 2 edition. New York: Chatham House.

Scott, James C. 1987. *Weapons of the Weak: Everyday Forms of Peasant Resistance*. Reprint edition. New Haven: Yale University Press.

Shafer, Michael. 1983. "Capturing the Mineral Multinationals: Advantage or Disadvantage?" *International Organization* 37 (1): 93–119.

Shepsle, Kenneth A., and Barry R. Weingast. 1981. "Political Preferences for the Pork Barrel: A Generalization." *American Journal of Political Science* 25 (1): 96–111. https://doi.org/10.2307/2110914.

Shih, Victor. 2007. "Partial Reform Equilibrium, Chinese Style Political Incentives and Reform Stagnation in Chinese Financial Policies." *Comparative Political Studies* 40 (10): 1238–62.

2008. "'Nauseating' Displays of Loyalty: Monitoring the Factional Bargain through Ideological Campaigns in China." *The Journal of Politics* 70 (4): 1177–92.

Shih, Victor, Christopher Adolph, and Mingxing Liu. 2012. "Getting Ahead in the Communist Party: Explaining the Advancement of Central Committee Members in China." *American Political Science Review* 106 (1): 166–87. https://doi.org/10.1017/S0003055411000566.

Shih, Victor C. 2009. *Factions and Finance in China: Elite Conflict and Inflation.* New York: Cambridge University Press.

Shleifer, Andrei. 1998. "State versus Private Ownership." *Journal of Economic Perspectives* 12 (4): 133–50.

Shleifer, Andrei, and Robert W. Vishny. 2002. *The Grabbing Hand: Government Pathologies and Their Cures.* Cambridge, MA: Harvard University Press.

Smith, Alastair, Randolph M. Siverson, James D. Morrow, and Bruce Bueno. 2004. *The Logic of Political Survival.* Cambridge, MA: The MIT Press.

Steinfeld, Edward S. 1998. *Forging Reform in China: The Fate of State-Owned Industry.* Cambridge Modern China Series. Cambridge: Cambridge University Press. https://doi.org/10.1017/CBO9780511625831.

Szakonyi, David. 2018. "Businesspeople in Elected Office: Identifying Private Benefits from Firm-Level Returns." *The American Political Science Review* 112 (2): 322–38.

Takeuchi, Hiroki. 2014. *Tax Reform in Rural China: Revenue, Resistance, and Authoritarian Rule.* New York: Cambridge University Press.

Teets, Jessica C. 2015. "The Politics of Innovation in China: Local Officials as Policy Entrepreneurs." *Issues and Studies; Taipei* 51 (2): 79–109.

Teets, Jessica C., and Reza Hasmath. 2020. "The Evolution of Policy Experimentation in China." *Journal of Asian Public Policy* 13 (1): 49–59. https://doi.org/10.1080/17516234.2020.1711491.

Teets, Jessica C., and William Hurst. 2014. *Local Governance Innovation in China: Experimentation, Diffusion, and Defiance.* London: Routledge.

Thireau, Isabelle, and Linshan Hua. 2003. "The Moral Universe of Aggrieved Chinese Workers: Workers' Appeals to Arbitration Committees and Letters and Visits Offices." *The China Journal* 50 (July): 83–103. https://doi.org/10.2307/3182247.

Tihanyi, Laszlo, Ruth V. Aguilera, Pursey Heugens, Marc van Essen, Steve Sauerwald, Patricio Duran, and Roxana Turturea. 2019. "State Ownership and Political Connections." *Journal of Management* 45 (6): 2293–321. https://doi.org/10.1177/0149206318822113.

Tsai, Kellee S. 2002. *Back-Alley Banking: Private Entrepreneurs in China.* Ithaca: Cornell University Press.

2007. *Capitalism Without Democracy: The Private Sector in Contemporary China.* Ithaca: Cornell University Press.

Tsai, Lily L. 2008. "Understanding the Falsification of Village Income Statistics." *The China Quarterly* 196: 805–26.

Vickers, John, and George Yarrow. 1991. "Economic Perspectives on Privatization." *The Journal of Economic Perspectives* 5 (2): 111–32.

Wade, Robert. 1990. *Governing the Market: Economic Theory and the Role of Government in East Asian Industrialization*. Princeton University Press.

Wallace, Jeremy L. 2016. "Juking the Stats? Authoritarian Information Problems in China." *British Journal of Political Science* 46 (1): 11–29. https://doi.org/10.1017/S0007123414000106.

Wang, Feng. 2024. *China's Age of Abundance: Origins, Ascendance, and Aftermath*. Cambridge: Cambridge University Press. https://doi.org/10.1017/9781009444934.

Wang, Jian, Guo-hua Liu, Junyan Wang, Xianglong Xu, Yuting Shao, Qian Zhang, Yuchen Liu, Lu Qi, and Hongchen Wang. 2021. "Current Status, Existent Problems, and Coping Strategy of Urban Drainage Pipeline Network in China." *Environmental Science and Pollution Research* 28 (32): 43035–49. https://doi.org/10.1007/s11356-021-14802-9.

Wang, Yuhua. 2015. *Tying the Autocrat's Hands*. Cambridge: Cambridge University Press.

Weaver, R. Kent. 1986. "The Politics of Blame Avoidance." *Journal of Public Policy* 6 (4): 371–98.

Wedeman, Andrew. 2001. "Incompetence, Noise, and Fear in Central-Local Relations in China." *Studies in Comparative International Development* 35 (4): 59–83.

2005. "Anticorruption Campaigns and the Intensification of Corruption in China." *Journal of Contemporary China* 14 (42): 93–116. https://doi.org/10.1080/1067056042000300808.

2012. *Double Paradox: Rapid Growth and Rising Corruption in China*. Ithaca: Cornell University Press.

Wedeman, Andrew H. 2003. *From Mao to Market: Rent Seeking, Local Protectionism, and Marketization in China*. New York: Cambridge University Press.

Williams, Mark. 2005. *Competition Policy and Law in China, Hong Kong and Taiwan*. Cambridge: Cambridge University Press.

Wintrobe, Ronald. 1998. *The Political Economy of Dictatorship*. Cambridge: Cambridge University Press. https://doi.org/10.1017/CBO9781139174916.

Xu, Jin, and Zuxin Xu. 2022. "China Sewage Treatment Engineering Issues Assessment." *Journal of Cleaner Production* 377 (December): 134391. https://doi.org/10.1016/j.jclepro.2022.134391.

Xu, Jintao, and Yiying Cao. 2002. "Tuigeng huanlin huancao de kechixu fazhan wenti." *Guoji Jingji Pinglun* 3–4, 56–60.

Yang, Dali L. 1996. "Governing China's Transition to the Market: Institutional Incentives, Politicians' Choices, and Unintended Outcomes." *World Politics* 48 (3): 424–52. https://doi.org/10.1353/wp.1996.0009.

2004. *Remaking the Chinese Leviathan: Market Transition and the Politics of Governance in China*. Stanford, CA: Stanford University Press.

Yao, Shujie. 1999. "Economic Growth, Income Inequality and Poverty in China under Economic Reforms." *The Journal of Development Studies* 35 (6): 104–30. https://doi.org/10.1080/00220389908422604.

Yasuda, John K. 2017. *On Feeding the Masses: An Anatomy of Regulatory Failure in China*. Cambridge: Cambridge University Press. https://doi.org/10.1017/9781108185851.

Zakharov, Alexei V. 2016. "The Loyalty-Competence Trade-Off in Dictatorships and Outside Options for Subordinates." *The Journal of Politics* 78 (2): 457–66. https://doi.org/10.1086/684365.

Zhang, Houyi. (张厚义). 1993. "中国大陆私营经济的再生与发展." 社会学研究, no. 4, 41–52.

Zhang, Mo. 2008. "From Public to Private: The Newly Enacted Chinese Property Law and the Protection of Property Rights in China." *Berkeley Business Law Journal* 5: 317.

Zhao, Xin-gang, Gui-wu Jiang, Ang Li, and Yun Li. 2016. "Technology, Cost, a Performance of Waste-to-Energy Incineration Industry in China." *Renewable and Sustainable Energy Reviews* 55 (March): 115–30. https://doi.org/10.1016/j.rser.2015.10.137.

Zhou, Hao. 2009. "书记." "The Transition Period." www.imdb.com/title/tt1859619/

Zhou, Li-An. 2004. "The Incentive and Cooperation of Government Officials in the Political Tournaments: An Interpretation of the Prolonged Local Protectionism and Duplicative Investments in China." *Economic Research Journal* 6: 33–40.

2007. "Governing China's Local Officials: An Analysis of Promotion Tournament Model." *Economic Research Journal* 7: 36–50.

Zhu, Jiangnan, and Xueyong Wang. 2013. "Unveiling the Political Elite: High-Ranking Chinese Officials on Television Talk Shows." *Journal of Chinese Political Science* 18 (2): 117–37.

Zhu, Xufeng, and Youlang Zhang. 2016. "Political Mobility and Dynamic Diffusion of Innovation: The Spread of Municipal Pro-Business Administrative Reform in China." *Journal of Public Administration Research and Theory* 26 (3): 535–51. https://doi.org/10.1093/jopart/muv025.

Index

Printed by Integrated Books International,
United States of America